UNSHAMING

ALSO BY JOWITA BYDLOWSKA

FICTION

Guy (1994)

Possessed (2023)

Monster (2024)

NON-FICTION

Drunk Mom (2013)

UNSHAMING

A Memoir of ~~Recovery~~,
Relapse, and What Comes After

JOWITA BYDLOWSKA

LEBANON, NEW HAMPSHIRE

Published simultaneously in Canada by Penguin Random House Canada.

For information about permission to reproduce
selections from this book, write to:
Steerforth Press
254 Plainfield Rd Unit 11, #1063
West Lebanon, NH 03784

Cataloging-in-Publication Data is available from the Library of Congress

ISBN 978-1-58642-424-4

Printed in the United States of America

The authorized representative in the EEA is eucomply OÜ, Pärnu mnt. 139b-14,
11317, Tallinn, Estonia, hello@eucompliancepartner.com, +33757690241

1 3 5 7 9 10 8 6 4 2

To Hugo—

Kocham cię bardzo. Dziękuję że jesteś i że zawsze byłeś.

"Why are you drinking?" the little prince asked.

"To forget," replied the drunkard.

"To forget what?" inquired the little prince, who was already feeling sorry for him.

"To forget that I'm ashamed," confessed the drunkard, hanging his head.

"What are you ashamed of?" inquired the little prince, who wanted to help.

"Of drinking!" concluded the drunkard, withdrawing into silence for good.

—Antoine de Saint-Exupéry, *The Little Prince*

So when life fades, as the fading sunset,
my spirit may come to you without shame.

—Chief Yellow Lark (translator), "Great Spirit Prayer"

CONTENTS

PART 1

Clavicle

1.

I come to. I *wasn't*, then suddenly I *am*. I was riding my bike and next thing I know—

I'm in my boyfriend's high-ceilinged cottage studio, the familiar tousled green of a treetop visible in the skylight, the white room awash in the cheerful brightness of the morning. Outside, the buzz of insects marks the rising summer heat; in the distance, a sawing and hammering cracks the quiet and yet it sounds pleasant here, far away from the city where the noise is constant and threatening. My boyfriend is beside me, and he's awake. I reach for him and he looks at me, startled. Maybe it's the state of me or maybe it's my hand sneaking down his belly, I don't know. When I grip him harder his eyes soften with love or melancholy and something like resignation.

He moves above me; he is gentle, restrained, obliging. I shut my eyes. None of this is real. I focus on the pleasure, his skin against my skin. I pull him closer, bite his shoulder to signal he can get rougher. (When we talk about this moment in the future he'll say he worried about breaking me even more, but I seemed so desperate. I was.)

I am aware that something is very wrong. Sharpness where there was softness and order. Scaffolding coming apart inside me. I feel my face—it's sticky—and I open my eyes. Look at my fingers. Red. I'm frightened. The anxiety combines with the pleasure spreading from my core; it elevates it. I look into my boyfriend's impermeable, deep dark eyes, his face a mask of worry and tenderness.

Every couple has their cute story or two about a funny mishap or how they got lost in a big city or ran into Keanu Reeves. A story that showcases something about their bond and is told at dinner parties, shared with others.

Our relationship isn't an every couple's relationship. We have no dinner parties to go to, no one asks us how we met, do we have a funny mishap to share. We got together shortly before the pandemic and have since existed in almost total isolation, creating our own strange universe with its own rules. I'm not making excuses for my boyfriend's acquiescing to my sexual demand despite my state, but looking back when we tell this story—over and over and only to each other—we can't make sense out of it ourselves except that it seemed necessary.

In keeping with the pandemic slogan "We're All in This Together," this is our *This*—one that, despite its fuckedupness, bonds us. We don't yet have to acknowledge the reality of whatever's wrong, suspended as we are in a stolen ten minutes, holding on to the Before before we slip into the After.

Or maybe we're holding on to the fantasy that we're like those normal couples—normal people taking bike rides, going to sleep, waking up, making gentle love. What I remember well is a feeling of something ending from which there was no coming back. As wrong as it seemed later, the sex was our desperate need to reaffirm life.

Last night I died briefly on the boardwalk on the north side of Toronto Island, near the Riviera café. I was riding my bike and smashed head and shoulder first into a concrete wall, my eye an inch away from the corner. I crawled into a ditch. My boyfriend looked for me everywhere and twice passed the sack of bones I'd turned into before he went back and finally found me in that ditch near the restaurant, conscious but hurt, with one side of my face bleeding. I tried to convince him that I was fine. I have no recollection of any of that. In the end, I let him half-carry, half-walk me, first on the boardwalk, and then the road, then over the bridge, then the road again . . .

When I try to review the tape it's blank, right from when I first got on the bike. He fills in what happened next: he brought me back to the cottage, where he washed me in his big Jacuzzi tub and bandaged the gash on my face and then stayed beside me through the night waiting to sober up himself while watching me breathe.[1] With our relationship only a few months old at that point, it was the first time he clued in that I drank differently from most people. It was also the first time he considered breaking his promise to not read the book I wrote about just how differently I drank.

Is it bad?

It's bad, he says, our first conversation of the day.

I don't feel any pain.

We should call the paramedics now.

No, I say, and he closes his eyes and sighs.

1 Years later, he tells me there was another reason why he hesitated to call for help right away that night: he knew what this would look like. Or "the optics," as he put it, a hurt white woman and a drunken Indigenous man. Over the course of his life he'd been stopped by the cops and even arrested "for being Indian" numerous times; his was a reality that was different from mine.

Not yet, I say.

He knows not to argue with me; I always win.

I get up, stumble to the bathroom. There is blood on the towels lying on the floor. I look in the mirror and the monster looking back at me is naked and skinny and slightly scrambled, like one of those images produced by AI where something is definitely off even though it all looks human. The bandage on my face is dark brown. My shoulder is in the wrong place, as if weighed down by an invisible anvil.

I don't feel any pain, I think.

But I'm worried.

I pee, crying. I shut my eyes and again try to sift through frame after frame of film where what happened should be recorded. It isn't. And it won't be, no matter how many times I'll try in the future.

I don't know what I did but I know I did *it* again.

I did what I do because I am who I am.

A story forms in my head. A story I won't have to be ashamed of, that will match what I am not. Maybe a story we could even tell at dinner parties one day! When I come out of the bathroom, I tell my boyfriend the story and he finishes telling me the story that *did* happen as he hands me my dusty rose silk taffeta dress with a generous skirt and a tight bodice with spaghetti straps. My pink sweater. My pointy red flats. I am decked out as if for a party. I always dress for a party when I fall apart. It used to be a sexy funeral when I first relapsed—black furs, black faux leather pants, patent leather wedges—but these days it's a prom in an insane asylum. Silk slips and princess dresses, pretty, impractical shoes reminiscent of pastries, some variation on eclair.

I try to brush my hair but give up and ask him if he can do it for me.

I don't brush my teeth because some of them are not quite seated in my gums. A recurring nightmare I used to have was waking up to find that all my teeth were falling out of my head and today the nightmare threatens to come true. I touch the top back molars with my finger, gently, feel the crushed bottom one with my tongue. I try to add up the information I have so far—the bandage on my face, the bloody towels, the feeling of bones, fear—but I know there's more, a whole shattered constellation inside me.

My boyfriend makes the call and tidies the bathroom.

When the paramedics arrive, we give them the story I came up with and that we rehearsed together. I point to my red flats and joke about not having proper biking shoes: fashion victim. Ha ha. Two fingers on my wrist checking my pulse. Questions about lightheadedness, questions about today's date, the prime minister, my son's name. Headache? Nausea? Vomiting?

We went for a ride this morning. My front wheel got wedged between two planks on the boardwalk and to avoid falling I somehow catapulted myself into a wall.

Did you black out?

No, I didn't. I don't think so. I would know, no? We walked back here and I washed up. He helped me wash up. I wasn't sure what to do. We called right away. My front wheel got wedged—

I will repeat a version of this story many times. It passes the test; the paramedics don't argue with me. I'm assuming I don't smell of alcohol. Nobody asks me if I drank. Not till later, till I talk to the people to whom my morning-bike-ride story sounds suspicious.

(And even then, the question is more *Imagine if you were drunk?* and waiting for me to confess, which I don't, so then a headshake, never mind.)

I count five men inside the bright cottage room: the paramedics, a neighbour, and my boyfriend. And me in the middle of this weird party like Snow White with her dwarfs, the cheerful fir in the skylight window further confirming this to be a fairy tale.

My boyfriend helps me walk down the stairs to the ambulance and then we drive for less than a couple of minutes to the docks. We take a small utility barge back to the shore and my boyfriend snaps some pictures when I ask him to: me perched on some boxes in my princess dress and movie star sunglasses, my arm in a sling, men in uniform bustling about the boat. It's a difficult scene to decipher if you don't have the context; there's something absurd and fabulous about it, a whiff of a celebrity getting rescued and escorted.

Or that's what I tell myself when I feel the waves of shame accumulating and crashing within my adrenalin-spent body as I sit in the ER and scroll through the photos on my phone, mostly looking for some other, more innocent time.

When I get examined, the doctor comments on the gash in my forehead, how it's not a fresh one. I repeat the story about the morning bike ride. I can tell she doesn't believe me or maybe she's just tired, her sharp, yellowjacket face impatient as I blabber on. She decides against stitching the gash as the blood has coagulated already. I am sent for various scans and X-rays. Possible concussion. Something about sinuses and some of my teeth are definitely loose. My clavicle has splintered like a twig. My occipital bone and cheekbone have been broken and chipped too ("multiple facial contusions, fractures involving the zygomatic arch, orbital floor and orbital wall," reads the report).

There are bone fragments everywhere in the upper left side of my body ("a closed clavicle fracture that is comminuted").

The gash in my forehead is ugly. I want them to stitch it. But because I know it's all my fault, I also feel I deserve this, and I'm convinced that Yellowjacket *read* me, saw me catapulting drunk into the wall, and that she agrees that I'm a worthless piece of shit who should just live with a hole in her forehead. (But later, reading her assessment, I'm described this way: "She is a pleasant lady." I wish myself worse than anyone else possibly could.)

When I tell him about not getting the stitches, my usually calm boyfriend gets impatient with the ER staff; he demands to see a supervising resident, he stops nurses, they ignore him, they ignore me, he gets up, he paces, he leaves and comes back with treats—smoothies, chocolate bars—he blows up rubber gloves and pretends to milk them like udders, he asks me to remind him of my medical sex fantasy, he tells me I am the most beautiful woman on the planet. He's like most of the boyfriends before him: insane, loyal, and equally frustrated, a cross between a horny teenager, a stern but loving dad, and a fed-up Prince Charming—fed up with me, that is.

He goes to look for the ER doctor but Yellowjacket is gone, replaced by another resident who takes a look at me and the gash and says they can send me to Plastics, in another hospital where they repair broken faces.

We take a taxi to the hospital at the other end of the city. I don't know if it's still the morning or evening and does it matter?

It does not. I rest the good side of my face on my boyfriend's shoulder; he smooths my hair and occasionally kisses me on the side of my head as if to soothe my crying, which I'm not, crying. The only time I do feel close to it is when I text my son about having had "a little accident" and having to cancel our regular night. He texts back and then calls me but I don't answer because his "are you ok mummy?" threatens to undo me. The British spelling of the word always conjures him as a little boy, that need and unquestionable devotion to mummy only little boys are capable of. He is a big boy now but I remain his mummy, even though he doesn't need me like that anymore.

At the new hospital I'm seen by a young male resident with blond hair, very all-American looking, healthy, sporty. I feel old and fragile around him. I am old and fragile.

He lifts my chin gently and takes a look at the gash in my forehead. I complain about Yellowjacket, how she seemed so busy. I say nothing about my accident. He says nothing about the blood coagulating. And he doesn't ask, he's interested only in the gash, his eyes shining with excitement as he moves closer to see, so close that I'm suddenly on the moon of his face, stepping, admiring his poreless skin. I aged out of being younger than doctors a long time ago but now they seem too young, like children playing dress-up on Halloween with stethoscopes.

The baby doctor says he would love to stitch me up—he actually says the word "love"—and just as I'd imagined the sparkle in his eye I now imagine a certain vibration in his voice. For a moment I wonder if they don't let him practise such unimportant, minor needlework enough, or if this is his fetish.

He sews me up, turning me ever so slightly, his fingers steady and tender. I am a Tim Burton puppet and he is Tim Burton and this is Halloween except it's June and I've smashed my face and my clavicle into a concrete wall and I don't remember a thing because I never remember what I do after seven p.m. these days.

I close my eyes. He says something about how I might be eligible for a filler if it turns out the cheekbone is too broken—the zygomatic arch fracture can cause flattening of the cheek.

When he's done, he holds up a mirror for me to admire his work. He seems pleased. My face looking back at me seems pleased too, despite its one bloody eye.

He leaves and I look around the room. Behind me there are cotton balls stained with red and the suture kit is open, looking a little dishevelled, as if it's thrown up all its tiny scissors and thread and scalpels. This is a still life with trauma and I am its museum.

2.

Over the next few days the left side of my face swells and the white of my left eye fills with red. There's a deep black and purple bruise stretching along the cheekbone and spreading over my eyelid. A dark yellow stain pools below my eye. (I will not fully regain sensation in parts of my face for years to come—along the left temple all the way down to my upper lip—but I will get used to the permanent feeling of dental freezing.)

My left shoulder is pushed forward, the sling supporting the useless arm; there's something broken-wing-like about the way it's protruding. I also have to have dental work done or I'll lose three molars. That's not a priority but my shoulder is, so I go to get more X-rays and consult with a doctor who, after looking at the images, asks me how old I am.

Forty-three, I tell him.

Hmmm, he says.

The X-rays show the impact was so great that some of the bone has splintered and pieces of it are strewn about inside me; more frighteningly, there's a knife-like edge pressing against my skin from the inside. Till the surgery, I'll have one persistent fear: waking up one day and finding a bone tip poking through my skin.

Despite the severity of my injury, the doctor says something about how bones set themselves and surgery is optional and carries risks. I wonder if he says this because he believes I'm too old to worry about frivolous things like appearances and how a dress will look on me. In a monotone he explains the dangers: scars, bleeding, bruising, pain, and the risk of nerve damage to the top part of the chest. But with the procedure, the chances of the bone fusing back properly are 98 to 99 percent.

After Googling, I learn that the surgery is expensive, at least twenty thousand dollars, which is covered by OHIP, the provincial health insurance plan. Letting my bones try to grow back together on their own is free.

A friend posts in his mountain-biking Facebook group—a small population of people familiar with crushed clavicles—asking for advice about the operation, its risks and benefits. Everyone says get the surgery, it's worth it, and my friend is adamant that at forty-three I am far too young to give up on having straight shoulders and cute dresses.

As for my face, it remains distorted, huge, and almost square in shape. I recall the Plastics doctor saying something about how I could get a filler on top of the bone if it turns out that the dent is deep enough. Free plastic surgery! What a nice bonus. Since turning forty I've wanted to do something to my face, feed plastic to my lips or cheeks, slap on new brows or at least Zamboni my forehead with Botox, but I've never had the courage; I told myself that I've been lucky enough as it was when it came to appearance. That's because I was born pretty; I didn't do much to cultivate it. I was a pretty child, a pretty teenager, and I was still an attractive woman. I know we're not supposed to admit to those things but that's a fact, a genetic lottery just like mental illness.

I've always had a complex relationship with my looks, a back-and-forth of self-obsession and shallowness then rejection of it and then guilt, too, both for caring about it too much and for not capitalizing on it enough. I would accentuate my eyes or hide behind ugly glasses, eat like a pig or like an anorexic gymnast, swim two hundred laps a day or merely manage a walk between my apartment and the liquor store, wear only grandpa corduroys or just leather and corsets . . . I've used my looks as a bargaining chip more than once—getting meetings with powerful men in journalism school, skipping the velvet rope at clubs—but I've also despised not being taken seriously. I've always oscillated between provoking—as I do here, with my admitting to knowing I was pretty—and wanting to be invisible. I've tried humour and wit to distract from my ass, written books to impress men who would still comment on my author photo, gotten indignant when a professor told me I was hopeless as a journalist but at least I was attractive enough to marry rich or at least be on TV. So I've denounced beauty too, but truly I've always been a slave to it, worried about it, that it would pass and I'd be left with no more favours, the world would finally see that I'd always been stupid and empty with no substance other than my hysterical writing.

As I contemplate my face's fate, I think about all that and how maybe never again will I experience the rush I'd become addicted to—the rush of walking into a party and being the tallest woman in the room with a high ponytail and the shortest dress. The rush of seeing a lover's eyes cloud over as I unhook the garters and peel off the lace. The thrill of reading a journalist's description of my face as pretty and angular in a profile, or the pleasure of hearing a joke about yourself being glamorous and Eastern European, a Venus in furs with a cigarette, or of hearing your own mythology confirmed by strangers who've heard the rumours.

It's hard to let go of that rush, but now that I have no idea what the bones in my face are doing I become obsessed with coming out of this in a different container. I secretly wish for the cheekbone to grow back deformed, for the white of my eye to stay red, for the gash in my face to split it into a permanent distortion.

In my twenties, when I first knew I had a problem with alcohol, I tried to think of what my rock bottom would be—what's the one thing that could really shake me up, wake me up, make me stop? My face. My face was my rock bottom. The scene was always of me falling down the stairs drunk, head smashing into each step, an eye socket, a nasal cartilage, teeth spilling out like Chiclets from ground-meat lips. The worst rock bottom I could think of was the one where

I finally lost my face—figuratively and literally. So now, as much as I feel indebted to my beauty and am terrified about losing it, part of me is slightly thrilled about no longer having to worry about it. And then, of course, there is the thought of having fulfilled my own superstition and, with that thought, a relief that maybe I'll leave myself alone now—that I've given addiction the last thing I valued. That now I'm free.

Would freedom mean I'd stop or that I'd just get worse because now there was nothing left to lose? I don't know.

My boyfriend says I'm beautiful no matter what, and with that declaration he again confirms that he's just like any other boyfriend I've ever had—devoted and delusional. You have to be to stay with me, to stay with any alcoholic.[2]

As for everyone else in my life, they too continue to be gentle and worried and I recount the morning-bike-ride lie over and over, add little self-deprecating bits about how I'm so clumsy and how trying to be overly careful backfired. I even make jokes about how I had

[2] I use the term "alcoholic" (or "addict") to describe a person who is or has been dependent on alcohol or someone who suffers from substance use disorder (SUD). The term has been associated with negative stereotypes and societal judgments about those struggling with alcohol addiction. It can be used in a derogatory manner, perpetuating the stigma and Shame surrounding addiction. Rather than recognizing alcohol addiction as a complex health issue, the label implies moral or character flaws.

In recent years, though, there's been a shift toward person-centred language in reference to SUDs. The focus is on separating the person from the condition, emphasizing their individuality rather than defining them solely by their addiction. Some people who've struggled with alcohol addiction also prefer not to be labelled as "alcoholics" as they feel it can perpetuate a sense of helplessness and defeat. Others have embraced it to make it mean something the opposite: accountability. The current trend is to go with such terms as "person with SUD" or "person in recovery," but although I've started to identify in that way, my mind keeps saying "alcoholic" (or "addict").

such a "drunk" accident while sober, how ironic. I walk around with fancy scarves wrapped around my sling, I take lots of selfies of my left side, my dressed-up arm, and the little coy hairs peeking out of my armpit—I can't lift my arms so I let myself go hairy. Every few days my boyfriend washes my hair in the kitchen sink, pouring the water from a watering can, lovingly tending to each strand, then drying it all slowly and meticulously in a clean, puffy towel. It's all so romantic, the feeling amped up by the look of my apartment with its cabin-in-the-woods vibe, my dark kitchen opening on to a small yard densely shaded by a canopy of trees.

I can't bend either, and when I fold myself to lie down my body is a rigid chair, all wrong angles and bad design. To accommodate me, we put the mattress on the floor so that I don't have to climb into the bed. It stays there for a couple of weeks. Some warm nights I'm a panther, slinking into the kitchen naked and on all fours, crossing it to come out to the yard, where I lie down on the ground, letting the air cool my sweaty skin. I am sober and present and broken and feral. Because of the pandemic and the lockdowns the whole world is on pause; there's nowhere to go and no one to stand upright for.

3.

I research "clavicle plate and screw systems" online and marvel over 3-D images of stainless-steel plates with locking and nonlocking screw options; I make more jokes with those who ask about becoming a cyborg, and start looking forward to it all. The idea of surgery, but specifically the idea of being out, under anaesthesia, appeals to me as much as haircuts do to normal people. I recall a sober alcoholic friend telling me about going through a miscarriage and how they pumped her full of morphine for the pain; how despite the distress she felt happy that she got to be high on borrowed time, joking darkly that the miscarriage made it worth it. We both laughed because we got the joke. It's not the idea of being high, either, it's the boredom that every addict despises more than anything. An extreme experience means dopamine and dopamine is our God,[3] our real Higher Power. I think of the three-hour surgery and a bionic plate insertion the way some people think about zip lining.

My son stays with his father for most of that month. The accident has freaked him out and he doesn't want to see me hurt and in pain—at least not for prolonged periods of time. I see him for a few hours every two evenings or so, watch him play basketball, eat ice cream in the park, take pictures with my fancy camera. He doesn't stay overnight. And not because he doesn't want to see me hurt and in pain—it's because he still doesn't trust that I won't turn into a werewolf once it starts to get dark.

Ever since I can remember I've been sensitive to the time of day, anxious when it's light out and loosening up as night falls. A nocturnal

[3] Conducted by psychologist James Olds and his colleague Peter Milner in the 1950s, one of the most famous dopamine-hit experiments—still quoted at dinner parties and in TED talks—studied the mechanism of addiction in rats. The researchers inserted electrodes into rats' brains and allowed them to self-administer electrical stimulation to their brains' pleasure centres. The rats quickly learned to press a lever that would deliver the electrical stimulation, and they would continue to do so even when it required crossing an electrified floor or enduring other unpleasant conditions. The researchers concluded that the rats were experiencing intense pleasure from the stimulation, likely due to the release of dopamine.

animal, I find comfort in the darkness, respite in the shadows. And that's where the danger lurks. Every relapse I've ever had has happened after the sun's gone down. The night was a trap.

There have been many nights when my son would promise to come over, then change his mind at the last minute. And for a while now he hasn't felt comfortable staying with me when he knows he will need to get home after dark, after his soccer practice. He says it's not even that he worries about me being *notokay* (his euphemism for "drunk"); it's that, on two occasions in the past, he's found me wobbly, and now he has bad associations with coming home in the evening. That there were "only" two occasions is nothing to be proud of.

Still, it's frustrating that it's gone on for so long. I've said nothing, though. Losing privileges is a trajectory of every parent in recovery, and once you break your kid's trust no amount of sobriety or reassurance can bring it back—at least not right away.

I don't pressure him to stay. Too bad for me that I feel a little resentful about him going to his dad's. I mean, I've been sober since the accident. But there's no way to announce that information since I always say I'm sober—even, and especially, when I'm not. Besides, what used to be a celebratory announcement would sound cheap now and it never guarantees anything anymore. So I keep it quiet. I haven't given up on myself and I don't technically pray but I secretly pray non-stop that sobriety will somehow stick this time. *Please, please.* Maybe if I don't make a big deal out of it I'll fool my demons into not noticing that scent of an addict's desperate boredom, and then eventually I'll be too far into my sobriety for them to get me.

I know there are no demons and werewolves and that I'm not Odysseus having to tie myself to the mast to avoid sirens—my other favourite parable—or whatever other flamboyant analogy I come up with to explain the ongoing struggle of this addict's internal war that is actually just a story of sanity vs. non, or of making good and bad choices. And yet in twenty-five years of addiction, parts of its mechanism have felt truly wicked and out of my control; I've often thought of it as my curse, and I've always feared it. I love good psychological theory as much as anyone. I know about trauma and early childhood adversities and self-soothing and grief and loss of identity and brain chemistry. However, I also know that addiction knowledge is useless unless it's applied. Knowledge alone has never gotten anyone sober. But people claim prayers have and so I'm praying.[4] There are no witnesses to my praying—other than my

[4] Research studies exploring the effects of prayer in the context of AA or similar addiction programs have found that it may contribute to increased motivation, enhanced coping mechanisms, and improved overall well-being among people in recovery.

Other research has focused on the role of prayer in promoting positive health behaviours and adherence to conventional medical treatments by patients with chronic illnesses, for example. The findings in this area have been mixed, with some studies suggesting a potential positive impact and others showing no significant effects.

For me, prayers are less about spirituality and more about making a commitment, sending a message to the universe and saying it out loud so that I'll be accountable for it. *Please, please (let it stick, let it work, et cetera).* Who am I talking to? Myself, I plead with myself, the parts of me that are sane and reasonable. The idea is that when I'm in a situation where I'm tempted I'll remember the prayer and its desperation and will somehow move my hand away from reaching for a bottle. I will turn around and walk out of the liquor store. Of course, once I'm already in the store it's too late. My body is flooded with adrenalin—hands shaking, electric current in my chest, my heart a gong in my head—and my mind is in a seesaw of don't-do-don't-do-don't. My soul, or spirit, or whatever hears the prayers is outnumbered. I have never walked out of a liquor store empty-handed.

And yet. *Please.*

"The function of prayer is not to influence God, but rather to change the nature of the one who prays."—Søren Kierkegaard

boyfriend, who would never say anything—but I still hide it just as I hide everything I feel ashamed about. I am alone with my addiction and I am alone with my recovery, too; I've said nothing out loud about any of it; I've made no promises or proclamations and my boyfriend doesn't offer any comment. I want to ask him if he's hoping this time it will stick but that would mean we'd have to acknowledge the problem.

For now, I just don't drink and don't talk about not drinking. I don't teach in the summer but I have a lot of freelance gigs, such as ghostwriting, that I'm unable to work on, since with my arm in the sling I can't write. My savings are dwindling and there are no grants coming in but I'm in denial about my financial situation as much as I'm in denial about most things in my life. Maybe it's the pandemic but I'm not that alarmed about this bizarre, self-enforced vacation and all this rest. When I get sufficiently tired of reality TV—the only TV that holds my interest, as I enjoy watching others do embarrassing things that make me feel better about myself—I do what one does during the lockdown, which is go for long walks, and in my case, long walks along the train tracks. Sometimes alone, sometimes with my boyfriend. I take Polaroids of abandoned chairs, old mattresses, suitcases, discarded masks, ripped yellow tape blowing in the wind. I pass people and people pass me and we all stay six feet apart, sometimes nodding at each other but more often ignoring or even glaring at one another, suspicious of our viruses. We're all to blame and we all blame each other, the mistrust almost palpable, hanging over us like another virus, invisible but always there.

When I get tired I turn around and come home and take my clothes off and touch all the new dents and protrusions, alone or with my boyfriend; we marvel over all those new wounded surfaces, his body hardening, mine turning into liquid.

It's a beautiful, hazy zombie summer full of tension and pain and badly setting bones.

Pain because although I've been prescribed painkillers I don't take them all the time. I enjoy the rawness of shards grinding against each other—or at least I imagine I can sense it under my skin. I don't feel unhappy or scared; in fact, I feel more level-headed than I have in a long time. Only to myself do I admit my biggest superstition: that demons are attracted to joy; that it's what they feed on. And so I keep both my torment and my joy to myself.

I get a call telling me I have a date and time for a bionic plate that will support all the shattered clavicle bones. I can have it removed after two years.

During my pre-op X-rays I lie flat and stare up at a mural featuring a wild forest and a lake. Is this cruelty or kindness, letting broken people know that there's a world outside these walls they can never reach on crutches or in a wheelchair? I start to think how I'd love to leave here for good one day, how I'm trapped in my addiction and in dust and fumes and the ugliness of the city, how this is yet one more failure in my life, a cultural desert, a constant disappointment of shitty architecture and dysfunctional public transit. It's not just a broken clavicle or a broken sobriety, it's the wrong place, too, and a wrong boyfriend, and my once-promising future that turned the wrong corner a while back when my marriage fell apart and after we lost our house. I feel overwhelmed by my self-pity, brimming with tears that collect in my throat, threatening to burst. I stare at the flat trees and the never-moving paper lake, forcing myself to focus. I focus so hard on that lake that I hear a memory sound, a trembling, wavering call of a loon. A shitty city, a shitty body and mind, but at least I still have one saving grace, which is the ability to delude myself, if only for a brief reprieve.

On the day of the surgery my sister's partner picks me up and drops me off at the eerily empty hospital that, like everywhere else, is under strict lockdown restrictions, void of friends and loved ones. Besides an old man in a hospital bed, attached to various wires and tubes and a beeping monitor, I am alone in the pre-op. I take pictures—of my hand pierced with a catheter secured by medical tape, the linoleum floor, the taped-off chairs, the signs warning us to keep our distance. Always taking pictures. Documenting every moment of my misery. But I am not miserable. Everything is material. Maybe I'll write about this one day and tell the world the truth, which today I am hiding from everyone.

Here's the truth. I drank. Probably before I met my boyfriend at the ferry. I was always buzzed that summer. Sometimes I drank a whole carton of wine on the other side of the lake before getting onto the boat. Sometimes I'd show up early on the island and sit in a park and down a mickey of vodka before seeing him and then I'd gently twist his proverbial arm and we'd have more drinks at the restaurant's tiki bar. It would be fun for an hour or so, all those warm lush evenings, the smell of lilacs, and on the non-lockdown days, when the restaurant itself was open, the chatter of sun-tired beachgoers in flip-flops lining up to get seated. My boyfriend and I in Muskoka chairs on the lawn by the bar, with beers or ciders, watching and occasionally talking to whoever would stop by to say hello, sometimes the mandatory six feet apart but often not. These weren't my friends, nor anyone who knew me as the author of an addiction memoir. The pandemic and social media made it easy to keep tabs on each other, but there was little risk of anyone familiar seeing the poster girl for sobriety having a big ol' drink. When open, the bar was always busy, laughter and buzzed conversations, music playing Top 40 garbage, the island's usual feeling of permanent vacation in the air. Another cider and the day fading into evening, the music a little louder, the laughter more hysterical—theirs or mine, I don't know—and then more cider and the contours of trees, people, my feet, his face, all of it blurring, slowly losing the contours, bleeding into itself, my words gummier and clunkier in my mouth, my hands more erratic, my rage swirling somewhere in my belly, my long hair out and in my face or in his face, my steps stumbly, the stairs steeper, my ankles rubber, a splinter in my palm slipping on the railing, my balance a no balance, the evening a night, the night a pool of liquid no longer distinguishable from the one in my hand, my belly, the lake, the sky. I'm awake and I'm not, am I what? And then I am gone.

That night everything moved even faster than usual; it got too black too quickly.

At some point I got on the bike. I torpedoed ahead. When drunk, I'm often in a war. I challenged my boyfriend to a race except there was no race, just him trying to catch me as I lunged forward. I felt otherworldly, the way alcohol makes me feel sometimes, as though I had special powers, as though my feet were wings. The truth, of course, was that I was a heavily intoxicated forty-three-year-old on a bike in red flats and a princess dress and alcohol was fuelling every cell of my euphoria or my rage, it doesn't matter what you call it. Suddenly my feet did turn into wings but only temporarily as I flew in the air, none of which I remember, just as I don't remember the wings falling off, and then smashing into the concrete, then crawling into a ditch once I'd crashed. Did I crawl into the ditch to die? Die in a ditch—isn't that what happens to drunks?

My boyfriend rode past my abandoned bike near the wall, my body abandoned a few metres away. When he reached the end of the boardwalk he rode back, slowly, this time looking around until he spotted my remains.

He locked my bike and then picked me up and walked-carried me back to the cottage, over the little bridge separating the touristy area from the residential one. He said he walked me along like a puppet, then up the steep stairs to his studio. He sat me in his bed. I was conscious, talking and arguing as he took my clothes off and tried to wash me and dress my wounds. I begged him not to call an ambulance; I knew from experience that I'd have to spend the night in a plastic chair with other drunks in the waiting room instead of staying here and crawling into a nice bed.

This part of the story checks out: it's something I'd definitely suggest. Also, he'd been drinking too—he'd often drink too much to keep up with me—and he was worried about the optics and about my so-called reputation as the author of *Drunk Mom* who'd been officially sober for so many years. I didn't seem too hurt, I talked with him, and I bled and then the bleeding stopped. The point is neither of us was thinking clearly, and he was a man who was only just now realizing he'd been dating Chaos herself. I felt grateful for his acquiescence. I didn't have to fess up to being a drunk; I could continue the lie. The story of a morning ride and a front wheel wedged between two boardwalk planks and an unfortunate but sober impulse that propelled me to smash my body into pieces is the only story told up until now.

This is the real story.

And it's a story about Shame.

4.

I wake up from the surgery refreshed and not in pain. I'd stretch if I could but I can't, what with a shoulder that seems nailed to me like a fucked-up side cross. Everything is numb while at the same time I have a phantom itch that I can't quite pinpoint and that later I won't be able to scratch, ever. Instantly I "feel" the lost sensation in the upper parts of my chest and shoulder, a sensation that, as with the left side of my face, I won't regain for a few years to come. But at that moment I marvel at how nice I feel and how this experience mirrors the one from a few weeks ago, when one moment I was on a bike and the next day I came to in my boyfriend's bed with a broken body.

A nurse pulls a wheeled table in front of me and sets down a tray bearing fussy little containers filled with differently textured and flavoured mush—some kind of pudding, an applesauce—as well as a few crackers and a plastic cup with amber-coloured liquid inside claiming to be apple juice. I love hospital food as much as I love airplane food; I love that someone out there knows exactly what sort of portions are appropriate and nutritious. Besides my inability to stay sober, my other struggle is feeding myself, having spent most of my adult life either forgoing, restricting, or bingeing on food, which has always been another source of shame.[5] There have been many instances in my life when I would arrest my drinking only to switch to disordered eating; I've rarely had a break from both at the same time—a sober day in which I'd eaten three meals and hadn't felt a crushing sense of failure was a rarity for me. The only time I didn't worry about food was when I was pregnant—my body was a vessel for baby's body and I had no right to break it. Right now, I allow myself to ask for extra crackers since I'm coming out of a major surgery with a bionic plate in my shoulder.

When another nurse comes in to tend to me she reports that everything went well. She hands me a package with the dressing change and goes over instructions. I am jolly and talkative. I ask her about working during the pandemic and she patiently agrees that yes, we're all getting traumatized and it's hard to tell the implications yet.

I apologize.

She looks at me with blurry eyes. For what?

[5] There's a strong correlation between body dysmorphia and feelings of shame. People with body dysmorphic disorder (BDD) often experience heightened levels of shame owing to their preoccupation with perceived flaws in their appearance. I was never fat but I was always fat. I grew up in the 90s, on Kate Moss and a gap-between-thighs diet; when I read a feature on bulimia in *Seventeen* magazine at the age of fifteen I saw it not as a warning but rather as instruction. For me, bulimia was the perfect fit as I'm a person with large appetites–for food, for love, for sex, for oblivion–and my need for control clashed with those drives. But in my mind the type of eating disorder I developed wasn't a more noble one–anorexia–where I would've proven I had extreme self-control. Mine was ugly, and synonymous with disgust. I ate shame and I tried to vomit it only to fill up on it the next time.

I think of her Covid days and nights, masks and fear and infection and death. The coughing, sneezing, bleeding, moaning emergency waiting room.

Suddenly my baby sister is here, with those lemur eyes of hers and delicate face and tiny hands and shrinking body. She's lost a lot of weight and her naturally petite frame is even smaller. I get a little shock whenever I see her that summer, once secretly photographing her next to my son who, at eleven, is almost as tall and as heavy as she is, with some vague intention of showing her the pictures one day, which I never do. She says she has "a problem with lymph nodes," which is why she's losing weight so rapidly. I think that, like me, she does weird stuff with food, that she's restricting her eating. I confronted her about it once and have never confronted her again, since I'm the designated family nutbar and, considering my history, should be the last person to say anything. So I never say anything and especially now that she's here to push this wheelchair out of the hospital to the parking lot, where her partner is waiting to pick us up and take me home. I tell her I enjoyed the surgery, and we laugh darkly about doing what we're doing on a perfectly warm, summery evening when we should probably be on a beach somewhere drinking lemonade. We both know that we don't spend perfectly warm, summery evenings together. There was probably a time when we could've become those kinds of sisters but for the past decade or so our roles have switched and although she's younger I'm the one who is the real baby here with my addictions, my relapses, my many shames. I am not someone my sister would want to spend a perfectly warm, summery evening with and you wouldn't either if you were my sister.

I read the notes from the surgery: "The patient was placed supine on the operating table. After undergoing successful general anaesthetic with endotracheal intubation, the patient was positioned into the semi-sitting position."

I imagine getting propped up like a rag doll, my lifeless body being manipulated so that they can further expose me, and not just my nakedness but my viscera, my veins. I imagine a horror scenario with the young resident doctors and nurses looking at my small breasts and snickering; I picture someone lifting my gown to make fun of my vulva. And back further, I think of my boyfriend as he washed my mangled form, angry at what I'd done to myself, perhaps repulsed by the same breasts and vulva, considering the body that promised him pleasure but instead inspired pity.

Asked once what he thinks when he thinks of Shame, my kid replied, "It's getting your pants pulled down in public." And it's true: being seen, inappropriately, by the wrong people under the wrong circumstances is the quintessential experience of Shame. Nakedness and shame are interconnected and have been from the day Eve convinced Adam to bite into the apple in the garden of Eden.

The word shame originates from the Old English *sceamu* or *scamu*, meaning to disgrace or dishonour, and is related to Proto-Germanic[6] *skamo*, which is linked to the concept of covering or hiding. This etymological root suggests an impulse to conceal oneself, particularly the body, in response to exposure or judgment.

[6] Another fun fact: the German word for labia (*Schamlippen*) literally translates as "shame lips."

Similar words denoting this double meaning are also found in other languages, such as the word "aidos," which derives from Aidos or Aedos, the Greek personification of shame, modesty, respect, and humility; its plural form, "aidoia," refers to genitals.

So take this pathetic drunk here, who, subconsciously or not, creates experiences where she's naked—literally and figuratively—and gives up all control; as a result she becomes utterly dependent on others and vulnerable to ridicule. If Shame is a powerful emotion that arises from a sense of personal inadequacy, guilt, or humiliation, I have that in spades. Naked, exposed, a broken puppet—to continually put oneself in situations that reinforce those states is one of the many descriptions of an addict's special brand of insanity.

For the time being I continue to lay off the insanity, if only because I'm too unwell to hurt myself further. The next few weeks are the same as the weeks leading up to the surgery: sober, gentle, slow, and when my boyfriend is around, spent on the mattress that's back on the floor, making love. I'm fascinated by my own fragility, turned on by the intimacy it inspires in us both. He still washes my hair in the sink. I wake up throughout the night and, when it's too hot, move to my spot in the backyard and imagine I'm in the forest somewhere away from it all—and from myself, too. During the day I still walk on train tracks, still take Polaroids of abandoned objects and places. The pandemic naturally lends itself to the liminal-place aesthetic and I no longer have to seek it the way I used to, trying to find abandoned buildings or spaces and posing in front of my camera like an accusation, in various masks and costumes meant to hint at my increasing feeling of isolation.

My son starts staying overnight again, mostly reassured by my physical limitations and by the large dressing covering up my stitches that proves I've been fixed, at least on a surface level. When he's over, I go to bed at the same time as he does and wake up early enough to make breakfast. I still haven't filled my prescription for Percocet and, overall, I feel proud of myself. I'm still keeping my cautious joy secret, still worried the demons will sniff it out. If it could just be like this it would be fine, a new chance. I've said a version of this to myself so many times before that it's hard to take myself seriously, but I do believe I can spellbind my sobriety and make it stick this time. This is also something I've done repeatedly, even though by now surely I've run out of spells just as I've run out of chances with my son. Yet, somehow, my son is back, a child's trust almost impossible to break altogether, even though I've chipped at it enough, eroding his childhood, which, like all childhood, *is* measured in trust. But the spells feel fresh, and I've the fervour of someone newly converted, or just a fervour of early sobriety that in many ways feels like a high, as though I've purified myself with all that alcohol, hollowed out all my transgressions.

Now that I'm empty I can begin again, and I want nothing more than a fresh start. I already have a fresh clavicle, hard and indestructible. In an X-ray you can clearly make out eleven screws holding it in place. The swelling in my face shrinks gradually, the red washes out of my eye, the black around it fades, turns yellow, then it's gone. My skull has fused back to its angular shape. I have not turned ugly, even the chipped cheekbone looks fine, unless I turn a certain way and then you can see the dent.

—

I buy makeup and expensive face creams. I buy a bathing suit and new sandals. I buy a champagne-coloured silk slip that moves like water when I walk.

5.

Sometime in July I book a hotel in the city for me and my son, where he plays in the pool as I sit and take Polaroids of him doing cannonballs.

At night we go out for food and pretend to be tourists here and for once I hate Toronto less, trying to see it through tourist goggles, the heat and the noise welcome now that the latest lockdown has been lifted. Canada in the summer is a whole event, a performance—our winter-exhausted bodies finally free of layers and gloom—with the lucky ones endlessly cottaging and barbecuing for friends or riding the lakes on Jet Skis and in boats. In the city everything is on edge this year, a little too frantic, sparkly; laughter and chatter, music and screeching wheels and buzzing heat; it all matches our giddiness and our nostalgia for a world with vacations in it, and it's a little bit like the old times when we used to travel to Europe, just me and my son and a backpack. In the old life we were the perfect team, taking planes and trains from Warsaw to Stuttgart, to the Baltic seaside or the Tatra Mountains. So many town squares, cathedrals, and castles that to my Canadian son were like magic come to life. Those trips were magical for me, too, breathers and spells that punctuated my difficult life post-separation. I had never fully recovered after my family fell apart and my ex sold our little house—the same house that for a while made it feel as if I'd finally found my place here in this country that had never quite felt like home. But with the entire world in limbo I feel less confused about my own dislocation, now that everyone else seems to feel the same way. A staycation is perfect. My son talks too much and giggles, his joy at this easy treat palpable.

After a walk we return to our hotel and put our bathing suits back on; he cannonballs into the deep end late into the evening, until the pool closes and they kick us out.

The next morning the two of us head to the island to meet up with my boyfriend. We spend a beautiful afternoon on the beach by the lake, the city on the far shore looking like a mirage. My son and my boyfriend are building a new friendship and I feel a fragile tenderness watching them play in the water. We take lots of pictures together. It's been six months since they met and it's the first time my participation isn't necessary for their enjoyment of each other. This warms my heart; in fact, I've been feeling so much happiness and gratitude that it chokes me up watching this new family form in front of my eyes, the loss of the old family finally tolerable with the new hope. They laugh and I laugh. I've let the joy out and damn the demon hounds.

That evening at the island restaurant we order burgers and salads, a round of ginger ales. My son is even more chatty and sunburnt, and my boyfriend and I crinkle our eyes at each other when he's not looking. This is special. Once supper is over the two of them set out for a barbecue in the city. We were all invited but I want to stay on the island and relax, so when my son asked if it was okay to go without me I agreed right away. Let them bond even more. At this point my heart is no longer warm, it is on fire. I haven't felt this happy in a long time.

I'm in the red of happy; the dial is still going and about to burst out of the thermometer. But I don't pay it any attention, I can handle this happiness, I deserve this happiness, I am good with this happiness.

As soon as they leave, I order a bottle of wine.

My son will never stay on Toronto Island with me and my boyfriend again. We add it to the list of places where we'll never go, at least not as whatever configuration we were in when I drank all the joy out of it and turned it into a distorted, trauma version of itself, a dark alternative dimension existing in parallel to the human world.

Sometime mid-week after that night, I get a bill from the Toronto Paramedic Services. I have no recollection of whether I was ferried back to the mainland on the same utility barge they used the morning after my accident. I have no recollection of anything much. It's the same time travel as before: one moment I'm pouring a glass of wine and the next I'm coming to in the ER. I am unattended. I slip out and make my way back to the island. At this point my memory goes in and out of a blackout—here I am nodding off on the ferry; here I am stumbling in the darkness, wet grass, wet-breath night like the inside of a lung; here I am walking up the stairs, here I am. Here I am not.

The one thing I do remember clearly is being unable to look my son in the eye the next morning and then his overly cheerful demeanour throughout the day as we head back to my place, trying to be tourists again, although this time we're all pretending too hard, we're in a play we all put on for each other to avoid mentioning the night before. My son's incessant talking seems forced; I want him to shut up because this is breaking my heart. It's also breaking my heart to write this now.

The next time I get an X-ray it shows that one of the screws in my plate has come loose, probably when I slumped off my chair and landed on the hard stone floor of the patio only metres away from the concrete wall I smashed my face and shoulder into just weeks before.

You've literally got a screw loose, my boyfriend says when I tell him, and neither of us laughs.

6.

At the end of the summer I post a GoFundMe link on my Facebook page for what promises to be expensive dental surgery, several thousand dollars at least.

I'm back on the rickety rollercoaster of sobriety and hurtling inevitably toward a slip. I would like to say that it's up to me to stop this trajectory but it's not up to me; I am strapped and stuck and as days go by I feel more dismissive about my problem. Yes, I want to stay sober forever, but like every alcoholic, sober or not, I'm obsessed with the idea of being able to drink with impunity. Maybe not *all* feel that so close to the surface of their skin—I'm thinking of sobriety dinosaurs with thirty, fifty years clean—and *none* would say they miss it, but all see their life through a prism of a rainbow breaking in a glass. Or more accurately: people who are not alcoholics don't think about alcohol.

And it's not that I consciously try to come up with reasons why I can drink again or even that I crave it, it's that I am . . . romantic. For me, alcohol is a mystery that used to open doors to experiences, to people, to adventure, to love—often, when I think about it, it's not the bad that comes up but the good, or the exciting at least. Romantically, I'm stuck somewhere in my late teens or early twenties, when being buzzed made me more interesting, funnier, sexier, more beautiful. I was always shy,[7] and as it is for many others, alcohol allowed me to break out of my insecurities, at least temporarily. (In that way, I can say that from the beginning I drank because of Shame.)[8]

[7] Also, extremely anxious. Alcohol blocks the GABA (gamma-aminobutyric acid) receptor in the brain, inhibiting the activity of nerve cells. In other words, it calms the mind, reducing the excitement by making fewer neurons fire. By the time you're a few drinks in, it's also said to block glutamate, which is the brain's main excitatory transmitter, controlling anxiety. Less glutamate means less anxiety. The drunker you get, the more blissed out you get. Except the next day when you pay for it twofold—as you stop drinking, your GABA function is at a low and your glutamate spikes, leading to heightened anxiety (and occasionally to seizures). Studies have shown that for heavy drinkers it can take years to return to regular GABA levels—years for their brains to snap back.

[8] Shame is a specific emotional response to a perceived failure or discrepancy between one's idealized self and actual self. Since I aspired to be a person who was comfortable in social situations (my idealized self), my shyness (my actual self) was another source of shame. Shy people fear judgment or criticism from others, leading them to avoid social interactions or to feel uncomfortable in them. For example, I had no idea how to flirt or show interest in a boy, and the thought of kissing one would send me into a state of panic. I wanted to meet boys and I wanted them to like me, but I worried they'd ridicule me and reject me. Using alcohol removed the stress of judgment. I became bold, loud, a daredevil. I got attention and the validation I craved. From that point on my choices were always: avoid or get trashed. It wasn't until my first stint in sobriety, at twenty-seven, that I learned I could engage with people in the way I wanted to engage without completely falling apart. From having dinners with my AA friends to going on my first sober date to posing nude for a fashion shoot, I slowly taught myself how to relax in situations that previously would have required drinking or otherwise made me hyperventilate or bolt.

Not all shy people necessarily experience shame. Shyness can be influenced by a range of factors, including temperament, upbringing, and social experiences. Some shy people may have a healthy self-esteem and a positive self-image, while others, like me, may experience shame as an underlying emotional component of their shyness.

It was alcohol that made my clunky English softer and more seductive; when drunk I felt proud—instead of ashamed—of my accent, played into the Eastern European stereotype of the cold girl, a cigarette between my blood-red lips, unwavering eye contact, a *Killing Eve* assassin on a mission to hang out in a dive with replaceable boys.

It was alcohol that dressed me in fur and tight clothes and painted my eyes and lips and made me bold, made me dance on tables and speakers, made me get into taxis speeding off to after-parties, made me charming. It was alcohol that made me get on a plane to Paris once to spend a few days with a beautiful stranger I'd met in a club who bought me the ticket on a whim, who promised not to touch me unless I wanted to be touched.

It was alcohol long before those Europe trips, too—when I was fifteen and ran after a married man, throwing myself at him with my sweaty teenage body, letting him know I was ready to lose my virginity that night after all, and it was alcohol that made me go to a fancy hotel room with him at the end of an evening at the disco where he'd fed me shots of vodka until my legs turned to jelly.

It was alcohol that redeemed sex for me a year later, alcohol that made me sit on a beach with a boy my age I did want to kiss and who wanted to kiss me, who told me he was in love with me. Later, in the tent, it was alcohol that made me agree we didn't need a condom, and it was alcohol that convinced me there was no other way to prove my love. I proved my love.

It was alcohol that made me date his best friend. And then fall for another boy the next summer after the best friend left. I could not be alone for more than a week or two, and as long as there was alcohol, there was . . . love.

More accurately: every lover was a bottle. All I ever wanted was to have love. All I ever wanted was to drink. Do you see how hard—how impossible—it would've been to get what I wanted without it?

It was alcohol that introduced me to the future father of my son. We lived out our romantic, intense, sexual love story; there were techno clubs, galleries and dinner parties and cottages, and a broken heel after I kicked a wall as we fought in the street, the snow falling, the sharp winter air in my nose.

It was a love story destroyed by alcohol.

It was alcohol that mercifully took me out when I didn't know how to handle his numerous betrayals.

It was alcohol that helped me not think about everything alcohol took from me. Because it always helped me deal with what it destroyed. Eventually the line blurred, destruction and salvation forever intertwining in the same glass or bottle—one that, as time went on, I had to hide more often as it became obvious that destruction was winning, that my nostalgia was my downfall, that my romantic nature was nothing but my alcoholic nature.

Because every alcoholic is a romantic.

I know all that and yet I can't help feeling nostalgic as I pass clusters of hipsters drinking IPAs in a park near my apartment, making it all look so carefree and cool. I've never drunk IPAs with hipsters in my life—it would be torture to have to pace my monster thirst like that—and yet I feel I've missed out terribly.

Still, I stay tied to the mast; I ignore alcohol's siren song, my bionic shoulder proof that if I let myself listen to it I'll fall and shatter.

But it's hard to ignore it entirely. And there seems to be more of it than ever before. The jokes about the pandemic inducing everyone to drink too much are true, meaning I'm stressed every time I leave the house but also somehow relieved that I'm no longer the only one who struggles. Everyone drinks in secret now, hiding: whether from themselves, or lovers hiding from lovers, or parents hiding from children, everyone cooped up in their fortresses, leaving only to line up at the liquor store—it's New Year's Eve every day, the lineups snaking round corners, but the eyes are darting, holiday camaraderie not a part of this deal. This deal is a back alley transaction, hands shook and shaking.[9]

When the restrictions loosen up most restaurants set out tables on the sidewalk; whenever I walk around downtown it feels like stepping into the steady current of an alcoholic river, glasses and bottles and pints all floating by. I used to joke about how one never just walks into a bottle of vodka; you have to make the effort to procure it. Now it's like being in a video game trying not to touch poisonous objects that keep popping up everywhere as you go. And it all looks

[9] Google any statistics about alcohol and drug consumption during the pandemic and you'll see. Here's one: in the U.S., "a 2021 National Library of Medicine study shows a 23 percent increase in alcohol abuse and a 16 percent increase in drug abuse for people who had consumed those substances before the pandemic. People in self-isolation reported a 26 percent higher consumption than they would normally use to cope." It's not just alcoholics who are trying to cope, it's almost half of us: four in ten as reported in my city, Toronto. This also tells you all you need to know about the relationship between trauma and drinking.

so pretty and European. I'm constantly reminded of my native Poland, my "romantic" sickness spreading inside my shattered and unbroken bones, those memories of every sexy, boozy summer activated again, every block I drank through, every sidewalk table I sat at, surrounded by crowds of beautiful sweaty strangers, our youth infinite . . . at least for the night, now resurrected and shimmering like ghosts. And I am thirsty in my soul and the thirst clenches it tighter and tighter.

I'm barely holding on to my private rollercoaster's safety rail. I'm sober but shakily sober.

The truth is I don't require either triggers or excuses to heed my calling; as I move through the summer, it's just a matter of time—days or hours or minutes even . . . soon it will be like this:

Now I am here.

The next moment I will be coming to.

7.

Every night I check the GoFundMe page, but as money accumulates the rising amount parallels the guilt I feel. A dignity, a dollar. I didn't lie about my injuries but I whitewashed my dirty story. In it, I'm a victim of terrible luck and a few bad decisions but none of them corrupt, which is how we see drinking too much—as a moral failing. I've told people about wearing the wrong shoes, riding a bike in a dress, going too fast. But it's as if I put my audience into a selective, collective half blackout and they're missing the most important details. I rattled my head and my teeth in it but not because I unscrewed the red plastic cap of a Smirnoff mickey. There was no plastic cap of a Smirnoff mickey. I merely miscalculated a step, although not the first step I made in the direction of a liquor store. Because let's be honest: Would anyone donate a cent knowing I'd smashed into that wall while drunk? Would *I* donate to someone like me? I probably would not. I'd want them to learn a lesson. If they have to lose teeth maybe that's what needs to happen. Tough love. I've gone from manipulating my loved ones to manipulating strangers. It's been five years since my first relapse—five years that could be divided into elevations and dips, sober, drunk, sober, drunk, the rollercoaster speeding faster, the sober periods shorter until I'm reduced to days and not months, until one week feels like a monumental achievement.

I'm on week four, walking around not sober but drink-free, what's known in recovery circles as "dry drunk." I'm carrying all those lies on my fucked-up shoulders and nobody sees this weight crushing me. Sometimes, at night especially—when my guilt[10] is

[10] Guilt and shame are intrinsically connected. But whereas guilt is associated with a sense of personal responsibility for a specific behaviour or action perceived as morally or socially inappropriate—here it's me feeling the ick over the GoFundMe fibbing—shame is a more global evaluation of the self. Guilt is often accompanied by remorse and a desire to make amends or correct the wrongdoing, but when people internalize and personalize their feelings of guilt, attributing them to their core identity rather than specific actions, those feelings can develop into shame. My guilt over lying to people is proof that I'm inherently an awful, deceiving person—an alcoholic who pretends to be sober and whose ongoing deception is required to maintain that lie. My desire to walk into traffic stems from wanting to stop feeling guilty, but it's also a misguided fantasy of atoning for what I feel guilty about. I could, of course, come out and say that I drank and had an accident, but that would mean admitting to a much larger lie (that I've been sober) and the risk of getting ridiculed and shunned.

too much—I want to run into the busy road in front of my house and scream into oncoming traffic, taking my chances, hoping for it to end. This isn't just me being dramatic—I frequently fantasize about some drastic action that would stop the torment. Another fantasy, less bloody, involves leaving the house in a nightgown and walking barefoot like a lunatic into the night until someone stops me, takes me away, saves me from myself. What a relief that would be—to be properly certified and locked up so that I could finally have some peace, just me and my lies and my delusions and none of those mental gymnastics I need in order to avoid imploding from Shame.

For now, I'm a quieter kind of crazy. Maybe a cutter. Yes, I'm a cutter cutting myself up on the inside, the cuts dividing me not just from others but also from myself.

The pandemic means a lot more unhoused people are visible in the streets, and when I pass them I feel rage. Not because of their unfortunate circumstances and not because the world is falling apart and they're the most obvious proof. But because I'm jealous. No one expects anything from them anymore; we've given up on them or they've given up on themselves. We leave them alone. Isn't indifference true freedom; theirs, ours?

This realization hits me as I hide in a doorway, frozen in a strange trance, near a Starbucks on Front Street, at the foot of the city. It's a beautiful day. Sun, sundresses, sun-kissed hair, the heat broken by an evening breeze.

I've just spent hours talking with an old friend, and then we wrote side-by-side—she her novel, I pretending to do the same—as though I'm normal and this is what I do on the regular, meet with friends to write.

Front Street is dangerous. At some point the usual map flashed in my head, and on this map is a red dot that alerts me to the liquor store just a few blocks away. I always feel some anxiety when I'm in an unfamiliar neighbourhood, the liquor stores like beacons, or better, like tourist attractions I must check out. In the state I'm in that day the imaginary red dot is mocking my sobriety, calling me, the compulsion to go so intense that my skin itches.

After we walked out of Starbucks my friend was talking, possibly making plans to meet again, but I couldn't quite hear. I watched her mouth move and guessed my responses. Words words words. My skin wasn't just itchy, now it was crawling. I really had to go. We said our goodbyes—hurry, hurry—and I walked away fast.

And then I stopped. I saw *him*.

And now there he is, his huge, sweaty form curled up around a parking meter, his ass crack peeking out of oily, dirty jeans, no shoes. At first I want to go up to him and see if he's okay but he's okay—I watch as he briefly flips over onto his back and his face is shiny, eyes closed but mouth open and black. He opens his eyes and they swim briefly, then go blank again. He turns back onto his side. I stand and watch him, feel the tension accumulate somewhere in my core, the realization nailing me to my spot in the dark doorway where I ducked to be able to see him better.

The liquor store is only a couple of hundred metres away.

That day I don't go. But it's not the sight of him that stops me; I don't see him as a warning. What I see when I look at him is freedom. An absolute and final fuck-you to the world, shamelessly mooning us all just as we deserve. I don't go because I still think there's another way to be free, although I'm pretty sure that the more Shame I feel, the more I'm moving away from that freedom. And the only way to feel less Shame is to stop moving but I can't because I'm running away from it too.

I write a sad update on my recovery from the surgery and post a picture of a perfect smile (not mine). For contrast, I post another picture—of my face that first week, my black-and-blue eye with that block-like jaw. When I first set up the GoFundMe page it took only hours to collect more than half my goal—my story resonated with people; I can write pretty sentences. The money keeps coming. Some of the donations are anonymous but many aren't. A former friend and her husband donate $100 along with well wishes. My discomfort deepens when I read her name under the donation. I want to send the money back but I don't know how. This is someone who stopped being a friend over petty jealousies. But what really pisses me off about her now is that she was always on me for my drinking; that she predicted four years before my accident that I would die from alcohol; that I now suspect she was right. And my GoFundMe proves it. I bet she can read between the lines of my front-wheel-caught-in-the-boardwalk lie. If we were still friends she wouldn't be convinced of my story. The $100 mocks me; it's as if she paid for front-row tickets to the Jowita Clown Show. I send a thank-you note and I never hear back.

Another friend sends $1,000, and when I object she makes fun of how well she's getting paid for not doing anything (this isn't true;

she's a lawyer working in child welfare) and jokes about my shitty luck. She's trying to make it seem as if it's a normal thing to drop a grand on a personal charity case. My hands shake when I try to text her back in the same jokey manner, and I'm funny and I'm dead serious and I wish I could just die, that this would stop, the guilt and the generosity of others. Maybe because of the amount I want to tell her the truth, offer her at least that as a repayment, but I lose my nerve; I need the money. The money shuts me up and I'm humbled by her generosity—I'm humbled by everyone's generosity.

Humbled or humiliated, it's the same to me. An arts organization helping artists in medical emergencies writes to say they're going to match the donation—the news of my accident has now spread across the country.

My lie has become a national cause.

I develop a chronic stress headache, my temples tight and throbbing, keeping me up at night. Some mornings I'm almost delirious from exhaustion and humbleness.

Besides the headaches, I'm often nauseous or worse, barely in control of my bowels, which loosen every time I open the GoFundMe page to check the progress. I sit on the toilet often, trying to shit out my Shame. I'm losing weight rapidly, my face the opposite of swollen now; it's shrinking, dull skin draping over bone. My eyes are haunted when I actually manage to look at myself; most of the time it's too much; I feel as though I've got nowhere to hide from me. I joke to my boyfriend that I look like one of those decorative Mexican skulls. When I walk or sit my muscles are tense, something I tell myself is from the accident. But that's not why.[11] I'm always drawing in my shoulders and rounding my back, trying to make myself smaller as the charity money pile grows bigger.

And then, one morning, I wake up after another chaotic two-hour sleep, covered in raised red, painful bumps that won't go away—they're spread in long clusters on my chest, my belly, and in the groin area as well. I Google my symptoms, immediately accuse my boyfriend of cheating, and set up an emergency appointment with my physician. My boyfriend is baffled and jokes how it would be physically impossible even if he wanted to be unfaithful, since he's with me 24-7 and technically there's a lockdown. It doesn't matter; I need something like this flash-flood fight to wash out the tension. I shout at him a little, without conviction, then give up, the accumulated pain doubling me over, putting me in my place. I rarely raise my voice and we don't fight that often, so it's almost as if I'm trying it on for size. Not for the first time I catch myself

[11] One study examining the association between shame and physical health outcomes found that people who reported higher levels of shame also reported poorer overall physical health, increased symptoms of physical illness, and higher levels of pain. (Guilt, meanwhile, was not significantly associated with these outcomes.)

Another study also found that higher levels of shame were significantly correlated with poorer self-rated health, higher levels of bodily pain, and more physical symptoms. The study suggests that chronic experiences of shame may have a detrimental impact on overall physical health.

A third study examined the effects of shame on cardiovascular health, assessing shame proneness and cardiovascular reactivity in response to stress. The findings revealed that those with higher levels of shame proneness exhibited greater cardiovascular reactivity, including higher blood pressure and heart rate, during stress-inducing tasks. Chronic experiences of shame, then, may contribute to cardiovascular health risks.

thinking we're only playing a couple, that in reality we're just two strangers stuck together because of sex and the pandemic: that we're toxic and perfectly matched in our toxicity.

We call an Uber and sit in the back seat without talking all the way to the doctor's office. Continuing with my angry-wife performance, I act out a loud angry silence, as if I did indeed discover him with another woman. He strokes my arm once, gingerly with love, and I swat at it gently. He chuckles. There's something dog-like about my boyfriend's insistence on helping me, or maybe it's his having grown up with two people who drank through his childhood and taught him how to disconnect and hide in plain sight. He is the perfect boyfriend for this addict, unwavering in his support, or . . . maybe just enabling me. Right now I'm in no emotional or mental condition to be able to see how much we're hurting each other; we probably mistake our desperation for love.

The doctor runs tests and double-checks my current medications, which I haven't been taking in my deluded repentance, in my attempt to stay clinically, martyr-level sober. We talk about the past two months. At this point in my life as an alcoholic I'm an expert in reporting some facts while omitting others with a high ethanol percentage. This is a skill many addicts possess—knowing how to navigate conversations with doctors,[12] whom we tend to see often owing to our wobbly disposition.

[12] For those doctors who deal with addicts, someone needs to develop an app that could interpret the meaning behind these patients' more common complaints or explanations.

- "I have really bad insomnia" = "I drink in the evenings and pass out, mistaking that for sleep. I suddenly come to at two a.m., stone-cold sober and withdrawing."

When nothing shows up in the first round of tests, she tells me that stress—cortisol and adrenalin—tends to weaken the immune system and can often cause changes in the skin. In the second round of tests, she checks for the varicella-zoster virus, VZV, which is responsible for shingles. Since I had chicken pox in my teens, it's possible that the virus remained dormant in the nerve tissue near the spinal cord and brain, and that my weakened immune system triggered its reactivation.

Bingo.

- "I'm really anxious in the mornings" = "I've an increased heart rate, restlessness, irritability, and general feelings of unease due to acute alcohol withdrawal."
- "I'm feeling depressed" = "I've been drinking to cope with my pain and alcohol has disrupted my brain chemistry, leading to chronic inflammation in the brain that worsens my depressive symptoms."
- "I'm under a lot of stress" = "Alcohol has dysregulated the hypothalamic-pituitary-adrenal (HPA) axis system in my brain, which is responsible for elevating my body's stress response."

I know that doctors are trained to gather information about a patient's history, symptoms, and behaviours to make informed diagnoses and treatment decisions. They ask open-ended questions, use validated screening tools, and observe physical and behavioural signs that may indicate substance abuse or addiction, but they also understand that patients may intentionally or unintentionally withhold or misrepresent information about their addiction, whether from fear, shame, denial, or the desire to maintain access to medication. And, unlike me, doctors can't project their own personal hangups; they have to give their patients the benefit of the doubt and consider all possible explanations. But I'm just saying: addicts are brilliant manipulators. I've sat in many doctors' offices feigning bafflement over things like anxiety attacks and easy bruising. I once assembled a whole team of fascinated neurologists who couldn't figure out the reasons for my ataxia—a group of disorders that affect coordination, balance, and speech—which was a result of mixing benzodiazepines with diet pills in an attempt to cope with a traumatic event while avoiding *drinking* drinking.

Or, you know, that time I smashed into a concrete wall on *a morning bike ride because of shitty shoes.*

It's rare to get blisters in the groin area, but that summer I win several unusual prizes in the medical lottery. The shingles are mild and relatively manageable, or I just manage to manage; it blends in with all my other distresses. I have an inhuman tolerance for discomfort; there's something about finding safety in what you know, and what I know is misery.

I adjust my story of shingles to fit the ongoing narrative and tell people the rash was due to delayed trauma from the accident. The friend who sent $1,000 marvels at the shittiness of my luck again. I can't repay her but I'm glad that at least I'm entertaining. I imagine I make good fodder for dinner party conversation, although given the pandemic I don't know who's having those these days. Still, as the world gets smaller we all fixate on whatever's at hand; we all become gossips. I work on my accident story day and night, polishing corners, adding little touches here and there. I build a little shrine of it, and in the middle there's me and my lying, tired, sugarskull face.

8.

Do I drink because I'm a romantic?

Do I drink because I'm an alcoholic?

Or do I drink because it's fun? (As much fun as a rollercoaster. As much fun as a rollercoaster that doesn't stop.)

Do I drink because I'm in pain and because I'm exhausted and need to sleep and need to check out and not think?

Because I need to die a little more, hide better than I can while sober, hide all the way at the bottom, where nothing and no one can reach me, not even my own conscience?

Or do I drink because it's hot outside and I kind of like my sugarskull face and I have a champagne-coloured silk dress? And because sometimes I feel manically happy for no reason I can decipher, an unearned euphoria that kicks in randomly despite all the shit and stress, or even because of the contentment that—in that moment I do not recognize—happens because I'm sober? Do I drink because—because I just drink, because that's what a person like me does, breaks out in drinks; that's what sits dormant in us like the varicella-zoster virus of the soul tissue?

As a journalist, I once interviewed the author and addiction expert Dr. Gabor Maté about the words we use to describe ourselves. We were sitting in a small room in my publisher's office, me fidgeting with the recording app on my phone, trying to pay attention despite my nervousness as he calmly answered my questions about addiction and guilt and labels and love. He was relaxed and serene, his gaunt, lined face tired but soft somehow, his large, deeply set eyes unwavering and patient as I stuttered, suddenly too aware of my chaotic energy, my inadequacy in the presence of a great mind.

Finally I asked him what he thought of the word "alcoholic." He answered immediately and with a question, the way he answered all my queries, challenging each one as if they were little puzzles to solve that I'd gone about in the wrong way. It was frustrating and illuminating, but before I figured out his style I felt as if I were stupid, possibly wasting his time. *Oh the wise one!* I rolled my eyes internally. I wanted the interview to be over; I was not worthy. I was sweating, overwhelmed by talking to the man who understood more about addiction than I ever could, whose book on the subject

I once used like a weapon to quote from and defend my inability to stop drinking. Reading his book was the only time I felt that my addiction wasn't a moral failing, that I could be forgiven.

And now that we were here he was forgiving me one more time. "But why define somebody even if they stand up and say, 'I'm so-and-so and I'm an alcoholic'?" he said. "That's just a behaviour they indulged in because they were in too much pain. So it would be a whole lot better for somebody to stand up and say, 'My name is so-and-so and I have so much pain in my life and I didn't know how to deal with it. So I've been using alcohol to escape from the pain and I have been doing it for a long time.' That would be more accurate."

From where I'm writing this, I know that that summer I was in pain, but not from smashing into a cement wall—no. The pain came from within, and I drank over it the way I drank over it every other time.

9.

But what kind of pain exactly? What is the thing or things that happened to me that made me want to escape so badly that I'd risk my health and my life to do it repeatedly?

Does it matter? Almost no one escapes trauma. My childhood in Poland was traumatic. My parents were unhappy in Canada, and because of it, abusive. I met some weak men who liked to prey on vulnerable women.

What matters is that *I* was the one responsible for my demise. When I joke about never having walked into a bottle of vodka, what I really mean is that there was never a time when I drank by accident and there was never a time when I was forced to drink until I got drunk. Every time I let my feet walk me toward the red-capped bottle it was my brain that sent them the signals to do so. Not once had my feet been operated remotely by goblins and tricked into changing direction.

I know I was in the washing machine of bad choices and bad outcomes that led me to those bad choices but I refuse to believe that there was ever a point when I had no choice.

This is good news.

Because if I'm the one responsible for my demise, it also means that I'm the one responsible for my salvation.

10.

I don't like the dictionary definition of relapse—"a deterioration after a temporary period of improvement"—because it's a lot more complex than falling into old habits, and "improvement" can't be dismissed so easily just because it's interrupted. Recovery isn't a linear journey. You can't dismiss what you've learned already, even though you might've forgotten momentarily—sobriety is a marathon, not a sprint, and for most of us it means having to build up muscle before we can run its full course.

But a relapse is always dangerous, whether it happens once or twenty times, and not just because it can end your life (behind the wheel, on a subway platform, at home in the bathtub) but because it fortifies the parts of you that are the most self-destructive. For an addict, a relapse is a threat to their very identity. Repeated relapses bolster that threat—and addicts are people who like repetition.

We're also extreme people: black or white, zero to a hundred, no middle ground. That's why even one relapse might suggest to us that we're a catastrophic failure. It's evidence that yes, you were able to recover despite the odds but it's also proof that it was all for naught because there you are, defeated again, unworthy of your own efforts and the people who supported you. If you relapse, you're a relapser, and if you relapse like me you're a chronic relapser. And for those of us who've relapsed while under the aegis of the twelve steps, there's also this, from *Alcoholics Anonymous* (nicknamed *The Big Book of Alcoholics Anonymous*), read out at the beginning of most non-secular meetings: "Those who do not recover are people who cannot or will not completely give themselves to this simple program, usually men and women who are constitutionally incapable of being honest with themselves. There are such unfortunates. They are not at fault; they seem to have been born that way."

I've been in recovery for twenty years and have never stopped wondering if I'm one of those "constitutionally incapable" individuals; if I am, in fact, doomed because I was "born that way." I'm sober now, and yet since 2006, when I first went to AA, I've declared "This is the last time" on almost two dozen occasions.

But who cares what AA has to say, right? Except that AA says: only those who do the program recover. To me this reads as "AA or death." And for me, not being able to do AA successfully is another source of shame. On the other hand, this is a conundrum only for me and anyone else who went to AA in the first place, since the people who do recover without it[13] have no idea that supposedly only AA can help them do so. In this way, what they don't know doesn't hurt them; actually, it's the opposite. Ignorance is bliss.

There is one element, though, that unites *all* recoveries: other people. Even in a place like non-secular AA—where members are urged to find God in order to achieve sobriety—skeptics are encouraged to see the Higher Power as the connections we make while there. (In AA this is sometimes referred to as *group consciousness*.)

Hope is the other thing we all have—it's there the moment the idea of recovery pops into your head for the first time.

Hope and people are what will get you to and through the doors of recovery—whether that's a door to rehab, to a church basement, or to a hospital room—*repeatedly*.

In the context of addiction, the mystery of the Higher Power is solved once you realize that the only way to rid yourself of Shame—which lies at the core of all addiction—is to share it with others.

I keep coming back to AA[14] because it's where I tried to get sober for the first time and where I know most people stay sober. So

[13] While AA has been a valuable support system for many, it's not the only approach to recovery. Various alternatives and methods—professional counselling, therapy, support from friends and family, self-help programs, treatment centres—have also assisted people in achieving sobriety. Given the variety of available methods, and the decentralized nature of recovery in general, it's challenging to accurately determine the number of people who recover from alcohol addiction without the specific aid of AA. For now, AA is the most popular and most studied program of recovery, although it's not without controversy.

[14] Despite the many criticisms leveled at it, AA is still by far the most successful in helping people get sober. At the time of my relapse, in 2020, a new meta study—comparing thirty-five other studies—from Stanford University had just been released, showing AA to be at least 60 percent more effective than any other intervention.

it's familiar to me, and the perfect place to practise not only connecting with people—subconsciously ridding myself of Shame—but also developing faith that what I hope for is possible.

And any recovery plan that allows for all those things to happen—hoping, connecting, believing—is a good plan.

Beyond AA, the medical field and addictions research claim that relapses[15] are part of the whole deal. They're also addiction's most inconvenient aspect, one that gets trumped only by death. Furthermore, relapse interrupts our favourite narrative of addiction: the story of redemption. I was a bad girl and now I'm a good girl and all of you watching can not only root for me but also use my example to help yourselves. Sober addicts are heroes: their stories strengthen our faith in humanity; they're the modern prodigal sons and daughters. Look at them go, with their oat-milk lattes, their meditating and their yoga, their winning their families back and restarting their careers and becoming Oprah Winfrey!

A nice addiction story allows a bit of room for a relapse, but a repeated relapse is a lot less cute. I don't get to add chapters to my

[15] Addiction is a complex and chronic condition that involves changes in the brain's reward and motivation systems. Studies suggest that relapse rates for substance use disorders can range from 40 to 60 percent within the first year of recovery (and some estimates place this number much higher, at 90 percent). Relapse is viewed as a temporary setback rather than a sign of failure.

Research also suggests that factors such as stress, social environment, co-occurring mental health conditions, and inadequate coping skills can increase the risk of relapse. Finally, individual factors like motivation and readiness for change play a significant role in maintaining sobriety, which complicates things if you think about it because it's not as if we addicts don't want to live and don't want to change, but rather that, just like anyone else, life sometimes gets in our way.

memoir as I fall and get up.[16] I've used up everyone's patience already by admitting to being a drunk mom—so to come back and tell you that the bow we've wrapped my story with unravelled not just once but multiple times? I'm also aware of the responsibility implied in putting out a book with a happy ending (albeit a realistic one—I never promised I'd *stay* sober).

Yet I'm here to tell you that a repeated relapse story can be a recovery story. You can decide whether my story is worth your attention, knowing very well that I drank—again and again—after I told the world I was done drinking. Stubborn as I am, all I know is that the help offered in places like AA, where there are other people, is precisely what gets people like me better. And it's not about the program itself, or what's wrong with it and what's right—it's about giving yourself a chance, *again*.

11.

At this point in my story, no one's celebrating when I get those few pathetic stretches of sobriety either. If you have an addict in your life who's like me, I know your heart has been broken so many times that you can't will it to open once more. Where's the guarantee that

[16] And I'm aware of AA's rules and warnings about being anonymous "at the level of press, radio and film" because each public relapse means bad press for the establishment. I'm not a spokesperson for AA and have never claimed to be, and yet my having relapsed after telling the world I got sober with its help could possibly mean that there's something wrong not just with me but with the help I received. This is how it was explained to me by some of the old-timers who were against public declarations of sobriety. Except, remember, for me AA is also the only place where I do get sober.

it won't be broken however many more times in the future? You feel angry about your naïveté, you blame yourself for your love and your desire to help, and you hate how your addict has robbed you of goodness, how they made you build an armour that stifles your movement, how they turned you into someone you're not—perhaps even a person you feel ashamed of.[17]

Although there could be a celebration. If I were to get serious about being sober again, I could rise up from my seat in an AA meeting, march in front of the entire room of (how I think of them: *smug*) alcoholics, and get my twenty-four-hour chip, a token signifying my desire to stop drinking again.

Were I to take that token, everyone would clap and congratulate me; there'd be hoots and hollers and fellow alcoholics shaking my hand as I return to my chair, cheeks burning. The first couple of times I did this it was special; I felt proud. My son was there when I got one after coming back from my most infamous relapse. He took one of his first walks in an AA meeting room, there was something profound about both of us starting anew there.

Officially, the ritual is meant to mark an alcoholic's new beginning, the token something they can put in their wallet so that the next time they reach into it to peel out a tenner as they stand in a liquor

[17] But helping can turn into enabling when the line between supporting and prolonging gets blurred. At first you offer assistance, guidance, and encouragement to someone in need, but the dynamics shift when you begin shielding the person from the negative consequences of their actions, unintentionally reinforcing their harmful behaviour and perpetuating a cycle of dependency. Never mind how duped you feel when you realize you've been deceived or tricked, with all the embarrassment and self-blame that follow.

store lineup, they'll hopefully remember their humbling march and the cheers of those in the room. They will recoil and run.

Getting the chip is a small act of courage and a show of commitment. But for me, over the years, it has become something else—a reminder that I'd failed once again, that I couldn't commit.

Every time I had to march in front of people it was nothing but a walk of Shame. I did not feel proud. I didn't want to be accountable. Please for fuck's sake stop clapping. For me, the twenty-four-hour chip became one more deterrent to coming back.

It's been a while since I picked up a chip. But even if I had, there's no lucky amulet to protect me as I walk home one day and for no particular reason keep walking past my street until I hit the red dot on my internal map. There's a lineup but it's not bad. Here too I perform a walk of Shame, except no one knows me as I snatch the familiar red-capped bottle, my heart pounding in my ears as I approach the cashier. Bag? No bag. Receipt? No thank you. (No evidence, no crime. Clean getaway.)

It will go how it always goes: I'll drink without a mixer. I no longer perform my old rituals, designed as they were to pretend this isn't what it is. There's no point in stopping, mixing, sipping. I don't want to walk around carrying this thing, worrying about where to dispose of it, obsessing over whatever little amount is left as I divide it into two gulps. That's another thing: I get the smallest mickey because I have some kind of delusion that I'm sick and this is medicinal, that I just need a little pick-me-up. With my prize I'll duck into one of the alleys—always empty these days—or a public washroom if I'm near one, and then I'll gulp my first gulp. My second an hour later, or sooner. If it's during the day and it's nice, I'll walk. If I'm near a park I'll go to the park. If I'm suddenly feeling social I'll make a call.

As it always has, alcohol makes me feel *more than*: more than me, more than happy, and later, more than sad. Something unlocks inside me—my drawn-in shoulders relax, my body warms up, occasionally there's a gentle pulse between my legs, everything softens and goes electric. The colours sharpen, the dust from the street disappears, the pulse spreads, my hips like butterfly wings, my step bouncy and light, and suddenly I'm in a movie about a pretty artist wanderer, shot on 8 mm film, and even God loves me. For at least thirty minutes the world is perfect; I want to be in it, lull myself inside its safe, muscular arms, or make out with it and tell it how I didn't mean all those things I said.

More often than not, at some point I go and get another mickey. The first one helps make this step smoother, and the second helps elevate me higher, although I always crash.

I won't bore you with too many details of my drinking gymnastics. I don't remember specific instances unless something happened and most of the time nothing happens. I just get drunk, stay up too late, talk to friends I normally feel too anxious to call, or force my boyfriend to entertain me, which means going on late walks "for a drink" if places are open.

There's also my son but he stays with me only half the week, which means I won't do this every day, which means that for a while I can tell myself this isn't a relapse; in fact, I consider myself to be sober. I tell myself every day that tomorrow I'll stop and when I don't stop I tell myself that tomorrow I will. I haven't exactly relapsed yet.

Except, of course, I have. At this point in the story I see my latest relapse as a weakness, as cowardice, as proof of a lack of character. It's all inexplicably connected to Shame.

Shame is often referred to as "inner torment," often in relation to a failure to cope successfully with a challenge. It's been said that it's also the most central affect[18] in the development of identity. A person with Shame, like the person I was in 2020, is a person who's strengthening an identity that tells me I'm inferior, that unlike many of my peers who've gotten sober—and unlike many of the readers of my first memoir—there's something wrong with me because I can't *get* this thing. I wrote about it, I talked about it, I paraded it around like a proud parent. And yet.

This is beyond the feeling of being faulty that many addicts often talk about (a popular line in AA is about being "born without the proper instruction manual"). I've had twenty years of reading that manual and following its instructions, and yet I keep failing, over and over.

[18] In psychology, "affect" refers to the subjective experience of emotion or feeling, often described as the immediate and direct experience of emotions such as happiness, sadness, anger, fear, or disgust. It involves the internal experience of emotions as well as their outward expression through facial expressions, body language, and vocal tone. Affect plays a crucial role in human behaviour, cognition, and interpersonal relationships, and is studied to understand emotional states, mood disorders, and emotional well-being.

12.

We may not be born with it, but research shows that babies as young as six months experience shame. No one is immune to it, which isn't a bad thing—healthy shame is part of the moral compass[19] that helps us coexist with our fellow human beings and navigate social interactions.

In psychology, it's viewed as an emotion intrinsically connected to stages of development. For example, the first shame is evidence of having formed a healthy attachment, as when a baby averts their eyes when seeing an unfamiliar face. Up to that point, the baby has known only their caretakers, and this reaction signals that they've formed their first emotional bond—a precursor to trust, which is crucial to our survival. The strange face triggers shyness, an expression of shame; it signals caution and establishes a boundary. With time, most little humans begin to grasp the concept of autonomy and independence, and with it they begin to understand how their actions affect others, and they learn to react to the reactions they receive. In later years, shame can also prompt self-reflection, empathy, and growth when people recognize and take responsibility for things they do.

The most overt and recognizable expression of shame is the hiding of eyes, meant to guard a child against being seen. It's not

[19] Healthy shame arises when we violate our own moral code or engage in behaviours that are harmful to ourselves or others. It can serve as a signal that we need to reflect on our actions and make changes to prevent similar situations from occurring in the future. However, if we rely too heavily on shame alone to guide our behaviour, it can develop into self-criticism and negativity, which can turn toxic. Exercising for your health is a great thing, but working out obsessively—and begrudgingly—to align with unrealistic, even draconian beauty standards is something else entirely.

how becoming invisible works exactly, but it's an attempt at it—becoming unseen—and at avoiding the pain of shame. Nor is it exclusive to children; we all avert our eyes when we're ashamed. And for many the overt display of shame occurs on or around one's face—not just looking away but also blushing, along with burning of the cheeks and eyes. It's no wonder shame is sometimes referred to as "losing face," as it literally distorts it.

As they age, children test behaviours that elicit praise or punishment and learn to internalize their feelings—this is where "I did a bad thing" can sometimes turn into "I am a bad thing." Not all guilt turns into shame, of course—most childhood shame teaches us about the limits of our behaviour; learning to become a social creature means learning about shame.[20] Charles Darwin believed that

[20] I frequently find my dog Misiu's little bed filled with impressive collections of random items—underwear, hats, shoes, his own harness, my son's dirty socks—whatever he's able to reach and whatever has a smell. "What did you do?" will often elicit the most impressive display of Shame—averted eyes, giant ears folded, and pancaking or cowering, trying to make himself smaller. Yet research has asserted that shame is primarily a human construct. Although dogs are capable of experiencing a range of emotions—happiness, fear, excitement, even guilt to some extent—the specific emotion of Shame is not something they possess.

I want to agree to disagree—social media is littered with reels of golden retrievers feeling (?) horrible about sinning; my own dog will often do his version of tiptoeing while looking guilty, which is what usually alerts me to a new "collection." There are even "dog-shaming" websites where featured dogs wear written "confessions" next to the damage they've caused. But apparently, when a dog exhibits such behaviours as lowering their head or slinking away it's usually a response to the owner's reaction rather than a genuine feeling of shame.

A study conducted by Alexandra Horowitz, a cognitive scientist and dog behaviour expert, explored how dogs respond when they're caught disobeying a command. The study involved training dogs to leave a desirable treat and then tempting them with the treat while the owner was out of the room. When the owners returned and

blushing was what separated us from all other animals, and thus defined our humanity ("Blushing is the most peculiar and most human of all expressions"). And yet, even something as innocent as blushing can lead to distress when there's too much of it, further developing into anxiety when we're unable to control it. Underlying its crippling effect is the fear of being exposed or being inappropriately seen by other people. And so, without positive outside feedback, even the healthiest shame can grow cancerous; shame begets Shame.

Shame is a universal feeling, present in all cultures, although not all consider shame to be an individual thing. In Mexico, China, and India, for example, shame is associated with cultural values; conforming to those values helps one avoid feelings of shame. Those who misbehave bring shame not only to themselves but also their communities. Consider "honour killings"[21]—where in order to save

---

discovered that the treat was gone, they were instructed to act in one of three ways: scold the dog, act neutrally, or display positive reinforcement. "I found that the 'look' appeared most often when owners scolded their dogs, regardless of whether the dog had disobeyed or did something for which they might or should feel guilty. It wasn't 'guilt' but a reaction to the owner that prompted the look," Horowitz told the Associated Press. She concluded that the study demonstrated not that the dogs were feeling shame but rather that they were responding to their owners' negative cues.

[21] These can be regarded as a horrific attempt to restore honour by eliminating the source of shame. The act of killing is driven by a misguided sense of preserving the family's reputation, as the shame associated with the individual's perceived transgressions is believed to taint the entire family's standing within the community. In one instance, Qandeel Baloch, a Pakistani social media celebrity, was murdered by her brother. Baloch had gained notoriety for her provocative and outspoken online presence, one that challenged societal norms and traditional expectations. Her actions were seen as bringing Shame upon her family; in 2016 her brother strangled her to death.

face family members exterminate those who've violated cultural values and thus tarnished their family's reputation. At the other end of the spectrum, in individualist cultures like the United States, Sweden, and Norway, the self is considered to be independent; shame, therefore, belongs to the rule breaker only.

Most languages have multiple words for shame, allowing for a more nuanced understanding of the complex emotional experiences related to shame within a given cultural context.[22] In English we're limited to one word, but in a way this is a good thing since its progression can be tracked in degrees, from healthy to problematic to "toxic shame" (this last denoting its effect on our health). Problematic shame develops when whatever leads to it becomes significant enough that it interferes with our well-being, beginning to rule our life in the same way toxic sludge gets into a river and grows unimpeded until the river becomes the toxic sludge itself. What was once shame turns into Shame; no longer an occurrence, it becomes a current.

A few ingredients are necessary to develop Shame to the point that it takes over your life. With guilt saying "I did a bad thing" and Shame saying "I *am* the bad thing," the first ingredient of shame is

[22] For example, in Japanese, the word "hazukashii" is commonly used to express a general feeling of embarrassment or shame. It relates to situations where one feels a sense of discomfort or awkwardness after violating social norms or expectations. Another term, "zange," refers to the act of deep repentance or confession, especially for a moral or ethical failing. It often implies a sincere desire to atone and improve oneself. It's often associated with a sense of lingering guilt and a commitment to making amends or improving oneself. A third word, "haji," describes a more profound sense of shame, disgrace, or humiliation. It can be associated with actions or circumstances that bring significant dishonour or loss of face to oneself or others.

always guilt. In my case, it's the guilt over drinking but more specifically over lying about drinking—which brings me to the second ingredient. Lying, of course, means there are witnesses around, whether potential or real; essentially, the people who you believe would condemn you for what you've done. That would be my son, and all the people I've disappointed over the years, including the strangers who've read my memoir. Lying and potential witnesses lead to the final ingredient needed to cultivate Shame: a place or a state where it can flourish and spread—and, to continue the metaphor, I see a dark, festering stream, maybe the River Styx, that mythical underground passage ferrying the newly dead to their final destination. But an even better word for it is hiding, which is not a place but a state. It encompasses what you do to prevent people from seeing your Shame; and what ultimately helps you avoid being seen. Shame cannot exist without hiding; without hiding, Shame has no chance to grow—it gets exposed, and when it does it loses its power. The currents change, the water clears.

And yet, for most people, exposing their Shame is worse than death.

Think of a time when *your* Shame was exposed, the moment you got caught and confronted about the bad thing you were doing. The humiliation that burned your skin, that made your heart pound in your ears, that made your stomach churn. The people who looked at you in disbelief, and possibly in disgust.

Maybe there's something you're holding on to now, a thing that, said out loud, could possibly alter everything. The kind of secret that springs your eyes open in the middle of the night. And this is somehow tolerable, because admitting to it would be much worse.

Worse than death, since unlike death the punishment for it would go on, mercilessly. And although you can't really predict the consequences of such a revelation, they'll most likely be dire. You will be humiliated, and possibly finished.

For me, it's being the poster girl for sobriety who's slinking in alleys, my hand getting all sweaty around the smooth shape of a mickey. Inside the mickey is the guilt fuel I'll down in a couple of gulps that taste of scalpel. Hurry, hurry, drink it up—I don't want anyone, most of all *you*, to find out what I'm doing. If I drink fast enough maybe I can outrun it, maybe it'll be as if I hadn't drunk it at all. Out of sight. Then I'll walk home in bouncy, chaotic steps, trying to expend my demon energy. Right now I live in a small apartment with a bus stop in front of it and a shaded yard at the back that makes me sometimes imagine I'm deep in the forest where nobody can see. Except I can't stop thinking someone might see, and that once they do they'll condemn me. This person, my witness, has to believe I'm not drinking, or they hope so hard I'm not that they've given me countless chances to prove them right.

Unfortunately for me, I forgot that tonight is my night with my son—my son who freezes when I waltz into the room mid-song, words getting stuck to my lips like toffee then suddenly falling out of my mouth all wrong, setting an alarm off in his head.

We both pause, look at each other without speaking. If I admit to what he's about to ask me it'll be a long time before he'll stay with me again. Maybe after this he'll never stay with me ever. Once more I'll lose whatever trust he has left in me. If I admit to my Shame he'll see that I'm not only a pathetic selfish drunk but the worst kind of a hypocrite there is. He knows about the memoir. He's heard me rave about my sobriety to friends, and we've had many chummy chats together about it, too.

He's watching me. He's witnessing me. Seeing me.

So I gamble. I steady myself internally, I speak slowly, the words perfectly polished and measured now. I tell him I'm not *notokay*. I feel indignant when he looks at me with suspicion. But it's too late to come clean.

That evening he's unusually quiet when we watch our regular TV shows together. He doesn't ask me to lie down with him after I turn the lights off, but he does ask for Blue, his old stuffy dog. I got Blue when I was four months pregnant, the day I first heard my son's heartbeat. Once I close the door to his bedroom the house is silent and dark—except in my head, where there's a neon arrow pointing to a place behind the cornflakes box where there's the only thing that can stop me from clawing my eyes out.

This kind of emotional state of Shame-led confusion goes beyond guilt or regret. It deeply affects your sense of self-worth and can lead to a pervasive belief that you're fundamentally flawed or inadequate. That's how it is living with Shame—it makes you feel as if you're pretending to be someone you're not. This constant anxiety about being found out is a vicious emotional drain, and it contributes to a cycle of self-doubt, self-criticism, and diminished self-esteem.

People experience Shame when there's a discrepancy between their idealized self and actual self. It's not uncommon for people living with Shame to feel like imposters, waiting to be unmasked—if only to relieve the pressure of always having to pretend to be someone else (the poster girl for sobriety, a not *notokay* mom, a sober mom).

The wait is intolerable. The wait is tolerated.

Until it isn't.

13.

"Shame for an alcoholic is a language in which we converse with expertise," wrote Heather Brooke Armstrong—known as "Dooce"—in her final blog entry on April 6, 2023. A month later she was dead from suicide. As always, people asked why—the way we ask why when anyone takes their own life, especially and despite "having everything," but also despite the fact that everything isn't everything at all, that sometimes everything is not enough.

I didn't know Armstrong but we occupied the same space, first when I tried being a mommy blogger myself and then later when we both wrote about mental health and then drinking, too. Things were a little different in the beginning, but by the time Armstrong took her own life, writing about such subjects was no longer taboo. For me this attitude shift is perhaps most apparent in my journalism students, who frequently pitch mental health features, the kinds of stories that would have been considered shocking just a decade ago.

Today there's also nothing unusual about admitting to struggling with depression or anxiety on social media, where we broadcast to hundreds of friends and strangers. My Instagram is peppered with people posting quotes about feeling sad or anxious, about having dated narcissists, or being happy about having healed. I constantly notice ads for mental health services; even AI is in on it, advertising intelligent bot-led therapy. My Facebook prompt nudges me toward confession every day, asking "What's on your mind?" as soon as

I log in. Most of us have a lot on our mind. There've been shares about being neurodivergent, an informal umbrella term that characterizes people whose brain development or functioning deviates from what's considered typical and that covers most mental health issues, from autism to anxiety disorder to dyslexia. Some people use it to explain how facing distinct challenges interferes with their performance, but also how their lateral (irregular) way of processing information and the world in general sets them apart from normies.

We've been having important discussions about what we used to be mum about, and this goes beyond what you read in your social media feeds. A number of studies have found an increased acceptance of mental health issues in academia and the workplace, with greater awareness and understanding of their impact on people's well-being and how that correlates with their performance.

Media has finally played a role in raising awareness and reducing stigma, especially in giving coverage to public campaigns. These have included World Suicide Prevention Day, Bell Let's Talk, ITV's Britain Get Talking, CALM's Suicidal Doesn't Always Look Suicidal, the NFL's My Cause My Cleats, and the Indianapolis Colts' Kicking The Stigma. There have been celebrity endorsements, among them Prince Harry talking about depression, Michael Phelps discussing ADHD, and Lena Dunham speaking up about addiction. Organizations implement initiatives like mental health training and employee assistance programs, and many workplaces and schools have policies that support mental health accommodations. When I once looked through my then fourteen-year-old son's assignment folder, I wasn't too surprised to find a raft of worksheets on managing stress and anxiety and a quiz on mindfulness meditation.

(In that folder I also found a test titled Substance Use, Addictions, and Related Behaviours. My son scored 83 percent on it; the only question he answered "wrong" asked for three long-term health risks associated with alcohol use. He wrote "Relationships with friends and family" and put down "?" for the other two risks, the question marks incising deep, shiny grooves from his pencil pressing down hard and repeatedly. The teacher helpfully crossed out his answers and listed "organ damage," "anxiety & depression," and "cancer," oblivious to my son's having given the answer most correct for him.)

In one of the journalism courses I used to teach at my alma mater, I once had fourteen out of twenty-three students with academic accommodations, meaning more than half the class might ask for extensions or other arrangements owing to something (usually a mental health condition) that prevents them from completing a task on time. I've had students who suffer from social anxiety ask to be excused from speaking in class. I've had students with inconsistent attendance due to depression. Others have a hard time finishing work on account of ADHD. I can't help wondering what these barriers might mean for their future work performance. Then I remind myself that they'll most likely end up in a place that will accommodate them even further—although maybe not the student who has a phobia about speaking on the phone.

I also think about how, back when I was a student, I had to, you know, walk uphill in the snow to school, with no shoes on. Joking aside, I do think about when I once had a mini stroke from staying up three nights in a row to study for an exam, or when I intentionally burned my thigh with a cigarette tip to relieve stress, or when

I scored Valium off another kid because my eye and my mouth wouldn't stop twitching before an oral presentation.

I don't know if my younger self would fare better today, but it wouldn't have been so lonely and paranoid, always thinking there must be something wrong with me when everyone else seemed to be doing so well. They probably weren't, but no one talked. Today we talk. This doesn't mean the stigma is gone, but at least we're more open about it.[23]

Or are we? This is what I wondered about when I learned of Armstrong's suicide. What was it that this woman—a pioneer in airing dirty laundry, one with no apparent qualms in talking about anything taboo, whether it was depression, religion, parenting, or marriage—felt was worse than death to admit? What was her Shame?

14.

Over the years people have said they found parts of themselves in my story, and many have talked about being shaken up by what they read. I didn't set out to shock with my memoir of being a mother who drank alcoholically. My main motivation was to write a book that I myself had been searching for in the first year of motherhood,

[23] At the same time, there's already some pushback against using your past and your trauma as excuses for poor behaviour; personally, I recoil at the constant pointing to a mental health diagnosis as the sole explanation for why you're fucking up in life. Perhaps it's my own rigid attitude, but I do believe that a constant focus on problems is as detrimental as the problems themselves. We are not our Trauma. Still, acknowledging and talking about them is the first step to finding solutions to those problems, and being able to relate to others is key to getting help ourselves. As with anything else, and pardon the cliché, balance is key.

as I wandered the city with a stroller looking for garbage cans where I could discreetly deposit my empties.

I wasn't surprised that when I spoke out publicly about my problems, I experienced public shaming, was accused of oversharing, or as one journalist remarked, "making a career based on spilling my guts." On the morning of the memoir's publication, I opened the Arts section of the biggest national newspaper in Canada to a picture of my forlorn face spread over the entire front page. "This is a memoir," the text read, "that pushes at boundaries—what is private, what should perhaps be kept private, what we need to know, what we don't, what is insightful or just exhibitionism."

My first-ever media exposure. Many other condescending gems would follow: "She says she wrote the book, in part, to take away the stigma of her disorders. It's unlikely anyone will read *Drunk Mom* and want to hug an addict." Or this, regarding my sexual assault: "And what of her son, who will read someday that his mother woke up in a Montreal hotel, black bra sodden with breast milk, panties gone, no idea if she'd had sex with the two strangers she'd met the night before?" In 2013, that sort of attitude, especially toward women, was not unusual. It came on the heels of a time when famous young women were getting sloppy in public (Tara Reid, Paris Hilton, Lauryn Hill), shaving their heads (Britney Spears), stealing designer clothes (Winona Ryder), passing out drunk (Lindsay Lohan), fellating powerful men (Monica Lewinsky), or dying (Amy Winehouse, Anna Nicole Smith). They were all being ridiculed for their conduct.

Women suffering from addiction and mental health issues, victims of domestic assault or sexual and other forms of abuse—all served as punchlines for comedians and late-night talk show hosts. I wasn't a celebrity by any means, but with *Drunk Mom* I did get a taste of that dubious honour, derided as I was by some media outlets for admitting to my struggles. Today that kind of openness would, in many circles, be considered refreshing and in bad taste to joke about.

Yet I couldn't help feeling empowered by the book. A year before my memoir came out my ex-husband published a long-form personal essay in which he mentioned my addiction and recovery. The essay wasn't a surprise to me, but I still felt uneasy about someone else—someone I trusted deeply, then—revealing my biggest secret. With my memoir, I was able to not only better control the narrative but also to out myself, and there was a great liberation in that. Having to hide my addiction and later my recovery had always been a burden, but weirdly, now that it was all public knowledge, I no longer had to stress about getting found out. What was the worst that could happen? I'd already lived through that worst, and now I owned it. There's freedom in being in charge of your own narrative. No one can use it against you once you do.

Drunk Mom would've been received differently today than it was in 2013; I can't imagine journalists commenting on my appearance, my romantic relationship, or especially the sexual assault in the same snarky manner. Even the way we think of addiction is different now, with people readily and publicly admitting to their struggle with it, taking pride in becoming sober, and telling the same war stories of shameful behaviour (drinking around babies, losing careers, going to jail . . .) formerly reserved for the rooms of AA. Admitting to your worst actions is for many a way to elicit support and sympathy.

We haven't become immune to shaming, but we have turned Shame on its head; we've made it into a source of pride. Posting about our vulnerabilities gives us a sense of ownership—we can't be hurt by others when we're first to get to the place of shaming. We take away that power; we regain control.

But even though admitting to your so-called failings—drinking, being a "bad" parent, being crazy—tends to get applauded these days, I wonder how much of this applause is performative. After all, it's trendy. At least for now. Do we *really* admire it when someone admits to their vulnerability? Yes and no, depending on when you came of age. My late Gen-X cohort grapples with it, having grown up in a world where it wasn't safe to do so. Our parents were raised by parents traumatized by the Second World War, and I imagine there wasn't a lot of compassion for feeling awkward about speaking in public or for being too sad to get out of bed. Growing up around two, sometimes three generations of the "I'll give you something to cry about" school of compassion will naturally quash any urge to be openly vulnerable, especially with others.

Despite having workshopped my mental health to death—publicly and not—I've often felt impatient about my own vulnerabilities. (But not my son's, and not just because I unintentionally most certainly did give him lots to cry about.) Still, I'm outspoken about these internal conflicts because I do believe silence is death. Shortly after *Drunk Mom* came out, the first-ever mental health column I pitched told the world "I'm writing this because I don't want to die" in a screamy headline above my goofy melancholy smile. The boomer ghost in me cringed as Generation Z applauded.

Seeing others' vulnerability gives us permission to examine our own situation with more compassion. Relatability—the degree to which we perceive a similarity between ourselves and others, particularly in terms of experiences, emotions, or circumstances—encompasses the ability to empathize with another person's thoughts, feelings, and behaviours. It plays a crucial role in group therapy as it helps foster a sense of connection, support, and understanding among group members. When new members realize that others have gone through or are going through similar struggles, it can create a feeling of validation and reduce feelings of isolation. Sharing relatable experiences can lead to a sense of camaraderie and bonding, fostering a safe space where we feel seen and accepted.

This is why places like AA boast large memberships and why, as I mentioned before, they're considered by some to be the most successful place of recovery.[24]

Not everyone responds well to a group therapy setting—or to groups in general—when seeking help and trying to find support. This was something I too was at odds with when I first joined AA. Groups freaked me out. Having grown up Catholic and in a communist country, I was wary of too much conformity. Repetitions, rituals, and rules were suspect, and although I was no anarchist I recoiled at having to be indoctrinated into a human centipede of groupthink. I'd flinch when anyone tried to welcome-hug me at meetings.

[24] Yet some critics contend that the organization's success rates are difficult to measure accurately, and that its reliance on self-reported outcomes and anonymity make it challenging to conduct rigorous scientific studies. They argue for the need to evaluate AA's effectiveness using more stringent scientific methods.

AA slogans—about letting go, putting the program first, not making things complicated in general—struck me as unintelligent.[25] I often wondered whether giving up drinking meant giving up thinking, too. But when I'd bring up feeling brainwashed, more than once some wise old soul would jokingly remind me that maybe my dirty brain needed washing, ha ha.

Still, AA was where I talked about my drinking without feeling like a complete freak, where people *got* my particular affliction and I instinctively got theirs. It was also the place where I learned empathy; where I saw that the people in my life who'd hurt me had been hurt themselves; where I learned that I didn't need to instantly react to situations. And, ultimately, I learned that I probably wasn't alone in how I felt and processed Shame, which is what made me drink in the first place.

As I opened myself up to the possibility of recovering within the group, I began to feel more at home in AA and eventually identified with most of their recovery dogmas. My least favourite slogan was "You Are No Longer Alone," which at first I read as a threat and would joke that it made me think of stalkers. But I came to understand its intention, and appreciated having a place where I could share my troubles and find some compassion and understanding.

I mean, to some extent. I've always struggled with those parts of the program that to me meant suspending my inquiries and getting my dirty brain washed. Not being able to find "God" was an ongoing

[25] Some feel that AA's spiritual component, with its emphasis on God or a Higher Power, can be exclusionary for those who don't adhere to traditional religious beliefs or who identify as atheist or agnostic. As an alternative, they advocate for secular recovery approaches that are inclusive and accessible to a broader range of people.

source of confusion, especially since I was surrounded by people who spoke of "spiritual awakenings" and seemed to have that God on speed dial. They spoke of talking to "Him" and leaving things up to "Him." "He" would sometimes appear in showers, or send messages by arranging numbers on the alarm clock, or provide answers through the television or through someone's comment in a meeting that would perfectly address someone else's conundrum.

Maybe the problem with my problem was also that I didn't believe the "give yourself over to this simple program" approach was key to my survival and my sobriety. But I tried to do it right. I threw myself into it the same way I threw myself into anything I threw myself into—as if my life depended on it. Where my commitment to drinking was suicide in installments, I started to see my commitment to sobriety as resurrection on a repayment plan.

I got the books, I read the books, I quoted from the books. I made coffee and sandwiches, I greeted, I stacked chairs, I made posters. I organized speakers. And every Wednesday for two years I went to a detox called Women's Place along with a sober friend—both of us like overeager elders from the Latter-day Saints. There we talked about the program to the two or three women who'd show up only to relieve their monotone day or take a nap on the couch. (My friend and I would meet beforehand in a restaurant for lunch and had an ongoing joke with the cute waiter that we were attending a professional pillow fighting or Jell-O wrestling group. In retrospect, I can see that we both had some shame attached to the whole business of seeming like zealots promoting what was possibly a cult.)

I also waited outside meeting rooms for any young people who'd be streaming out afterward, a way to catch potential "sponsees"—newcomer women who might've been looking for someone to take them through the program. I became fanatical and enthusiastic—insisting on people writing my number down and acting all easygoing and chummy—but that's because I knew my own life was at stake here; I'd been told several times that in order to keep what I had I had to give it away. That was what step twelve said specifically ("Having had a spiritual awakening as the result of these steps, we tried to carry this message to alcoholics and to practice these principles in all our affairs"); plus, passing on the message was as close as you'd get in the program to graduating.

But even completing all twelve steps didn't mean I was done; you were always encouraged to repeat them. The analogy given was that of fine-tuning your car, getting your oil changed. So I went through the steps a number of times: I admitted, I confessed, I apologized, I carried the message. Year in and year out I wrote lists of resentments and of people, places, and things that had hurt me and that I hurt over; I tried diligently to find "my part" as I filled notebooks with names and causes. I often struggled in finding my part, especially when it came to more serious perpetrators—such as men who had assaulted me sexually. But whenever the program would get too muddled for me, I could speak to a sponsor about it. And I had many wonderful sponsors[26]—women who took me through

[26] And not so wonderful—like anything, AA is full of people who have all kinds of quirks, some more dangerous than others. Like the sponsor who suggested I get off Prozac and pray my depression away, or the one who made me write an apology letter to one of my abusers. There was a "going to any lengths to get it" philosophy—in other words,

the steps, women who'd had some time in sobriety and were people I looked up to for how well their lives were going. The logic was that you'd choose a sponsor who had what you wanted, namely sobriety, but also whatever mattered to you: mental stability, joyful disposition, financial security.

As for the rest of the members, there too I found ones I could relate to. In the beginning that meant young adults who looked like the fun, attractive types I'd only recently partied with, minus the whole overdose and death vibe: they were bright-eyed, Adidas-wearing kids who knew DJs and talked about fucking; there were very few taboo topics. We were like *Vice* but without the drugs. When that got old, I found a group of witchy women who loved fashion, art, and sex. Then, when I finally grew out of my social-approval years, I just found people I simply liked to be around without obsessing over our commonalities.

Different things mattered differently over the years—my first two sponsors were former models and artists whose beauty and beautiful lives impressed me so much that all I wanted was to join their cool club. My last sponsor was a fellow writer and the sort of human in whose mouth the word "fuck" sounded like a flower.

I chose Ruth, my first sponsor—who later became my best friend—because she spoke from a podium about giving up her lucrative,

---

proving that you were willing to do anything to stay sober. Like the time a sponsor visited me during my lunch hour and demanded I drop to my knees in the middle of a busy sidewalk to prove my faith. So we kneeled and prayed, holding hands, which is when my supervisor at the ad agency where I'd just gotten a gig walked by, blinking in disbelief before entering the building. I'm not saying I got fired because of that, since I did have some trouble writing copy for a pasta-and-powder-cheese company.

Ford-agented modelling career because she was no longer willing to starve herself. She told jokes and swore and deposited a quarter in the swear jar immediately after doing so, then she swore again and joked about not having any more quarters.

I stared at her. I couldn't believe someone that stunning and funny and sober on top of it all existed in my universe. When she became my sponsor a few weeks later, I said to my boyfriend at the time that if this was how all cults got you—by sending out attractive baits like Ruth—then I was in. I wanted what that girl had. There really seemed to be no downside to joining this cult—it promised not only sobriety but also friends and happiness.

Eventually, AA became one more place where I'd experience Shame. But first: the more time I spent in AA, the more I identified as a sober alcoholic. (I didn't realize it then, but any diversion from that identity would become not only a threat to my sobriety but also a threat to my sense of self.) Being an alcoholic was shameful; becoming a sober alcoholic was less so—even though the "Anonymous" half of the organization's name signifies that our membership was not to be broadcasted.[27]

When AA formed in 1939, this part was crucial to the organization's success—people were worried about being shunned socially or getting fired if their employers found out. The town drunks had an easier time being known as town drunks. No one lauded those hiding out in church basements with a bunch of like-minded members—people who'd destroyed their families and careers but were trying to

[27] Sorry!

restore peace—because belonging to AA meant officially admitting to being what you were (er, the town drunk). To this day the word "alcoholic" itself denotes Shame, an outdated label that reduces you to your condition and that depersonalizes you.

Still, when I first joined, I was fine with being both Anonymous and an Alcoholic. I opted for sober alcoholic—not a term I shared without internal cringing, however, even when I described myself as such in the media. But the media, too, had no other name to call me.

I was happy in AA for a long time. I was proud of my membership there, proud to be associated with people who'd rebuilt their lives, many of whom were successful, intelligent, and healthy. People who were in touch with their emotions, who tried to live their lives with intention and honesty, and whose brand of humour was similar to mine. They could laugh about the darkest shit. It was no accident that I gave my memoir the title I gave it: it was both honest and morbidly funny.

My sobriety was never an easy thing. But I've never been as happy as I was when I was sober. Before becoming a Shame-based chronic relapser—the last thing I called myself in meetings—my ongoing struggle was with finding "God," who suspiciously sounded like the same bearded white guy I used to grapple with back in my Catholic days as a child. An AA friend once looked at me blankly and shrugged when I told her I wasn't sure about this God. "Well, God either is or isn't," she said, "and until you decide which it is, you won't fully recover."

"God" is mentioned in five of the twelve steps, so she was definitely on to something. And that's how I became troubled over not *getting it* in AA and paranoid about failing. Ultimately, this is not the fault of AA; it's simply how I, a person prone to experiencing Shame, managed to find it in an institution that promised to relieve me of the one thing that brought on Shame in the first place.

15.

But when it comes to Shame, do any of us really stand a chance? Is there a way to exist in this world—with all its shoulds and shouldn'ts—and not become a victim of it? Possibly. A person with high self-esteem, integrity, and a solid value system; who's grown up convinced of their worth, having been raised in an encouraging environment where every criticism, doubt, and threat to identity is refuted before it manages to sink its little claws in; who's been educated in institutions that foster growth and celebrate difference; who's had solid, supportive friendships and, later, entered workplaces that value their input and skill—yes, that sort of person could perhaps avoid Shame.

Another type of person for whom Shame is a foreign concept are those who, unlike the general population, are born unable to experience it. These people are characterized by such traits as a lack of empathy, shallow emotions, and a disregard for social norms and moral principles. Compared to non-psychopathic individuals, they often exhibit a diminished capacity for guilt and remorse and lower physiological and emotional responses associated with

Shame. They may also have difficulty recognizing or understanding Shame in others.

The rest of us? Tough luck.[28]

For many people the stigma associated with Shame is internalized, a result of the prevailing attitude in past decades whereby vulnerability was mocked and considered a weakness. The writer Heather Armstrong, who killed herself, grew up in the same world as I did: one in which skinny was praised, marriage was a sign of a successful life, and telling people you struggled with depression or an eating disorder and sometimes hated parenting meant you were a bad person.

In 2001, when she started her blog, Armstrong wrote about all kinds of taboos, and her frank, unfiltered style sometimes attracted criticism from those who found it to be overly irreverent or even offensive. In 2002 she gained notoriety after getting canned from her day job for publishing a funny post about her experience working for a corporation; for a while the term "dooced," after her nickname, trended as slang for getting fired. Over the years she received copious amounts of hate mail and dealt with it the way she dealt with all harassment—by creating a separate page called "Monetizing Hate" and posting it.

Eventually, though, as the tide turned for unapologetic confessors, her honesty was applauded. If you threw Shame at her she'd either throw it right back or admit to it so that it would lose its

[28] I don't like making definitive statements like that and I know there are always exceptions to most rules and I believe that there are people out there who simply don't feel a lot of Shame and they're neither sociopathic nor have been raised in ideal conditions and thriving. But they are in the minority, Shannon.

power. It's hard to know how much of that was intentional, but I suspect most of it was. That's exactly how I dealt with writing about my own "usual sordid dealings"—thank you anonymous commenter. If Shame is synonymous with being exposed, exposing Shame sometimes makes you a little . . . shameless,[29] which is almost a good thing.

We like our heroes shame-free. We're happy to restore some formerly controversial people back to glory or admit they were right all along, as was evident in Armstrong tributes, where, for example, the branding of her writing as "mommy blogging" was acknowledged as dismissive. Except that, despite being described as revolutionary and a pioneer, and someone who'll be forever ingrained in the fabric of social media and internet culture, there is a little *bu-u-u-t*—specifically in relation to the 2022 controversy where, in the wake

[29] The word "shameless" connotes a lack of shame in a negative or immoral sense, and is thus considered derogatory. Yet this can contribute to stigmatization and further perpetuate harmful societal norms. Besides, we can never eradicate shame, and some of it is good. (It would be unwise to, oh, I don't know, defiantly walk around naked or do other rule-breaking things, as much fun as it is to give in to our more anarchist attitudes.) Drawing from the word "undoing" (or my personal favourite, "unfucking," which has become synonymous with "fixing"), I came up with "unshaming"—which can be understood as a more positive and empowering concept. For me this made-up word emphasizes the process of freeing oneself from shame and challenging the societal constructs that impose it; it also implies a shift away from judgment and condemnation and toward understanding, empathy, and support. By promoting unshaming, we can create an environment that encourages open conversations, self-reflection, and acceptance of oneself and others. It's a cousin word to "unfucking," just more specific about what it is you'd like to fix.

Language has a powerful impact on how we perceive ourselves and others. By choosing words like "unshaming" instead of a more problematic one like "shameless," we can contribute to a more compassionate and inclusive dialogue around experiences related to shame and personal growth.

of her younger child's identification as nonbinary, Armstrong argued that gender is defined by biology, a position considered to be anti-trans. Following the public outcry Armstrong took down the post and replaced it with a poem prefaced with this: "Your children are asking you through their behavior, 'Why are you agreeing with me when I am telling you that I hate myself?' Remember that and consider it every day for the rest of your lives."

In 2001, when she started her blog, she was shamed for being too open and having the wrong opinion . . . and with that post twenty-one years later, she was shamed for the same thing. Many commenters said the year 2022 was when her reputation suffered the greatest blow of all.

Armstrong died a year after that. She was found by her boyfriend, Pete Ashdown, who "told the press that she had been sober for more than 18 months, and recently had a relapse. He did not provide further details." I thought it was telling that he'd felt this was worthy of note; maybe I'm reading too much into it, but I don't think so—from the partner of an addict, the part about the recent relapse was not a subtle hint.

I'm baffled by people taking their own lives. I've read lots about suicide and I've written about it hoping to understand it better, but I'm aware that whatever realizations I come up with will be tinted by my own experience with it. What I mean is that for me drinking hasn't been only a coping mechanism. It has also stemmed from a desire to not have to deal with hardship. To check out.

I think of that passed-out drunk I saw on Front Street: of how I felt jealous of him, how for a moment he represented a version of freedom. I'm also reminded of Julian Barnes's novel *The Sense of an Ending*, in which a character who kills himself considers suicide to be an ultimate human freedom. Or of the Albert Camus quote "There is but one truly serious philosophical problem, and that is suicide. Judging whether life is or is not worth living amounts to answering the fundamental question of philosophy." (Writing my own column on the topic back in 2014, I provided the most underwhelming conclusion of all time: "I won't ever understand it but I know that it helps to be heard.")[30]

In the context of Shame, suicide is an effort to save face, from judgment specifically, whether it's your own or others'. A dead person doesn't care. There's nothing in the world that can make them care.

Heather Brooke Armstrong was indeed no mere mommy blogger; her writing is, as they say in her tributes, visceral, funny, smart. Over and over she offered her tender belly to the world, too much of it perhaps. But also maybe not enough—at least not about the last frontier of her hurt. The one that possibly took her life. And as I read endless Reddit threads about Armstrong and the usual internet speculation about why she ended it all—depression, unhealed trauma, religious upbringing, too much public exposure—I came up with my own guess.

Perhaps her death was related to some of those things or none of those things. Most likely what she died of is what lies at their

[30] Except that when I think about it now, I like how that aligns with my current philosophy, whereby I choose to favour solutions (being heard) instead of problems (trying to understand something).

heart, meaning that most likely she died of Shame . . . over a relapse. I'm wondering if she felt overpowering stress at having to disclose her failure to remain sober. If she was too tired to fight.

What I'm not wondering about is that in the end, the woman who was famous and infamous for speaking up succumbed to silence.

Maybe I'm giving her final blog entry ("Shame for an alcoholic is a language in which we converse with expertise") too much significance,[31] treating it as a clue. Maybe.

It could have been "just" depression. Armstrong's case was so serious that she sought the most extreme of all treatments, electric shock therapy, to reset her brain. I think about her children (that final blog entry was about her firstborn) and mine. How my son's sweet face, his skin smelling of sunshine and dirt, his inquisitive mahogany-brown eyes would always stop me from even the most insistent ideations; I think how lucky I am to have always had the grace of that thought. How Armstrong wasn't as lucky, or if she was, how the burden got too heavy to carry and nothing, not even the thought of leaving her children behind, could prevent it.

Whatever it was that made her take her life, I relate to Armstrong a lot—and maybe for that reason keep coming back to Shame as the most likely culprit. I too have offered too much of my own

[31] Of her drinking, Armstrong wrote, "I had isolated myself entirely from the outside world because I didn't understand what was happening to me. And I was embarrassed. Here, two years into this often frenzied and wandering dance with life, I understand that I couldn't hold anyone's gaze because everywhere I looked I saw nothing but my own worthlessness. And so I chose loneliness. I couldn't handle the idea of anyone else knowing just how bad I felt about myself."

tender belly, but despite putting my own insecurities on blast, I almost let my Shame and my silence kill me.[32]

16.

When I began to relapse—slowly, then instantly—I had a big conundrum. Most addicts, unlike me, haven't told the entire world of their sobriety and then published a book about it. Still, this doesn't mean my situation wasn't relatable—I later realized that I chose that as my unique excuse only because it was the easiest explanation. And I did genuinely feel Shame about first going public about my recovery and then relapsing . . . repeatedly.

Shame, however, does not discriminate. Consumed as I was by the fear of being considered a hypocrite, I also let the Shame about it eclipse everything. Crippling shame is a universal experience—you don't need to deceive thousands of witnesses to live it.

Coined by the sociologist Charles Horton Cooley, the term "looking-glass self" encapsulates how you develop your concept of self by how you think others see you. You don't need evidence that they see you in a certain way, you only have to *believe* it. When my memoir came out and I was ridiculed by some for my "confessional" writing, I actually didn't feel shamed because I didn't feel bad about the book; I was proud of it. It was stressful and unpleasant to read some of those comments, but no amount of outsiders'

[32] When I heard the news about Armstrong's death I was three months sober and all I could think was that I'd been lucky one more time. When I think of my sobriety now, I have an image of a train speeding away and a person running to catch it, jumping at the last minute onto the caboose. That person is me.

negativity could shake how I thought about it because that negativity didn't align with my own beliefs.

However, having kept up a sober facade, I believed people would condemn me for my repeated relapses. I believed this despite the lack of evidence. Not once had anyone confronted me about being a hypocrite. It didn't matter.

Being shamed doesn't necessarily result in internal shame, yet the presence of internal shame can significantly influence one's experience of external shame. In other words, when we feel a sense of shame within ourselves, it can greatly affect how we perceive and respond to external sources of Shame or judgment—whether they're present or not.

My own relapse-Shame-relapse trajectory is complicated in that I've managed to stay continuously sober sometimes for years at a time[33] (I've never had more than six of those). But if I count individual instances of drinking as relapses, my relapse-Shame-relapse trajectory began two years after the publication of *Drunk Mom*—coinciding with personal trauma—and intensified in 2020. And when it began I was still going to AA meetings. It was always other people who were instrumental in my managing not to drink

[33] Because I got sober in AA, I tend to see sobriety as an all-or-nothing thing. I'm aware that all-or-nothing is not for everyone, though. I'm also aware of the various new ways of seeing sobriety these days, as conveyed in the terms sober-curious, soberish, mindful drinking, and no-and-low—all of which refer to a grey-area middle ground between abstinence and drinking less harmfully (a.k.a. no bingeing). Most of my relapses weren't dramatic at all. Some lasted a short time. But middle-ground sober doesn't work for me in the same way that having Medium Shame—as opposed to Big Shame—doesn't. I can't be a little bit addicted. This is why the goal, for me anyway, is always to stop; full stop.

for prolonged periods of time, so when I saw them as Shame-exposing—as when I imagined they would judge me for relapses—that perpetuated the trouble. Conversely, when I leaned on them in exposing my Shame—by sharing how I worried about that judgment—that could circumvent the trouble. This is why I call myself the architect of both my demise and my salvation, something I learned only after twenty years of this journey.

I can't pinpoint the exact moment when I started hiding, but I know now that although addiction is about many things—whether it's a reaction to trauma or really anything we believe it's about—addiction is about secrecy.

And so is Shame.

They are intertwined.

Before I got trapped in that final, years-long loop, there was one other particular situation that almost inevitably led to my drinking again.

If I had to draw a trigger pie chart, 80 percent of the pie would correspond to that situation. The rest would be some other emotional imbalance (postpartum woes) and only a tiny portion would be opportunity (I was at a party where everyone around me was drinking).

The 80 percent slice was all about Shame—specifically the Shame of being in a relationship that I wouldn't leave, and more specifically the Shame of being a woman whose partner cheated on her.

There was a time when I thought of the correlation between my drinking and his cheating as a spell or a curse. It's a wild theory, and not exactly a logical one. Yet I became convinced that my drinking was triggered by this thing that was happening, even though back then I had no proof it was happening. Sometimes the only proof I had was . . . that I was drinking again.

It was like voodoo. Someone else doing something indirectly that would hurt me directly.

I wonder today if the uncertainty of the situation fed my need for drama on some subconscious level. The idea that I was with someone whose presence caused anxiety, whose commitment I could never be sure of, had an addictive element[34] to it, the classic highs and lows of a toxic relationship.

But this isn't a story about who did what to whom and how I was a victim of infidelity. I'm only examining that particular trigger

[34] Studies have demonstrated how uncertainty (think gambling or taking a weird pill at a club) triggers the release of dopamine, addiction's best friend, a neurotransmitter of pleasure and reward. The anticipation associated with uncertainty activates the brain's reward pathways—dopamine on fire—leading to a pleasurable sensation (later, relief) that people prone to addiction seek to experience repeatedly. The uncertain nature of the outcome creates a strong association between the behaviour and the anticipation of reward.

Other, related research on addictive behaviour and gambling shows that intermittent unpredictable rewards (such as occasional wins) can reinforce the behaviour and increase the likelihood of its continuation. Uncertainty also engages our cognitive processes in that it requires problem solving, adaptability, and critical thinking, which can be intellectually stimulating and rewarding in its own way. The process of navigating uncertainty offers a sense of accomplishment and satisfaction.

I used to be a person who was almost perpetually bored unless I was in good (men) or bad (men) trouble or had an impossible deadline. It might not have been conscious, but trying to solve the mystery of a lover's disappearing-in-plain-sight act was thrilling to me on some level. The so-called emotional rollercoaster created a sense of *rabid* excitement that kept me emotionally, *rabidly* invested.

because it informs my other point about hiding. Between exposing the situation and hiding, I chose hiding.

Unlike with some more serious cases of abuse, I wasn't a victim—I had a choice. The choice was to speak up. To leave. But I didn't. Because speaking up meant I'd have to confront myself as not only a woman who allows cheating to continue but also one who's in denial about it. A woman who causes terrible fights and accuses a possibly innocent man of wrongdoings for which she has no proof—until I do, until I'm the last person to find out what *everyone* else knows, which is a whole other level of humiliation as I feel betrayed by an entire group of people I used to call friends.

Before the cheating eroded me and then filled me up with the rosé wine I drank during that time,[35] I believed I was interesting, intelligent, and fun, and that he was lucky to be with me.

Later my looking-glass self became a reflection in a funhouse mirror. I saw what I thought a woman in my situation looked like to others, were I to admit to what was happening. She was pathetic.

I didn't want to be a bleeding Frida Kahlo with *a few small nips* and I didn't want to be Sylvia Plath with her head in the oven. I didn't want people to wonder if he was the way he was because there was something terribly wrong with me. Because I was ugly or stupid, because I didn't know how to please him, how to listen, how to keep him. I don't now believe I'm any of those things, nor is anyone else who gets cheated on. But at the time I had no one to disabuse me of that.

[35] In classic alcoholic logic, I believed that if it was rosé it wasn't really a relapse.

And even after I no longer felt I was any of those things, in the most amusing twist, I went along with the "he-cheats-because-you-drink" rationale. At least I had an explanation (which was also his excuse once he finally admitted it).

When you must deal with a persistent feeling of deep humiliation—stemming from the discrepancy between your behaviours or characteristics and your moral standards—toxic Shame takes root and can become a part of you.

In short, I had an ongoing identity crisis—from denial to discovering I was the sort of person who'd check her partner's Sent folder and try to guess his new lock-screen password. And later, after my suspicions had been borne out—it wasn't paranoia after all—the crisis only deepened when I kept doing nothing about my situation other than drown it in pink wine.

I have a friend in another country who was once a successful romance novelist and who later escaped an abusive relationship with a controlling man. She'd left her husband for this man, and as these stories sometimes go, everything was fine in the beginning—until the new man gradually began to destroy her life. It started with rages and then escalated to demands that she change the way she dress, that she quit her writing career, and eventually that she work for his company, in effect robbing her of her financial independence. The physical abuse wasn't "that bad," she told me, although he'd once knocked her out cold.

Once she decided to leave she began "stealing" small amounts of money from the payroll, and over eight months accumulated enough to escape with her son. Over the three years this was going on, all I knew was that she'd started to disappear from social media, posting only a Christmas tree during the holidays and a very rare meme about not having enough coffee. We had one phone conversation that I later learned was being monitored.

We talked two months after she was out of her predicament. I happened to be the first person to whom she'd told the whole story, and it was a story of her own disbelief. Disbelief that she'd stayed so long, that she'd allowed it to happen despite being brilliant, sensitive, and a feminist. That she'd been silent about it. But intelligence and sensitivity have nothing on what she was really coming up against—not the man, and not even the danger she was in, although that too. I knew how it happened.

It came about in the same way I endured my own situation—because I was ashamed to tell anyone. And the longer I was ashamed the more I had to hide, and the more I had to hide the more I had to deal with it. And I dealt with it how I dealt with it. I kept it *all* secret.

17.

Addiction cannot exist and thrive without two essential ingredients: Hiding and Shame. Yes, there's a genetic component to it, and an emotional one (for example, it can be a reaction to a tragic event). It can be related to trauma, and it can even develop accidentally (what in recovery circles is referred to as "educational variety," where it progresses slowly and sneaks up on you; think nightcaps).

But for addiction to grow and flourish, you need secrecy. Secrecy is its conduit, or better, a fertilizer for its underground zygote that will let it spread. What's underneath is what kills you and what's on the surface is a lie. You're not who you are. And with that sort of secrecy driving your existence you're no longer known—to anyone, yourself included. (Which explains how baffled many twelve-step addicts are when they try to pinpoint why exactly they relapsed, even when they come up with a neat conclusion: "I wasn't praying hard enough," or "I wasn't doing the steps," or "I stopped talking to my sponsor." These are only speculations. They don't truly know, and they don't know because they don't know who they are. They've become their own enigma.)

When I went to meetings during my relapse, I felt exhausted by others' energy. Their enthusiasm and their belief in the program annoyed me. We were different: they took my surface to be my actual self, and they were all stupid for that. I was in pain yet I was superior because I knew something they didn't—even if it was only about me and even though it caused me Shame. There was a gap between us, and the wider it got the harder it was to find my way back to what it used to be like.

I don't remember my last in-person AA meeting, but it probably resembled many others before it, where I'd socialize briefly beforehand and never afterward. And if I shared anything it would've sounded cool or provoking: how I hated when they all hugged at the end, say, or how I was probably a misanthrope. In my home group people knew about the memoir; they knew I was funny. And when I shared everyone listened; as one of my friends there said, "It's entertaining to watch you stick your neck out."

I gave the people what they wanted. It was a performance and I was an actor. My AA membership was no longer authentically about me—there was no me. The woman who showed up in my place wore my skin and had my laugh, but that's where the similarities ended.

After that last meeting it's possible that once we said our goodbyes I went east instead of west, where I lived. It's likely that I walked the two blocks to the Manulife Centre with its cinema and bookstore and, downstairs, my own Christmas-in-July with its bright warm lights and a discreet clinking of bottles ferried in small, whispery shopping carts. It's likely that after leaving the store I headed to the gleaming-white public washroom and locked myself in a stall and unscrewed the red cap and took an oily, razor-sharp gulp that went in smooth and sizzled once it hit my feverish soul. A final toast to my AA lie, a relief that it was all over—at least the part where I had to squirm for an hour twice a week in a plastic seat in a classroom on the second floor where I went to lie to people I believed would ridicule me for showing them how much it all hurt.

18.

While researching this book I asked a lot of people to tell me about Shame. I often had to probe. No one ever volunteered an anecdote; their answers were always general: "It's present in my kink[36]

[36] One of my interviews was with a professional dominant, but the world of kink probably needs a whole book of its own. My interviewee said this about shame and the

community" or "Oh, I think about my Catholic upbringing." Rarely would they relate a personal story, unless it was some funny party blunder where it was obvious they were talking more about embarrassment than Shame. Still, the stories were all related to the person's identity and involved doing something out of character, or breaking a social norm, or acting in a way that was considered morally flawed.

Shame, pride, guilt, embarrassment, envy, empathy, and jealousy are all part of the family of self-conscious emotions, closely tied as they are to our sense of self and self-awareness. The stories volunteered by my interviewees were often a result of circumstances. Rarely did they portray them in a bad light.

Embarrassment is a feeling of discomfort, awkwardness, or self-consciousness that arises in response to a situation or event that threatens one's self-image or social identity. Something as small as being caught with food stuck in one's teeth, tripping and falling in public, or calling someone by the wrong name can all be sources of embarrassment.

---

clients he works with: "While not all bring shame into this space, it's absolutely present, and for some clients it's at the core of what we discuss and specifically curate our sessions to include—to directly aim at that shame to regain that power. For some, it may be shame related to trauma. For others, it's shame that they're turned on by and want things done to them that 'society' says is shameful and wrong. The most important thing in my work is creating a safe space where my clients can be completely vulnerable. Once that's achieved, it's incredibly powerful the work we can do to remove ideological barriers around what sexual desires should look like versus what they actually are. Some clients involve kink in their everyday lives and would be considered lifestyle kinksters. Others keep it very private, and in some cases, only I know. I don't judge anyone for how they manage their private lives, and I reaffirm to them that it doesn't matter to me. If I can create a safe space for them and they can't find it elsewhere, I feel privileged to allow them to break down some of those barriers."

To me this is all about connecting with another person, letting them *really* see you.

Shame, on the other hand, is a much deeper and more pervasive emotion, characterized by feelings of worthlessness, inadequacy, and self-disgust. Shame arises when a person believes there's something wrong with them. It can be triggered by a variety of embarrassing situations, such as making a mistake, being rejected, or failing to meet one's own or others' expectations. For Shame to emerge, these situations must be repeated and reinforced in order to be interpreted as evidence of a much larger character flaw. There have to be witnesses present, and those can be imaginary (as they were when I feared being perceived as a pathetic, cheated-on woman by the world at large). And unlike those to whom you willingly disclose your Shame—your therapist, your AA group, a trusted friend—these witnesses are unwelcome, accidental, judgmental. (Which is why they can be imaginary: for those witnesses to exist, you need only believe they do.)

Shame is also characterized by certain absolutes that announce it to be a permanent condition: *always*, *never*, *I am*. Or in the case of how I thought of my relapses: *chronic*. The key difference between Shame and embarrassment, then, is the intensity and duration of the emotion. Embarrassment is typically a mild, temporary feeling, whereas Shame can be much more intense and long-lasting. Or better yet: embarrassment is a feeling, whereas Shame is being.

For example, repeated romantic rejection can signal to someone that they're unlovable or unattractive. So the next time that person—who at first might only suspect there's something "wrong" with them—gets ghosted, they'll start to form a belief: "This always happens to me because I *am* unlovable."

Drinking and smashing into a wall when I was supposed to be sober—and then lying about the circumstances—was my final confirmation of Shame, drawing as it did a direct line to feelings of worthlessness and self-disgust. And by following up with a GoFundMe announcement[37] I doubled or tripled that Shame; no wonder I got shingles from all the stress of the facade. My subsequent march to the liquor store was just me succumbing to the strongest emotion I operated on. Relapsing once was embarrassing, twice was stupid, thrice was a habit. And then it became me.

When Antoine de Saint-Exupéry's little prince comes across a planet occupied by a drunkard, through a series of questions he learns that this unhappy man drinks in order to forget his shame about drinking.

I love this exchange because it perfectly describes the mechanism underlying addiction.

We don't know why the drunkard started drinking in the first place—was it childhood trauma, was it genetic, was it because he gradually became dependent on having Scotch in the evenings, which then became Scotch in the afternoons, which eventually turned into Scotch all day long? Does it matter? We don't find out his name, nor do we learn his history or anything else about him other than that he's already in the throes of addiction to the point where it's the only force in his life. We know it's Shame that drives his addiction and that he drinks because he doesn't know how to deal with that Shame. He's in a loop and there doesn't seem to be a way out.

[37] Where, in the end, I collected more than $6,000, which covered all my dental surgeries. I got my perfect smile. I had very little to smile about for some time.

A lot of research focuses on Shame as it relates to self. The more events that bring on Shame, the more likely an individual is to become Shame-based. Some research indicates that Shame-proneness is a result of an abusive childhood, where the abuse—especially by someone who's seen as superior—eventually leads to a person feeling inferior, the Shame-associated situation metaphorically shrinking them until they feel so small that it's the size they end up identifying with most often.[38]

A proneness to Shame doesn't develop only as a result of abuse, but it does always develop when the person's safety and sense of self are threatened, and threatened repeatedly. When a child is ridiculed (bullied) for something they strongly identify with, whether it's a visible handicap, having been adopted, or being gay, their difference informs them that there's something wrong with them, that they're worth less because of that difference. This sets the stage for later in life when they become ashamed not just of that thing but also of themselves. Some spend their lives feeling that inferiority and sinking deeper into the bog of self-disgust; others try to cope with it in ways that numb or overcompensate. Many addicts talk about Shame in relation to their use, which they consider the basis for their Shame but also something they employ to cope with it. You don't need *The Little Prince* to understand this analogy—go to any AA meeting and listen to how most addicts perceive the later stages of their use. Shame is a constant companion.

[38] And who hasn't been shamed by their parents or some other person responsible for providing a safe and loving environment where children should feel emotionally supported and nurtured? Who hasn't been called stupid, fat, or lazy by someone whose job is to teach such values as self-respect, kindness, empathy, and responsibility?

I've wondered whether calling myself a chronic relapser meant I was more prone to a relapse, as in "I relapse because I'd relapsed and had relapsed because I relapse." But that's not the entire story. There were periods in my life when I drank because I felt ashamed of being a drunk—although more specifically ashamed of the behaviour caused by me being drunk—but usually I didn't have a reason. Other than being a romantic, of course.

And yet for me, Shame—as bad as it was—has also been a motivator; without it I would've succumbed to some version of that dubious freedom of mooning the world while wrapped around a parking meter. I was closer to death when I weighed my feelings of Shame against telling the truth—with telling the truth seemingly a worse option than suicide. But, at the same time, if I still had Shame—and as long as suicide remained too drastic—I had hope, which is the only magic we have as human beings.

What's the first thing you think of when a debilitating headache comes on? How to get rid of it, right? In that way, pain is ultimately a good thing, not only informing us of something being wrong—which is secondary to simply wanting it to stop—but also motivating us to get better. In the context of my addiction, that pain was my Shame—over relapses and my hypocrisy—and its presence was uncomfortable enough that I wanted to do something about it. As for hope, the proof was in the number: I had relapsed at least twenty times, which means there were at least twenty times when I believed I'd one day be sober. That is *a lot* of hope.

The little prince leaves the drunkard and we never find out if the drunkard manages to get sober. Unlike me, he lives on the planet alone and hasn't confessed to the world that at one point he was a sober drunkard. And yet! There is hope.[39] As long as the drunkard feels Shame, he could possibly sober up one day. He's been *seen.* Maybe it's shaken him up so badly that he'll get sober in the hope that the little prince will visit him again and find out who the drunkard was before he started drinking.

Later in the book there's a parallel episode about becoming known (seen) when the little prince befriends the fox, who explains that attending to someone, getting to know them, is what creates connection and a bond. ("It's the time you spent on your rose that makes your rose so important . . . People have forgotten this truth, but you mustn't forget it. You become responsible forever for what you've tamed. You're responsible for your rose," the fox tells him.)

And the drunkard has already told the little prince his Shame, thus laying a foundation for their connection.

39 Shame can be a great motivator. In one study, the participants who felt strong negative emotions of shame, and reported a general sense of dissatisfaction with their behaviour, felt that changing it would allow them to gain a new sense of who they were, a desirable outcome. Although as fully formed adults we can't completely alter our personality, it *is* possible for us to change our negative behaviours. As the study put it, we're more "successful when [we] are motivated by strong negative emotions and [can effect] a change in [our] sense of identity."

In another study, researchers asked participants to think of a shame-inducing event and measured their responses based on Repair ("I felt like I should apologize for what happened), Distance ("I wanted to be completely unassociated with the event"), and Change Self ("I felt the urge to be a better person"). Finding that the strongest desire was for lasting change, the researchers theorized that since guilt is closely connected to apologizing and making amends, these actions can lessen the sense of personal or moral conflict caused by the event and thus may diminish the motivation to change. In other words, apologizing and moving on wasn't enough to elicit different behaviour. Shame, by contrast, was a much stronger predictor of a different behaviour because it offered much more of a redemption.

19.

People love a good comeback story;[40] it resonates with the common human experience of failure followed by transformation. Such stories inspire hope and demonstrate that change is possible, even after significant setbacks. They're a powerful reminder of resilience and the capacity for renewal, encouraging us to believe in second chances and the potential for positive change in ourselves and others.

My story of redemption was so repetitive that I no longer had visions of a triumphant return—I was too tired and mostly just wanted the cycle to end. And occasionally, I still believed it was possible. But even when I didn't, I just remembered that things were always better when I didn't drink. Sometimes that was enough to motivate me to pick myself up after yet another fall.

Besides my fateful bike ride, I've had plenty of metaphorical falls—including every time I woke up feeling like the worst piece-of-shit parent on the planet, having yet again broken my son's trust.

But I'd also repeatedly get back up, namely when I'd rejoin AA, but also twice when I entered rehab. I used to believe rehab was the absolute last resort—it was also prohibitively expensive—but because it was the last resort, its significance was even greater in my life.

[40] The Prodigal Son, that well-known biblical tale of a wealthy man and his two sons, is one example. The younger son asks for his inheritance early, leaves home, and squanders his wealth on reckless living. When a famine strikes, he falls into destitution and takes a job feeding pigs. Realizing his mistake, he returns home, repents, and asks his father for forgiveness. His father welcomes him warmly, rejoicing that his son has come back, while the older brother feels resentment. The father explains that they should celebrate his brother's return, that he who was lost is now found.

The good news for someone like me is that I'd not only admit what made me behave in those ways but I'd also know what to do to redeem myself. And belief in redemption is a crucial part of the recovery narrative.[41]

Go to any AA speaker meeting and you're bound to hear a version of the Prodigal Son tale, one that follows the "What was it like then? What happened? What is it like today?" formula. Every single one of them is a story of redemption. There's the Before, when drinking or using was fun, innocent, and without consequences. Then there's the "What happened?," when drinking or using starts to turn on you, when bad things begin to happen, sometimes when a very bad thing happens (getting in an accident, getting fired, losing a relationship). Finally there's the After, the life of sobriety marked by improvement, reunion with loved ones, new career opportunities, and a regaining of respect. To those coming to meetings for the first time, such a narrative is extremely attractive, demonstrating as it does that they too can

[41] One study that examined the power of addict stories has found that people whose narratives included self-redemption were substantially more likely to maintain sobriety in the following months compared to newly sober alcoholics who produced non-redemptive narratives.

Non-Redemptive Narrative: Meet John, a middle-aged man who regularly indulges in excessive drinking. His family and friends express concern, but John dismisses their worries and continues his self-destructive behaviour. Eventually his excessive drinking leads to liver damage, strained relationships, and job loss. The story ends with John isolated, unhealthy, and without any signs of personal growth.

Redemptive Narrative: Meet Sarah, a young woman who struggles with alcoholism. She joins a support group, undergoes therapy, and embarks on a journey of self-discovery and healing. Throughout the story, Sarah learns to forgive herself, rebuild relationships, and cultivate a healthier lifestyle.

dig themselves out of whatever hole they've buried themselves in and get their lives back.

My redemption story is still ongoing. The memoir I wrote and published wasn't a story of my redemption and neither is this book. That's because life isn't a memoir and I get my fix elsewhere, not through people reading[42] what I write and deciding I've atoned. (I get it through talking with people I trust.) Going public was a complicated triumph, one that brought on anxiety and more trauma. But it's also shown me how powerful the simple act of speaking up is. What sharing about my biggest Shame has done, and what I hope it will do again, is help me regain some control—so that I'll no longer have to worry about getting exposed by real or imaginary witnesses to my Shame. Remember, with addiction, I'm the architect of my demise *and* my salvation.

20.

I once heard Barbara Gowdy, a friend of mine, talk about a short story from her book *We So Seldom Look on Love*, about a woman who knows she's being spied on by a man who is not her husband. It's a classic story of a participatory voyeurism as the woman progressively reveals herself to the man who wants to watch. Gowdy said of exhibitionism, "It's wanting to be acknowledged. I think the best thing we can do to people in the world is to acknowledge who they are, who they're presenting themselves as, and it's a loving thing to do. The more we look, the more we attend to them, the more we

[42] Although this, too, is my attempt at being seen.

see them, the more empathetic we are, and the more difficult it is for us to do them harm. All failure in the world is failure of empathy and all failure of empathy is a failure of imagination and a failure of attending."

I didn't think I was an exhibitionist, and seeing the word in a review of my memoir was offensive to me. And like the word "alcoholic," it was meant in an offending way. But it's true that I wanted to be seen and maybe even understood. I was tired of the bad rep addiction had, and I wrote the memoir partly to explain its mechanism. Perhaps I gave myself a bad rep while doing it, or perhaps some people came to understand that a loving mother too can be a drunk. But more than anything, knowing that secrecy is the main ingredient of Shame, and that Shame is the basis of all addiction, I didn't want to participate anymore, passively, by staying quiet about it. I was tired of hiding. I needed to come clean.

On the morning I describe in my memoir, when I finally arrested my drinking, I gambled everything against the truth. At first my story was that I'd had a concussion falling off my bike the night before,[43] when I found myself dazed and without any shoes in the middle of the night, unable to tell my ex-husband on the phone where I was.

Concussion, he sighed that morning.

I knew he didn't believe me, but he was exhausted by the lies and we played the game of denial because stopping it meant we'd have to acknowledge the elephant in the room that was so huge it was pushing us out the windows and doors. I was on my last chance—a

[43] It's a pattern, I guess. I don't blame bikes.

graduate of rehab by then, a few failed addiction groups, and one pointless attempt to rejoin AA. We both knew that my admitting I'd been drunk meant he'd be kicking me out of the house and would begin separation proceedings, including taking custody of my son. That was his hard line, our agreement.

I went all in. My home, him, my ex, my son, a better life—against telling the truth. I didn't even let myself hope that the truth meant I could possibly win all those things back.

There was no concussion. I drank, I said. But you don't understand. This time it's different.

That's what you said last time.

I packed my bags.

PART 2

Poland One

(2021)

21.

I come to on the plane, awakened from the fog I've been drowning in by the pinging of the seatbelt sign above my head. Once we've landed I gather my things and move bleary-eyed through bodies and tight aisles, through wafts of perfume, fried food, sweat, hay, jasmine, musk, so many smells and thudding feet on the carpeted floors, Ma'am, sorry, sorry, Miłego dnia, dziękuję, dziękuję, You too, sorry, sorry. Then I'm out, stumbling into a large white corridor—I know this walk, left and then down to the baggage claim—and finally parking myself near a rubbery carousel with suitcases moving round and round like a sushi train, where I watch for an orange tie around a handle, there it is, "There you are," I think and grab it. Everything still fuzzy, I reach for my phone, except my pocket is empty. Where is the phone? Where is it? Fuck and shit, walk back, back, the door is closed, where do I go?

Zgubiłam telefon, I explain to the disinterested blur of a face at a counter in the Warsaw airport who says I'll need to go to Lost and Found *after* they clean the plane. I'm given directions and a scrap of paper with a scribbled number and told nothing can be done here and now. I'm still not quite with it, jittery too, but I feel calm; it's not the first time this has happened. In fact, it's almost comical how typical it all is: a drunk has landed somewhere in the world with all the usual drunk's woes.

A few minutes later I'm out in the Arrivals concourse, part of a moving river of people, bags, noise, sounds, and the aroma of espresso. I squint, trying to make him out in the crowd. He's been waiting for quite some time now. He looks like every other Polish man over seventy—bald, grey or beige clothes, thin lips, large nose, large hands. Except he's *my* Polish man over seventy, and I recognize him instantly, with his signature boyish awkwardness. Wujek (Uncle) Jacek. As usual, he appears embarrassed, pained almost, the way he always does when emotions are involved; he lets me hug him and laughs nervously as I do, follows my lead to land an air kiss near my cheek and I talk and talk and talk and tell him about the phone. He urges me to check the Lost and Found, although I explain how there's no point, they have to clean the plane, and yet I go anyway since at least it feels as if I'm doing something, giving myself an illusion of control over a situation where I have none and where I expect none to be regained. No phone will be found.

A former communist country, Poland is a place that delights in both bureaucracy and swindle, the first a legacy of its forty-four years under the Soviet thumb and the second a continuing chaos wrought by the Wild West of a struggling nascent economy, political reform, and the need to establish a new social order. A new and now lost iPhone X doesn't stand a chance. Still, I head to the Lost and Found, where a middle-aged man gives me another number to call—call how? Unfortunately, he says, other than that right now there's nothing to be done. I'm grateful to him for saying those words so decisively and yet so impassively. I am tired and jittery still, my hangover a distant road roller coming at me slowly but inevitably.

It'll be fine, I assure my uncle, who helps me with my suitcase as we get into his car. Once we're on the road he points to new buildings, complaining about all the construction going on. As always when I return home, a pinball machine activates in my mind, its ball scoring and missing points as I do and mostly don't recognize targets, bumpers, and other features on the playfield of my old memories. Later I'll visualize a different kind of topography: a map that lights up in familiar areas, unveils those dormant for too long, gradually fusing old and new, readjusting roads and landmarks, weaving a tapestry of physical but more importantly emotional connections.

Every one of us has a map like this, one that evokes the place and time of our origin, its blank canvas bearing a legend that lists not just geographical data but settings that mean something particular to us—the hospital where we were born, the kindergarten, the first best-friend pact, the first kiss, the last time I saw my beloved grandmother, short and wide in a purple skirt and white jacket, her tanned face with that sweet, coy smile I'll never not miss as she waved me off on my way to the airport we're driving from now.

22.

My first map is Warsaw, and I rebuild it every time I come back. The *You Are Here* point on the map is Ogrodowa Street, where I grew up in a communist-era block, on the eighth floor, in a small two-bedroom apartment with my parents, my little sister, and my grandmother. Right now it's only me here and our ghosts: me at fourteen, my sister at five, my parents just forty years old, my grandmother, and the family dog too. We're stuck between these walls and howling silently in the early morning when I wake up, startled and thirsty, suddenly sober and time-travelled, unsure whether I'm behind by only a few hours or a few decades.

The strangest thing about the apartment is that since we emigrated it's stayed almost the same; even the furniture remains in its place. For me, Warsaw isn't just an assemblage of buildings going up and buildings coming down; it's a living history inside of which I live my own, or relive it when I visit, here within my own little time capsule on Ogrodowa. It's as though I'm tucked inside a final matryoshka doll where all times are combined.

Imagine visiting your first home, where everything looks almost exactly the same as it was when you turned fourteen. When everything stopped.

At the moment, though, I just feel embarrassed—the way I've been feeling about the apartment since an old boyfriend, Marcin, came over for a visit a few years back and exclaimed in half horror, half fascination, "It's like a skansen[44] in here!" He marvelled over the gloomy brown meblościanka, a type of modular wall unit consisting of shelves, cabinets, and drawers that can be arranged in different configurations. During the communist era these were popular in Poland, considered to be modern and edgy. Marcin was

[44] "Skansen" is a Swedish word that refers to an open-air museum and zoo located in Stockholm. Poles use it as well, but often jokingly to describe structures and places that have been preserved in their natural state.

by then a vintage furniture dealer, but to me he sounded not so much impressed as mocking.

Now, in 2021, his words come back to me as I explore the apartment. *Skansen*. There are a few improvements, though. The wooden panelling—impossible to remove—has been painted over in white to modernize the look. And over the years my parents renovated the bathroom and replaced some of the falling-apart chairs and shelves, mostly to cater to the students they rented to during Warsaw's golden boom of the early 2000s.

Back then thousands of young people moved here from small towns and villages, creating a whole new working-and-partying sector known mockingly as Varshafka, a little Warsaw.[45] This ambitious crowd studied mostly business. They worked in retail and in coffee shops, restaurants, and bars, some of them saving up enough to open their own establishments. Some built homes or invested in the same modern concrete boxes in the sky as the young people born here had. Yet despite their acclimatization, they'll always be considered outsiders. (Even to me, if only because I was born here. But perhaps I'm Varshafka too now.)

The original Varshafka have since grown up and matured, flourished even. A friend from a small southern town who moved to the city to wait tables in the late 90s is now selling his steampunk-themed, top-rated, wildly popular tapas restaurant. It's not just Varshafka who are ambitious, either: another friend, a local, is turning his prewar

[45] This coincided with Poland's entering the European Union in 2004, when Warsaw experienced the biggest economic growth in its history.

tenement's former cult hipster dive—Second World War bullet holes pockmarking its walls—into a boutique hotel. And a buddy from elementary school has purchased a brand-new condo with a terrace the size of my Toronto apartment.

The few changes on Ogrodowa Street barely reflect what goes on outside.

My old elementary school, a block away from the block, has been replaced by a slick building with a medical centre upstairs where you can check your hearing or remove your varicose veins—and downstairs, there's a spa and a sushi restaurant.

But history is never far away. On my block's sidewalk is a thick line of polished stone incised with lettering; "1944" and "Ghetto" jump out at you. More than ten years ago the city commemorated the former Warsaw Ghetto with boundary lines traced in the ground to preserve the memory of that Second World War–era Jewish quarter. The building where I grew up didn't exist back then, but the nearby Grodzki courts, erected in 1939, did. They still operate to this day. During the Nazi occupation the courts were deemed "extraterritorial"—suspended between two worlds, with an entrance for Jews on Leszno Street and an entrance for "Aryans" on Ogrodowa. According to a Polish historian, Professor Jacek Leociak, "To enter the ghetto, you had to put on an armband [with the star of David] in the courthouse building; to get out, you had to take off the armband on Ogrodowa Street and then blend into the crowd." A portal between life and death. As a very young child I imagined it as a magical place, a macabre *Alice in Wonderland* doorway. I didn't understand that these entrances and exits weren't voluntary, that the ghetto was inescapable.

And to me the courts themselves were Mordor-like—dark, imposing, a cool, ancient breeze forever breathing out of impermeable stone walls. You could even climb onto stone elevations that made you taller as you walked beside an adult. Above it all were imposing Art Deco letters announcing the courts' maxim: SPRAWIEDLIWOŚĆ JEST OSTOJĄ MOCY I TRWAŁOŚCI RZECZYPOSPOLITEJ—"Justice is the bulwark of the power and durability of the Republic." The architect, Bohdan Pniewski, was famous for the dichotomy of his designs: buildings that from the outside looked like Judgment Day temples, monumental and restrained, but that inside dazzled with their spaciousness and rich, elegant curlicues of brass and marble.

Years later, those courts would become one of the most important landmarks on my Warsaw map. Yet still they would fade, as ephemeral as a fairy tale, then come back into focus as I continually trained my memory. At night, at fifteen, in the barely furnished bedroom I shared with my baby sister in Canada, I'd walk by them in my head—a meditation to lull me to sleep, a spell to remind myself who I was.

I was always in pain that first year. Both physical—from an infected molar—and emotional—from an infected heart. My father opted to have the molar extracted, which was cheaper than fixing it, except that brought on only more pain: it too felt like a betrayal, as though I couldn't count on being taken care of here. Until my late twenties I'd smile without showing my teeth, embarrassed about the terrible gap that never failed to remind me of *that* Shame. (Because of that negligence my teeth remained weak in general, but by 2021, if you'll recall, I'll have a perfect new smile.)

Besides my nighttime walks by the courts, in my mind's eye I'd play a special art film. In this one I'd look down at my feet, notice cracks in the Varsovian sidewalks, and try to remember the type of stone used in different parts of my neighbourhood—from cobblestones and mosaic to large flat cement pavement tiles. I'd trace my way around, constantly moving, checking, repeating, remembering.

I knew these games were making me impossibly desolate, but I had nothing else on which to hang my interrupted brain. And in a way, they were making me hopeful about the future too. It wasn't that I thought we'd go back; rather, it was just knowing that another place existed, with its buildings and its sidewalks, and that I hadn't just arrived in a horrid little Southern Ontario town out of nowhere. And that there was a way out, just as there'd been a way in. One day I could live somewhere else, find another home; there was a whole world beyond sad gas stations, rundown plazas, ugly malls with shelves stuffed with cheap crap. Beyond teenagers loitering around trash bins like rats. Beyond sloppily dressed, unhealthy adults whose cheerful hellos and fake friendliness were matched only by their disdain for outsiders like me who didn't speak English.

I know this is a harsh summary of my first impressions, and maybe an unjust one—there was a certain Ontario Gothic beauty in the area's farmlands and forests—but I was angry about leaving Poland and culturally shocked to the core.

We emigrated in 1992, ten years after our original plan to escape the communist regime during martial law. In 1992 the country was wild but full of promise. It had been three years since communism ended, but it seemed my parents had planned their escape so intermittently that it took that long to finally go. (To this day, we have a hard time answering why we left exactly—perhaps only because leaving for the mythical land of America used to be their quintessential dream and my parents felt obligated to fulfill it.)

It's an exaggeration to say we immigrated on autopilot but it's also not an exaggeration at all. The vague idea of improving our lives was always there, but by the time my parents were able to buy their own house—after four years in horror-show subsidized housing—we were disillusioned and lost. The people back home, meanwhile, seemed to have settled into the changes; many were succeeding in material ways far beyond what we'd accomplished.

A few years after leaving Poland, my mother referred to it as "the biggest mistake of our lives."

My own confused solution was to get a part-time job as soon as I could. And so by fifteen I was working in a fast-food joint at a gas station next to the highway near our town, saving up money for summers back in Poland. Which, my first summer back, became a magical place with no drinking age, a place where no one blinked at the sight of teenage girls with a bottle, falling off their very high heels.

As the bleak months full of longing moved closer to summer, I managed to accumulate enough money for a ticket. Then, a day after the final school bell, I got out of there.

For years I'd go back every summer. And for years it was the only reprieve I had from feeling stagnant and stuck and guilty about my parents' sacrifices and my ingratitude.

Now that I'm the age my parents were then, I understand a lot more about their own misery and tension, which I'm sure stemmed from a similar sense of guilt and perhaps failure. For them it manifested in bad behaviour—in their insensitivity, in their blind spots. They wilfully missed grave developments: how I was starving myself and becoming an alcoholic; my sister's growing anxiety that turned pathological when she, like me, escaped our home at seventeen.

People who are depressed and focused on their inner turmoil tend to be myopic,[46] emotionally shortsighted and unable to see beyond their own sadness or hopelessness. We were four unhappy losers clinging to a raft that was drifting in some unspecified direction. Looking back, perhaps it was my parents' myopia that prevented them from clueing in early on that immigrating had been a bad idea. However, knowing what I now know about the power of Shame, I believe that going back would have meant having to face all those people they'd left behind. It would have meant admitting defeat.

Maybe it's my hangover or maybe it's being inside a time capsule, but on that first day back in Poland I feel like a failure. Or more precisely, that no matter where I try to run, here I am. But I'm in no shape to self-reflect for too long on this; it's too painful. I intend to have a good time.

[46] The cognitive phenomenon known as myopia involves a narrowed focus whereby people tend to disproportionately magnify their perceived failures while downplaying or even ignoring positive aspects of their experiences. Their mental landscape contracts, intensifying feelings of hopelessness and self-doubt. As a result they may also have difficulty noticing and empathizing with others around them.

This is something that, as a parent, I too have been guilty of. In many ways addiction is a version of psychological myopia, whereby the addict's intense focus on immediate gratification is driven by cravings and impulses that overshadow any consideration of their consequences.

23.

In 2021, when I visit Poland, I am no longer an immigrant at sea but rather a woman who's experienced joy and stability in her second life along with a family of her own. It didn't work out, but ever since my son's birth I've felt at home there. Although it's funny that I still divide it into *here* and *there* and there and here and sometimes I don't know which one's which where.

When people ask, I make it sound as if there's a reason for my spontaneous visit. I tell them it's a last-minute escape from the pandemic lockdown. The lockdowns are on and off and nobody seems to know how to navigate our new reality exactly: when to stay in, when to go out, at what time and with what papers and what apps and shots, and whom to hug if at all, if it's six feet apart at all times or only inside, masks on, masks off, new variants. So when it was announced that the channel between Canada and Poland has opened for travel—albeit with endless, confusing requirements and goofily surreal protocols—it was as though I was a wild animal bolting for freedom. I was a wild animal indeed, still drunk when I landed.

On that first day, I do what I always do when I get here, no matter how long my trip, how hungover or drunk I still am, or how sober and simply tired: I decide to go out.

Once I am fully awake and all sobered up, I shower. I imagine I'm washing off the grime of Frankfurt or whatever German city we stopped in on the way here. If we did stop over. I don't remember but I know we were supposed to (is my phone in Frankfurt?). I wash and condition my hair. I moisturize and perfume my body. I dress in white. As excited as I'm beginning to feel, my movements are slow, deliberate, as if I'm being watched, as if I'm preparing myself for a ceremony. I caress my bionic clavicle, as always feeling strangely proud of this injury that makes me feel as if I'm some sort of half cyborg. Like me, the clavicle has two modes, sober and drunk. Depending on the mode, I see it either as an extreme body mod—a kind of bone tattoo—or as a sad reminder of being a total fuck-up.

I don't take a taxi; I walk. I pass buildings I grew up with—my school, my church, the courts, the postal office, the academic bookstore. I pass places whose construction I've missed entirely: a condo ("Moderna Living") possibly named after a Covid vaccine; a mushroom-shaped edifice with a cascade of fake pink roses spilling out its doors. The map in my head gets more complicated, digital. I open folders with files of places whose grids look the same but whose insides have been reprogrammed multiple times. The nail salon by the postal office used to be a burger joint that used to be a currency exchange shop that used to be a pet store. I superimpose budgie cages onto the walls lined with nail polish, a stack of pet rodent cages onto the fake marble reception desk. The two large pedicure chairs in the front window become a huge aquarium with a boa constrictor. After school we'd come over to stare at it. When the pet store owner once took it out of its terrarium for us, I was shocked by the boa's cool, silky skin.

Next door, the grey postal office, its massive windows and doors fashioned in the standard Socialist Realism style, closed a while ago. It's empty and dusty inside now, like an abandoned space station. But outside stands my grandmother's ghost in a lineup of other ghosts, waiting to pick up a care package sent by my mother. After we left, my grandmother transformed regular tasks into drawn-out rituals, picking up deionized water and her favourite snack, hazelnuts, in the neighbourhood farmers' market, exactly five slices of smoked ham at the butcher for her daily canapés, coming here to check for mail instead of waiting for its delivery.

I usually walk four stops north to the Old Town, which is probably Warsaw's best known tourist area. After the war it was rebuilt almost entirely, recreating the original buildings and streetscapes using surviving architectural fragments, historical documents, and period paintings. It features narrow streets, pointed arches, and intricate stone carvings characteristic of Gothic architecture. Baroque influences can be seen in curvilinear forms and opulent decorations while Renaissance influences are evident in ornate facades, detailing, and symmetry. Or just picture any Old Town in Europe and it should be close enough. Only newer, which makes it more Disney World than historical artifact.

My Warsaw friends avoid the area but I am a tourist here after all. It's something I'm mildly embarrassed about—not for being an outsider now but for indulging in outsider activities of the least-resistance variety. Still, I visit here first, always. I walk to my Old Town and then I walk to the Vistula River, which in the past ten years has been revitalized into boulevards peppered with bars and restaurants and public art. Dozens of new attractions now line its banks—a museum of science, a modern art museum, and Elektrownia, a historic power plant turned development with shops, restaurants, housing, offices, and a boutique hotel. Twenty years ago you wouldn't come here unless you were looking for some kind of dark adventure—running into rabid soccer hooligans drinking by the water, say, or petty criminals spotting your tourist vibe long before you spotted them.

Along the way I step into convenience stores where I buy tiny glass mickeys of flavoured vodka: raspberry, cherry, lime, three dollars per pretty sweetie. The drinks refresh and dull me both. I'm like Warsaw herself, broken and renewed at the same time.

I'm wearing a beautiful white summer dress and my summer hair is piled up on top of my head. I smell like diesel and stone and a fertile tea rose. Again, like Warsaw. I take another discreet sip and shove the last of three bottles into an overflowing recycling bin near the stone mermaid, one of the many mermaid sculptures in a city that boasts the half woman, half fish as its coat of arms.

I told myself I'd drink on the plane only because I'm afraid of flying and only enough to fall asleep. And I told myself that once I landed I'd be so busy visiting everyone and taking trains across Poland—I'm here for only three weeks—that I wouldn't even have time to drink.

But wherever I go my drinking follows. Plus, being here "na występach" (a performance tour)—which is how I refer to my Poland visits when I'm not exactly sober—creates an even greater disconnect. On tour you can be all kinds of extra: an actor of your own life or a cooler version of it, an approachable rock star, in a costume and with a different personality. You can be loud to your usual quiet, you can be promiscuous to your usual shy.

Aggressive to your inherent tame. It's no coincidence that even non-alcoholics binge-drink on holidays in foreign places. It allows everyone, but especially single travellers[47] like myself, to partake in their own tours; they can invent themselves, they can be anyone they want.

This występy of mine is going to be fast and hard, moving as I will between cities, people, bars, restaurants, art shows, and sometimes beds. It's no secret that alcohol is a great disinhibitor, a social lubricant as they call it, and under its influence I've often felt more than just psychological euphoria.

My euphoria is an open mouth, a golden liquid star inside it, sweet, hot, pulsating, moving down the esophagus, passing through organ walls—whoosh—and crashing, breaking into a thousand smaller stars that seem to activate all those nerve endings that suddenly pulse between the legs, closing them but only temporarily, a way to trap the tiny stars and to feel them better, more intensely. I know that the horniness is real but it's also fleeting, since the drunker you get the less sensitive you become—to a mouth, to pain. I've never been able to orgasm while drunk. Yet those *first drinks* feel golden and sexual, alcohol enhancing my arousal

[47] There isn't a lot of good research on infidelity during vacations, and any statistics that are available might be influenced by various factors, including survey methodologies and cultural differences. But, according to a survey conducted by Expedia, about 32 percent of travellers have admitted to cheating on their partner while on vacation. Another survey by the dating website Illicit Encounters found that August is the peak month for extramarital affairs in the U.K., which coincides with the summer vacation season. And we all know that people on holiday might be more prone to engage in unusual behaviour owing to factors like reduced supervision, increased alcohol consumption, and a break from routine.

through increased blood flow, hormonal shifts, and alterations in brain neurotransmitters.[48]

I mean, if you're not convinced that drinking is about sex, I recommend any of the dating reality shows I watch (I watch them all). The very first thing the contestants do is open a bottle of bubbly (or five) the producers ply them with. The second thing is somebody's tongue down somebody else's throat, and this goes on for 9,877 episodes. The only changes are the colour of bikinis and the slow dislodging of hair extensions and fake lashes. (The contestants' gradual deterioration makes for a nice metaphor—all those fun, sexy effects of alcohol are only good for the first while.)[49]

As for me, I'm in my own reality show now, moving toward oblivion at breakneck speed as I swing my hips, gliding gracefully across cobblestones, smiling back at strange men who pass and stare unabashedly.

[48] Additionally, since it lowers inhibitions and boosts self-assurance, alcohol leads to a greater willingness to engage in sexual activities. It acts as a vasodilator, meaning it causes blood vessels to expand and increases blood flow, including to the genital area, leading to heightened sensitivity and responsiveness. It also temporarily affects hormones like testosterone, which play a role in sexual desire as well. And it interacts with neurotransmitters in the brain, particularly affecting the balance between excitatory and inhibitory neurotransmitters; the latter include gamma-aminobutyric acid (GABA), which promotes relaxation and lowered inhibitions and can increase receptivity to sexual stimuli. Alcohol stimulates dopamine release too, contributing to feelings of pleasure and reward and potentially enhancing pleasure derived from sexual experiences. It even boosts serotonin, the famous Dr. Feelgood—in the beginning.

[49] Excessive alcohol consumption leads to a change in hormone levels, including testosterone levels, which impacts sexual desire. Things like erectile dysfunction can arise owing to alcohol's impact on blood flow and nervous system function. And alcohol's depressant qualities can delay orgasm and satisfaction. Finally, alcohol's dehydrating effects and fatigue can decrease interest in sexual activities.

The next day, I wake up back in my old home in the time capsule on Ogrodowa with no memory of how I got back. This feeling is also home.

24.

I'm on the train to Krakow to see Ania. I have my pink and yellow special sweeties tucked in the fancy green designer backpack I always travel with, a gift from a famous artist who had an affair with me when I was separating from my husband.

Whenever I wear this backpack I think of him. I don't miss him, but I remember our mischievousness. I also think of having affairs, which there's absolutely nothing wrong with if no one finds out. Just the other day I messaged Luke, a former lover, and told him I was here; within minutes he sent a winky face at something innocent I wrote—testing, testing which Jowita was talking to him. It was soon obvious that it was this one, the party one. I was here na występach. On a tour.

For now, on the train to Krakow, I drink from my pink and yellow sweeties not to feel horny but to feel brave and cool and interesting. Also, I drink because I'm excited—ecstatic, actually—given that I came to Poland mostly to see Ania, and now I'm only hours away.

Ania and I met almost ten years ago through an ex-boyfriend of mine, Marcin—the vintage furniture dealer—who was one of my great Polish summer loves, a beautiful maverick with a million ideas and all of them good. He's the sort of guy whose name can be mentioned in any part of Warsaw and people will have a story. He once inherited a warehouse from his eccentric aunt; it contained thousands of never-worn 1980s Italian boots that he sold to celebrities and fashionistas who'd line up around the block to get a pair. Over the years I've witnessed him open clubs and painfully hip dive bars where he'd host the most impossible-to-invite acts, and then do a complete 180 and get into running health food stores or printing art books. He finally landed on rare furniture, mostly from the postwar eras of former communist countries, and Italy.

But before all that we were two kids who fell in love one starry night in Warsaw. Our bodies were tanned and slim, our faces glowing with youth, and we made out in parks all over town, drunk on Grolsch beers. Our summer fling was slightly tragic, marked as it was by my impending return to Canada. But we kept in touch, and as adults I met his partner, Ania. Marcin used to joke that we were the opening and closing brackets of his great loves; he used to call us the Astral Sisters.

Ania and I had been born a day apart so it was an apt description, and although physically we look nothing alike—she's blond with blue eyes—there are enough parallels between us that there was something to it. An artist, a social justice activist, and a solo mom, Ania tends to live outside the nine-to-fives and definitely outside Poland's very traditional family values. Her relationship with Marcin is probably the longest one she's had, and over the years the two of them have created a number of artistic projects, from gallery exhibits to concept stores to ecological playgrounds.

Before meeting in person Ania and I did a project together, a small book of my photographs depicting dark truths of motherhood, most of them self-portraits that conveyed the sort of exhaustion and loneliness only a first-time mother knows.

During that time Ania and I would send each other visual references, documents, and clips of our previous work; we were getting to know one another, both as artists and as potential friends. We even planned to record our first actual meeting as part of another project we talked about, the idea being that she'd be shooting me as I shot her. It wasn't long before the woman I knew only as "Marcin's girlfriend" became someone with whom I could talk openly about being an artist without feeling like a fraud.

This was partly because she'd called me an artist as if it were a normal thing.[50] That gave me permission to see myself in that way as well, and although I still struggle with the label, its pinch makes me cringe a little less.

As for the project, Ania chose as its central image a startling self-portrait of me lying on the ground, skinny and exhausted, my child crawling over me.

My son and I are both naked in this photograph. You can see my bruised-up breasts and my pubic hair is a dark forest, in dramatic contrast with the soft innocence of my son's fat body. I've shown my photographs at small shows but never the more disturbing ones where I'm definitely *notokay*, where none of it has been staged—just as it hadn't been staged on the day the baby crawled on top of me.

[50] Despite producing art—writing as well as visual works—I've always felt shy about it, and that I had no right to it. Even the word itself, "artist," made me cringe, calling up an image of a Parisian mime or my former painting teacher with funky jewellery who once disclosed that she prayed to crystals. Incidentally, so much art is about Shame, and so sharing it is yet another way to name it—with our audiences as our witnesses. And not just to our Shame, but to human shame in general; an artist can convey Shame in ways we can all see.

It was one of those weeks when I'd holed up in the house with enough food for days, just to avoid going out—since the liquor store map in my head was emitting not just polite red flashes but sirens.

The whole experience of working with Ania was as if she had her arms wrapped around me when I wanted to bolt, holding me until I calmed down. When I finally met her in person, we recognized each other in the way people sometimes do, with an instant knowing: I've missed this person all my life.

Now in 2021, after years of friendship, we have even more in common. We've gone on a few trips together—Cuba, France, Croatia—and have stories that we joke have probably been written by the same cosmic screenwriter. Except that in 2021 Ania is in a brand-new relationship with a cool guy with a cool job and cool apartments, and I am a drunk. In 2021 Ania is studying for a new diploma and I have a manuscript that's late and falling apart without an editor. Ania's last book design was nominated for a prestigious award and I have an angry publisher who sent me a message ending with "Have fun choking on all your Polish sausages" after I told him I needed a change of scenery to finish the book.

As rude as he was, he's on to me. He knows I've run away. Alcoholics refer to this as a "geographical cure," meaning the belief that being somewhere else will fix the problem of drinking. It turns out, though, that changing continents and time zones is detrimental to my sobriety. I'm both on a trip and in purgatory, a place where I don't want to drink but have no idea how to stop.

When Ania said I should just come and work on the manuscript in Poland, I booked my ticket. She also suggested we do a project together involving Polaroids—a medium I still use and find strangely apt for the pandemic, as I no longer feel that anything is real, or tangible, and that I'm constantly missing something. I have hundreds of shots of people in lineups, abandoned buildings and empty storefronts, six-feet-apart signs at cemeteries, and always that ripped yellow tape flapping in the wind. I don't know what it is I'm missing even though I know I'm looking at it.

25.

At the train station Ania looks worried. A former model, she's always been naturally slim, a whippet of a woman with girl-like elbows and knees and a girly charm accentuated by her effortless style. She wears too-large geometric dresses and coats; actually everything looks too large on her and by default deadly fashionable, as if she's raided her very elegant cool aunt's closet.

I hug her and tell her she needs to eat more and she ignores the comment. I forget, of course, how much comments like this bother her, something she's heard all her life and that to her feels accusatory, as if she's a secret anorexic.

She gently hooks her elbow with mine the way she always does, and we walk and I talk and tell her all my most recent adventures, including how easy it was to buy a new iPhone the day after I landed. I take out the phone and show her as she manoeuvres me through crowds of people and then onto a streetcar and then we're in her apartment and I leave for a few minutes "to get some fruit juice." Then time blurs, contracts, and then it's evening and I'm not sure why we haven't gone out to eat the way we always do, the way

Cracovians do after it gets dark, but maybe we've talked so much we just forgot? Ania is wedged into a corner of the sofa, her knees drawn up to her chin, her eyes large and melancholy.

I smoke a cigarette on the dark balcony, where I know you can see the faraway mountains during the day. I've seen pictures of the apartment; it has a spiral metal staircase to the upstairs although I don't recall noticing it tonight, yet somehow we're upstairs. How do you miss a spiral staircase? It doesn't matter. At night only the nearby pine trees are visible, and I can smell their Christmasy smell through the cigarette smoke.

When I come back into the living room Ania has made a bed for me on the sofa. To make room I kick my backpack to one side along with some of its entrails, which are strewn all over the floor. Ania says something about being tired. She'd spent the past weekend entertaining her cool boyfriend's sister and had seen her off only this morning, right before she picked me up. I know she was stressed about the visit; she worried about making the right impression and knew the sister would be watching her closely since she's very protective of her brother. Truthfully, I don't recognize this new version of Ania, caring about first impressions so much and bringing up "Darek" a lot when she talks: "Darek would say," "Darek would want to." At one point I blurt out, Who cares about what Darek would say? Ania's forehead wrinkles and she says, I care.

Of course, I assure her, he sounds wonderful, and I mean it. It seems one of us has finally come to her senses and found not just a loving partner but one who can improve a life with his wealth and wisdom and his cool knowledge of cool places to vacation. But mostly with his wealth, really—although this is just me projecting after the past few years living on the brink of financial crisis and trying to combine writing and parenting and working but truly, just trying to fit those three around my drinking. In Ania I don't necessarily see myself, but I do see that there's hope for unanchored women. As much as we love it, it's exhausting, and I tell Ania I'm happy she's landed somewhere and then for some reason I break down about my own relationship. I'm not even sure why I'm crying, what is wrong exactly. I'm just feeling emotional about everything. It must be visiting Poland—it's like encountering your ex and seeing him doing well without you, and with a beautiful woman on his arm, too.

The next morning my head hurts but not too badly and I am in Krakow and I cannot believe I'm here. I pull out my new red iPhone—a few missed FaceTimes—and spontaneously book two tickets to Zakopane, a touristy mountain town a couple of hours south. I'm thinking of surprising Ania with the trip. We could go for a day, see my beloved Witkacy's[51] home, get some oscypki cheese, climb one of the gentler mountains, take some nice photos, and have an overpriced traditional highlander lunch. The pine trees in the window sway gently as I try to think of Zakopane activities. I feel only mildly anxious, the way I feel most mornings.

[51] Witkacy was a twentieth-century Polish playwright, writer, philosopher, and painter associated with the Formist movement, which sought to create a new modern art distinct from traditional styles. Witkacy's paintings often feature bold colours, distorted forms, and abstract designs, many of them created under the influence of various pharmaceutical concoctions. Witkacy was also known for his use of photography and his interest in exploring the subconscious mind. He was handsome, he invented a new language, he hated convention, and he loved women very very much. In 1939 he took his own life on the day the Red Army invaded Poland.

Jo, Ania's voice says somewhere beside me, and she motions for me to come back to the fold-out sofa. She climbs into bed with me. You're gonna have to go.

I understand instantly and am so mortified that I can't even look in her direction as she tells me that I stayed up quite late crying on the balcony and FaceTiming with my boyfriend, and that it kept her up way too long. She can tell there's something seriously wrong but she doesn't have the emotional bandwidth, she doesn't have the room—physically and otherwise—to help me with whatever it is I'm going through. Her daughter's coming back tonight and it's too overwhelming, and she's not sure what to do, she's not sure what's going on but she can't be the one to rescue me. She'll leave now and give me my space, and let's meet for a late breakfast later and figure it out.

Figure what out? Are you kicking me out?

She looks at me with infinite sadness in her eyes. I love you. But I can't, and she says other things, which I don't hear, which I block now, as I scramble to get up and collect my belongings, and she gets up at some point too and then I hear the door click gently somewhere downstairs.

I take a bath and dress slowly, my limbs heavier than the usual hangover corpse so it takes me a while. I am angry and humiliated and oh, so indignant. I recall bits of our conversations from the night before, my crying over a crisis in my relationship but what crisis, really, more just a general dissatisfaction with where I am in life and who I'm in this life with. I recall, too, crying over a less recent past, a miscarriage that has strangely haunted me, maybe because it was symbolic of a new possibility annihilated by my own self. It's been making me think about how I'm my own enemy, in my mind but in body too. I didn't want to have another child—more accurately, I didn't think I exactly passed the motherhood test—but I wanted *something* . . . to save me? . . . and that something kept not coming.

I don't think I said any of those things the night before but if I did I wasn't coherent and probably just burbled some nonsensical ends of them. I rarely cry so the tears must've been ugly, too, the way they are when they happen after a long time stuffing them in.

But so what? Isn't this what friendships are about? Ugliness and tears and drunkenness too? We can't just lie around on Croatian beaches and dance in Kazimierz clubs with sexy strangers, drink rum in Cuba, eat eclairs in Paris.

I wonder about her new cool boyfriend and decide then and there that it must be Darek who's responsible for this. Ania probably complained about me and he told her what to do. She's already letting her hair grow long and at least half of what comes out of her mouth is what Darek thinks. She's on her way to becoming a Stepford wife, smelling of the custom-made perfume he gave her on her birthday that combines frankincense with a scent of burning tire, which is something she prattled on about when she wasn't explaining how stressed out she'd been over the cool boyfriend's sister's visit.

I call an Uber and get it to take me to Central Square, where I make a stop at the convenience store and buy a couple of sweeties, drinking them while I look at the sculpture of some Polish king or composer or some other idiot I have a nice memory about.

The memory is of my son climbing it three years earlier as a group of local boys gathered around him, fascinated by my son's golden mane and his typical Polish-boy soccer getup—typical, yet somehow signalling that he's not from around here. I don't know how they knew but they spoke to him in half English, half Polish until they all found a common language of footie, my son reconstructing Lewandowski's famous five goals. We were visiting Ania and her daughter then, too, and spent the most magical week wandering the streets, having dinners in secret courtyard gardens, and swimming in a big turquoise quarry on the outskirts of town.

Right now there are no little boys climbing the statue. Instead it's swarming with dirty pigeons and their waste, which seems perfect, it seems apt, as though I'm living in a movie about things going to shit. It's very hot and I'm sweating in my jumper. I sit in the shade but it makes little difference. I know I should move somewhere even cooler, try to salvage this day somehow and not add heatstroke to it all. But I don't move.

Ania texts that she'd like to meet for a late lunch and talk and I accept. Despite all those big feelings, guilt, Shame, and anger, I don't want our friendship to end, or I want to at least talk it out, or something. I wonder if she'll ask me to come back and I decide that no way, I will not come back. Very quietly and secretly, I also hope she'll ask me back and that she'll sit with me and help me and—

I sip my sweetie and the world shimmers and blurs and I feel a little lighter and stimulated even, despite recent events.

I stand up and walk toward the shaded shopping passages off the main tourist strip, where I know it's cooler and where I hope to get inspired—to do what I don't know, but I still have some time.

I get inspired when I stumble onto a Thai massage spa and there's a masseuse who says she can see me right away and I know this is the best idea I've ever had. I deserve this little treat and in some way this is also a fuck-you to Ania, me having such a nice time in Krakow despite her.

I've never had a massage while drunk and it's even more pleasant than usual. I'm bendy and eager to be twisted and stretched, and at one point the masseuse and I are in complete tandem as we manipulate my doll body. I'm loving this so much I ask for another thirty minutes, mostly because I realize I should probably get sober.

At lunch both Ania and I are shy, having lost our bravado—I'm no longer ready to confront her, and she's probably less inclined to tell me how I've disappointed—

Well, I don't know what she wants to tell me. She says I left the bathroom in disarray, wet floors and messy sink, but she's jokey about it, she teases me about being a human version of that messy sink. Then her tone changes, hardens; she asks me what my plan is.

Because she asks this so plainly, without preamble, I answer as plainly as I can, too: I don't know. But I know I'm *notokay,* I add.

It's hard to see you like this, Ania says, and looks away, her voice breaking for the first time as she loses her put-on tough-love tone. I love you. And I don't want to . . . She waves her hand, looking away. I can't. I don't know how to help—

It'll be fine, I say. If she'd just ask me how she could help I would tell her, I would tell her that . . . what would I tell her, exactly? That I'd like to dry out in your lovely Krakow apartment with your sixteen-year-old daughter in the next room? It's gonna be a fun adventure! And maybe you could tell your cool new boyfriend to cancel your cool vacation next week to watch me sweat. It'll be like an art performance. Maybe we can record it?

But I'm not even sure if that's what I'd like. And as we sit there all I can think of is when this stupid lunch is going to be over so that I can get back on the train to Warsaw and do my thing in peace.

Speaking of which, where's the nearest convenience store? (I briefly worry about this because today is a Sunday, except that in Poland every convenience store sells alcohol. In fact, the only places guaranteed to be open twenty-four hours on Sundays and holidays are churches and liquor stores.)

I offer to pay for lunch and Ania lets me. We hug awkwardly but with relief that this—whatever this is or was—is over for now and we can go back to our: new lovers and family obligations, and: demons and Shames. I promise myself never to come back to Krakow, no matter what. I couldn't face it.

26.

Having returned to Warsaw, I message Luke. He agrees to meet me at some fabulous spot overlooking the Vistula River, a docked barque bouncing in techno and bare shoulders and white teeth and hands on waists and twisting hips and spinning skirts and me too. I look like a million dollars, sun-streaked hair, perfect makeup I spent an hour on while sipping a sweetie on Ogrodowa. I have on a tight black dress hugging my athletic curves, heels, but most importantly a galaxy between my legs full of twinkling and exploding stars as I meet my second vice, which is men's attention.

Luke is half in the bag as well, his charm full on. He flirts with his eyes and so much wit he could easily improvise a stand-up. There are compliments in there too, lines that would sound so very corny in somebody else's mouth, somebody whose eyes don't narrow at you seductively as he says his memories of you are like precious rare pearls, that he has a whole string of those pearls.

I used to joke with a mutual friend that Luke is the kind of guy who could seduce you, your mother, and your father while all three of you were in the same room, and all three would feel absolutely singled out and special. Having Luke all to yourself is like having a floodlight on you; it's that relentless and a little scary and exciting, too—exciting because you see your own beauty reflected back in his eyes, you do become a rare pearl and then you play up to that expectation.

The rest of the night is a montage of dance floors and cocktails and laughter and bodies moving closer and closer together, a dark back of a taxi, a hand, a tongue, teeth, throat, a hand between the thighs, an elevator and fumbling keys, then bodies doing what they've met to do in the first place.

We never, not once, talk about Luke's wife. I never, not once, think of my rosé years and the women I thought were pathetic losers for taking up with a man they well knew wasn't single.

27.

The rest of my trip is a string of sweeties and their different flavours and the different interesting backgrounds against which I drink—castles, parks, fountains, neon-lit clubs. None of my outings are really about those backgrounds; this, despite what it's supposed to be, is not really a trip. I drink with friends and I drink alone and I drink when at home. I try not to drink during the day and do my penance by dealing with my manuscript, trying to fix it but also so I've something to say when people ask me about this "working holiday" I insist I'm on.

Along the way I text with Ania to discuss what happened. She doesn't apologize and I don't expect her to—I don't know what I expect, but I don't want our friendship to end despite all the anger I feel about it. She tells me about losing a close friend earlier that year to addiction and how guilty she's felt about not saying anything, how she watched him drink and snort powder and laugh and dance and talk and dress in feathers and fur and kiss people and never sleep. How he was always at the best parties, and how one day he didn't show up at the best parties because he was dead.

I can't watch another friend go through this, she writes. I would never forgive myself for pretending. It was too much to see you like that, and I can't be in your life watching you die. I have to be well for my daughter, I have to be well for Darek. I'm sorry but I'm not sorry, she writes, and her steadfastness offends me and impresses me. Again, I think how if she were a real friend she'd offer to help me, and again I realize that I don't want her help, that I don't want anybody's fucking help, and that help would only interfere with my fun tour. It would interrupt this drunk, sexy body I've now shared with two different lovers whose attention is as intoxicating as my sweeties.

I assure Ania that I'm not Slawek, her friend who died. I will get help. As scary as this comparison is, inside I feel flattered that I have something in common with Ania's tragic Polish artist, that I'm almost as tragic myself, a writer drowning in vodka, dark and secretive, in service to her inner pain.

28.

Besides summer lovers and possibly ending friendships, I try to genuinely attend to one person I care about and that's my childhood best friend Agata, whose Catholic wedding I attended thirteen years earlier in Warsaw, as her witness, and whose first daughter was born the same summer as my son. With her married to a German and living in a small town near Frankfurt and me in Canada now, we try to coordinate our Polish excursions so that we can see each other, even if only for a few days.

We've known each other since first grade and have spent many summers together: first in Girl Scouts and later as teenagers falling in love with boys on Polish beaches or dancing in dark Warsaw clubs with other boys, and everywhere drinking till we puked (mostly me). And later in our twenties consoling each other over men who weren't worth it and picking up other men to get over it and to buy us more drinks in successively fancier places.

But our friendship wasn't about men—they were just part of what our friendship was about, which was growing up and navigating life and having each other to check in with. We were completely different in ambition and personality—she was bossy, business-smart, and rule-obeying, and I was not. But somehow it worked, maybe because we had that ancient shorthand all best friends have, where all you need to do is look a certain way or say a word and an uncontrollable giggle escapes you and there's no way you could ever explain the layers of those inner jokes to anyone who isn't the two of you. She loved my imagination and I loved her stability but also her willingness to once in a while break those rules she obeyed, and I loved her sensitivity too when she'd react in genuine and naive shock to things like my huge student debt or tumultuous home life. I was her bohemian weirdo friend and to me she was the weird one, with her traditional family values and a solid plan for the future. We live apart but when we meet it's always as if we'd seen each other only a week before.

It is exactly like that when we get together in 2021 and she invites me to spend a couple of days at a bucolic Polish eco farm in the Masuria, where she's staying with her entire family, her sister's family, and her mother too.

I arrive by bus, half-drunk already and dressed in a slinky silk nightgown standing in for a dress, along with ridiculous platform sandals that make me six feet tall. But these normal people I'm visiting expect a little eccentricity from me and I'm happy to entertain.

We met for supper once already in Warsaw, where I drew everyone's caricatures to the squeaky delight of Agata's younger daughter, over-the-moon enamoured of her artsy aunt with her long braids and sparkly personality—so avid for my spark, in fact, that I had to load up on it in the washroom more than once that evening.

Now, in Masuria, I make an instant excuse to visit a convenience store "for some painkillers," remembering at the last minute to grab a pack of ibuprofen for cover. Agata and her mother and daughters are waiting outside; four pairs of bright green and blue eyes looking up at me: You got everything you needed?

I'm so happy to be here with them and now to have stocked up so well, but, really, I'm so happy to be here with them, *that's why* I'm so happy and I tell them how happy I am and how beautiful it is here, so happy it's so beautiful here and so happy they're here with me.

We're happy you're here too, Agata says, giggling. You okay, gówniarzu? She uses the Polish parents' horrible equivalent for "brat" that translates to "shitling," which is what we affectionately call each other.

Absolutely perfect, gówniarzu, I say.

The little town of Mikołajki is crawling with tourists, mostly families with children, who crowd the pretty passage by the lakeshore, with its dozens of fish restaurants and its stands selling water toys and fridge magnets and Pop-It fidget toys that Agata's younger daughter says she collects. This is music to my happy ears—I'm so happy to have been invited here and to be able to reciprocate even a tiny bit—and the cool auntie buys two, one for me and one for her, both in the shape of a fish.

We eat overpriced fish dishes on a patio overlooking the famous Gołębiewski luxury hotel on the other side of the lake.

I try to make out its main building or anything else that looks the same way it did twenty-eight years ago. As a fifteen-year-old, during my first summer back in Poland, I spent a night there with a man more than twice my age. I had just discovered drinking.

I've workshopped that night so many times, and yet nothing about the hotel is familiar. And when I look at Agata's older daughter, who'll be a teenager next year, suddenly I can't imagine that long-ago fifteen-year-old either.

I look away when she catches me staring and I give her an apologetic smile, my ears burning now, my heart slamming against my ribcage like a flopping catch of the day. I feel a little sick, a little too hot, flooded with discomfort but on whose behalf I don't know—my own or that man's—or what wrong had been done exactly; I've always insisted it was my choice, from the first vodka shot that night. I haven't visited Mikołajki since the morning after, when I snuck out of the hotel room, feeling guilty, hungover, confused, and . . . proud. I'd lost my virginity that night, and I'd lost it to an adult man. I got on the bus back to Warsaw, and when I got off I marched like a robot into the first hair salon I saw and asked them to chop off my waist-long thick brown hair.

I understand the symbolism of that act,[52] its shunning of femininity, long hair being a weapon you can choose to remove so that others won't remove it for you.

And of course I know that cutting my hair off was related to what happened in the hotel room, that it was both a protest and a rejection. Maybe even a cry for help, although I was as delighted about my new do as I was about no longer being a child. The man had come on to me, but it was never assault—save for one stolen French kiss, which I let him steal—and he didn't force me to go into that hotel room. He just let me know he was interested, calling me "womanly" and "beautiful" and telling me with longing in his eyes that I could "crush

[52] Shearing hair to humiliate women, to shame them, has been used as a war tactic for as long as there have been wars—forever, in other words. During the Second World War, German women suspected of sleeping with foreigners would get their heads shaved, and during the Irish War of Independence both the IRA and British forces shaved women's heads to punish those suspected of collaborating with the enemy.

But women shaving their own heads, whether in self-defence or in protest, is another phenomenon. There have been accounts of Ukrainian girls, having heard reports of rape, shaving their heads to make themselves less of a target for Russian troops. And after the death of twenty-two-year-old Mahsa Amini—who died after being pulled off the streets of Tehran by morality police—women around the globe have protested by shaving their heads in public or while being filmed during rallies.

him like a little bug" if I ever chose to do so. I know today that he "groomed" me, that I wasn't capable of giving full consent at my age and in the state I was in. But I also know how proud I was to take my clothes off in that hotel room and let him do to my body what I'd read about in books. I also know how wicked I felt when I learned he had a wife, as if I'd one-upped this woman I'd never met.

I look for Shame in this story, too. But as it was with publishing *Drunk Mom*, this is one of those things that I know should've shamed me but hasn't; the only Shame I feel stems from the fact that I don't feel it—which must mean there's something seriously wrong with me. I'm also careful not to harvest that experience—to call it what I know it should technically be called. I do know the difference.

Yet back at the restaurant the memory gives me pause. And once the discomfort passes, for a moment I feel something quite unexpected: compassion for the girl-me who thought she had it all figured out. The girl-me who drank, who couldn't tell the difference between feeling happy and feeling pain.

29.

In the evening, at a gorgeous country house surrounded by green hills, forests, and ponds, Agata's family throws a barbecue. I down beers with her German husband, who seems delighted at having a drinking buddy, except that he drinks a little too slowly, like a regular person, so I have to get up twice or thrice to use the bathroom, where at some point I run out of my final sweetie. But it's fine, it's late, and it's the summer, everyone's on vacation and the conversation is so exciting that it can carry me for another hour or so.

At one point the talk turns to immigration politics. Then Agata's husband says what he says and suddenly we're on the precipice of a serious blowout.

Agata's adult nephew, whose English is fluent, sits like a referee, watching the ball being hit back and forth. I decide that his discreet smirk is directed at me, at my winning the match, so I up my rant. This seems to alarm the nephew, who gets up abruptly, announcing that it's getting quite late and it's time to go to bed.

When I wake up the next morning I'm twisted in sheets on a fold-out sofa in the living room, feeling and probably looking like a dying moth. Through half-closed eyelids I watch Agata's younger daughter cause an impossible ruckus in the kitchen as she makes herself a Nutella sandwich. When she spots me watching she bounces over and asks me how I slept.

I slept? I'm not so sure. My body feels as if I've pushed a boulder up one of the hills surrounding the house and my mouth isn't even a desert, it's an ashtray in the middle of a desert. In the shower I try to figure out how I'm going to survive the morning kayak excursion that Agata has booked for half the family.

For the first hour it's a beautiful journey down a gentle river flanked by the most idyllic countryside: patches of shaded forest, quaint secret beaches, fields where grazing black-and-white cows look up apathetically, old wooden farmhouses that somehow survived the last of many wars waged on Poland. I paddle and paddle, sometimes contributing to the conversation but mostly not, trying to sweat out the toxins from the night before as Agata chatters on and takes pictures and videos. I've told her I enjoy being athletic and it's no big deal, we kayak in Canada all the time; in fact, the word "kayak" probably originated there. (Actually I've never kayaked before, but in my twenties I did once canoe, beer in hand, an old boyfriend doing all the work as I relaxed into a boozy lull, my paddle jammed to the side.)

The trip down the river takes almost five hours, and by that time I'm exhausted, hungry, angry, and so very thirsty that I Google the location of the nearest convenience store as soon as we dock. I tell Agata and the rest of the group that I'll meet them at the restaurant we're supposed to lunch at and then run off like a maniac.

When I get back I'm calmer and happier—even grateful for that gruelling trip down the river. I'm jovial, energized. Generous. I tease Agata about not paddling; I pose for the selfies she insists on. I let her show me Instagram accounts of salad-eating women with healthy skin, which she obsesses over. I joke with her younger daughter and we race to pop our Pop-Its. I tell Agata's husband that we should never talk about certain topics again—he nods enthusiastically—and I talk to Agata's mother about how lin fish is superior to sandacz. When I'm quiet for a moment I look around and notice the beautiful lake we're sitting by, the kids playing in a sandy playground, the quiet Polish folk music coming from the gift store. Then, quite suddenly, I feel crushed, as if someone popped *me*.

This, I know from experience, is me reaching my quota of normalcy. I've arrived at the boredom point many addicts are familiar with, that place that makes us scream inside our heads.

Any fixation, whether it's an addiction to alcohol or some other vice that obsesses you, can lead to changes in the brain's reward system.[53] To put it another way, we can all become rats pressing levers for dopamine hits. This can make it difficult to experience pleasure in everyday activities, and as a result, those of us not used to sitting with our boredom will seek out drugs or other addictive behaviours to liven things up. And when I talk about boredom, I'm not just talking about having nothing to do and not feeling stimulated by our environment—I'm talking about being in any situation that isn't familiar, that we haven't learned to derive pleasure from. And for me, being among a family that is loving and close, content to be in a beautiful country restaurant, making small talk about the comparative attributes of lake fish, is absolute torture.

I remind myself that my trip will be over in a few days, and that later this afternoon I'll be getting a ride back to Warsaw. And soon enough I'm in a car with Agata's mother, niece, and nephew, who at my request makes a gas station stop where I help myself to a sweetie.[54] For the rest of the drive I entertain everyone in the car with fun anecdotes about Canada. A couple of times I meet the nephew's friendly but watchful eyes in the rearview mirror, and when Agata leaves me three voicemails after I get back to Canada, confronting me in the most loving way, I guess right away who it was that said something about my being a drunk.

[53] Additionally, if you'll recall, addiction can lead to changes in the prefrontal cortex, which is responsible for decision making and impulse control. This can make it difficult for some of us to resist the urge to engage in addictive behaviours when we're bored or experiencing other negative emotions.

[54] Yes, they sell vodka in Polish gas stations.

30.

My trip ends with a few blurry days and nights.

I have one spectacular but very sensual fall on the night when I've somehow managed to get two of my Polish lovers—who know each other, which I think is cool and perverse—meet me at the same bar. Afterward they walk me to an Uber, both terribly worried about the scrape on my shin but praising my newfound drunken balance on my roughed-up Louboutins (which I'd bought back when I still had some sanity, a house, and a family).

The second last day, I do what I do every time I leave Warsaw, drunk or sober.

If going to the Old Town is my touristy tradition of saying hello to the city, a trip to the National Museum is my way of saying goodbye to it. As a little girl I used to visit the gallery with my father, who tried to introduce me to serious, difficult art—Cubism, Rothko-like blotches, the terrifying eyeless faces of Beksiński's fantasy paintings. Eventually he gave up and took me to the sections of Polish art enjoyed by crowds, where I fell in love with the Młoda Polska (Young Poland) era,[55] an early twentieth-century modernist period in Polish visual arts, literature, and music that embraced Decadence,

[55] Young Poland artists sought to express the country's unique cultural identity, often drawing inspiration from traditional folk art, literature, and history. One popular subject was nature, with landscapes, animals, and plants rendered in a highly stylized and decorative manner, but another famous theme was mysticism and spirituality, with artists drawing on esoteric traditions and occult symbolism. And despite their interest in tradition and folklore, many artists were also fascinated by the rapid changes taking place in society and technology at the turn of the twentieth century and would often incorporate such modern elements as urban scenes and industrial motifs.

Neo-Romanticism, Symbolism, Impressionism, and Art Nouveau. I have tattoos referencing some of the better-known motifs by Stanisław Wyspiański,[56] who's probably the most well recognized representative of the movement.

I also have a special connection to Józef Mehoffer's *Dziwny Ogród (The Strange Garden)*, a huge painting done in the Young Poland style. It's a colourful scene showing a sweet family moment—but with a twist. In the foreground, a naked, cherub-like blond boy is out in the sun, carrying two heavy stems of red hollyhocks. To his right and slightly behind him stands an elegant woman in a massive hat, a rich blue dress, and a heavy bustle with a long skirt. She's about to step into the light from a shaded passage in the apple orchard where, in the background, another woman in a less elaborate dress is trailing her mistress. It's a happy scene, but looking at it, you get the feeling of walking in on someone's private moment. What makes the garden strange, though, isn't just its intimate vibe, one whose lack of specificity almost mocks the viewer, but rather the massive dragonfly at its top.

When you take in the work's confusing proportions all together, it's as though the dragonfly has flown out of the painting and is possibly sitting right on the tip of your nose. It's a startling visual experience.

[56] Stanisław Wyspiański died of syphilis at thirty-eight, a relatively short life whose legacy puts most of us to shame: he was a prolific painter, architect, and designer, a nation's pride playwright, an excellent poet, an inventor, a furniture maker. He even designed an intricate, functional model of his hometown, Krakow; had it been produced, it would have elevated this already beautiful city to the world's most futuristic metropolis.

The painting has delighted me for most of my life. I've smelled its sun; I've felt high from looking at the dragonfly. I've admired the gorgeous blue shades of the woman's dress, wondered about the blurred features of the maid in the background, imagined how the orchard's shade would feel on a hot day, how brightly the colours would have popped in that dim light, how bleached they'd become once out of the passage.

In 2008, when I came to Warsaw for Agata's wedding, I had a profound encounter with the painting. On saying goodbye to it, I looked away from the giant dragonfly and from the shaded orchard passage and focused on the blond boy instead. He's a focal point but I've never cared for him, so I don't know why he caught my attention then. But suddenly he became the most significant element of that fantastical scene. It was as if I could hear his laughter as he shook the hollyhocks and shouted at his mother to please watch. Then I had the weirdest thought—that I was looking at my son, who didn't yet exist, except that he did, in his own strange garden inside my body.

Now, in 2021, I go and cry a little in front of *Dziwny Ogród*, but I don't really mean it. I don't know why I'm crying, or whether it's for show, or who the audience is since I'm the only one here. I guess it's for me. *Stop it.* I avoid looking at the little blond boy, blurring him out. I know he's there in the centre, forever shaking those hollyhocks in the sun. The huge dragonfly looks slightly menacing, as if it's been sent out to our world to defend the people in the painting.

On the day of my departure I drink and then meet Agata and another friend for the fastest coffee ever, making it to the airport with two hours to spare. Once there I remember that I didn't get the required twenty-four-hour Covid test. Thankfully, right outside the airport hall is a makeshift medical centre, where I pay extra for instant results and then gun for the check-in, papers in hand, buzzed and dishevelled, imagining myself to be not a commoner who takes air travel seriously but rather an important person for whom running in airports is a regular occurrence.

Several hours later I come to; again it's the seatbelt's *ding ding ding* that wakes me. I'm in as bad a shape as I was at the beginning of this trip, but at least I don't lose my phone. I am, however, put into a two-week quarantine, having misplaced the printout of the Covid test. I curse Poland and swear to never come back, as if it was all Poland's fault.

31.

I won't vacation in Poland for another two years. I cannot face it.[57] I am hoping time will be enough of a buffer before I go back. The only trip I take is to New York with my son, where we explore Manhattan in sweltering heat.

For the most part, this is probably one of our best trips; however, by October things with my son are fragile. They've been fragile since the day we got back from our trip, but specifically since I took a few extra clonazepams for my fear of flying. On that two-hour return flight I swallowed enough to go on a space mission to Mars.

Later, my ex-husband showed me my son's texts:

Mommy is notokay.

[57] Losing face

I'm sorry buddy. That sucks. You'll be home soon.

I know. I love you.

I love you buddy. You'll be fine.

JFK Airport—like Toronto Island and a dozen other spots—becomes a new place we lock in a box and throw into the deepest well. If we talk about New York we talk about the heatwave, the hotel whose pool has a glass bottom, the inner city basketball game we stumbled upon, the horrible dry pretzel and the shitty hot dog in Bryant Park, the Broadway musical—where my son laughed a lot, spontaneously in pure kid delight, despite himself, despite being a teenager—and the turtles in Central Park. But we don't talk about the flight. And the gift bag I left on the plane. And how I insisted we wait for someone to retrieve the gift bag (they didn't) at three a.m. instead of saying fuck it and going home. I'm grateful we don't talk about that, although I would if asked. That's the only thing I have to offer as an addict—I'm a rare breed who, when confronted, will often fess up. In my experience, this isn't true for most addicts. So I try to offer at least that—not to shy away from the throat-clutching discomfort that confrontations bring, addiction's most immediate consequences.

I don't drink daily but I do drink, although not on the nights with my son. Except that night I do. I don't know why I can't wait at least till he goes to sleep but I don't. We had a lot of fun at the mall, where we donned cow costumes—complete with udders and a bell—and goofed around in the mirror and took ridiculous selfies.

Sometimes the urge to drink happens when I feel a sprout of happiness; for years now I've tried—and failed—to water this sprout with booze and pills to see if the happiness will grow bigger, grow leaves; it never does.

Or there are times when I fall into some sticky, murky memory that pulls me under the surface, grabs my ankles and won't let go: *There you are in your old garden on Wallace Avenue and it's May and it's so hot you took your top off and you're gardening in just your undies and big yellow rubber gloves, and you scratch your nose and the smell of young earth is wet, alive, and your son is two years old running through a sprinkler in the bright, fresh grass, and your husband is taking a photo, and he says he loves you.*

In the second memory: *There you are inside the house on Wallace that now resembles a game of Tetris, your boxes marked "J" and his boxes marked "R" and neither of you talking, what is there to say? So you're silent and you're both crying silently on the leather loveseat you bought together, where you've read your son all his first books, his favourite one Dr. Seuss's* Go, Dog. Go! *In this memory your son is seven and he pushes to sit between the two of you, and later when he doesn't think you're there you take a picture of him standing at the front window, his nose pressed against the glass, looking out onto the street that is no longer his, for the last time.*

Or maybe there was no memory, and I'm not particularly happy either after our afternoon at the mall; maybe there's just an extra mickey of vodka I forgot about, as if it were something I'd ever forget about, as if I probably didn't buy it the day before thinking maybe I'll just hold on to it, except when did I ever hold on to it before for more than a day?

I swallow it like medicine, let it coat my insides, recalibrate my happiness or dry out the sticky mud of some sad memory.

I don't do anything bad. I just open my mouth and my words are toffee. And my son-of-a-drunk son's ears know right away. This time he doesn't try to peer into my eyes to see the murk I've been drowning in, to ask me a question to confirm that he hears the extra stretch in my words. He simply gets up and says, I'm going to Daddy's, after which he folds the cow costume I ended up buying and shoves it in his backpack and leaves and I don't dare stop him.

Although how can he leave? Did we not have so much fun? The next day is Halloween. Tonight is my night with him except it isn't now.

And it won't be for three months. Which is the longest I've gone without having to wake up four times a week to prepare his elaborate school lunch in the morning. This is one of the few remaining activities that still make me feel like a good mom.

32.

All that happens around the publication date of my third book. If there's anything that's a natural high for me, it's the culmination of years or months of work and seeing it published, having tangible evidence that all the mundane sacrifices of time and effort and anxiety and self-doubt are for something after all. It's a cliché but it's no exaggeration when artists compare their projects to children: demanding, ever-absorbing, delightful, and terrible at the same time, spine-breaking and impossible to push out into the world but once pushed out absolutely miraculous and proud-making. As it is with children, here's the evidence of something that came out of me, a thing that originated out of nothing, a thought, a dream, a sentence.

But from the beginning, my novel *Possessed* proves to be my most demanding, difficult child, its gestation full of problems. By the time it's launched, my emotional exhaustion is analogous to the physical exhaustion I experienced when I was in labour with my son for more than twenty hours, an eon that ended with an emergency C-section and both of us nearly dying.

The editor who acquired the book got fired a year before its release, a date that had since been pushed back twice—both times demanded by me as I panicked about the lack of edits. The publishing house had been slowly becoming a ghost ship, losing eight staff just that year, including the publicist originally assigned to *Possessed*. I did get lucky when my friend and favourite author, Barbara Gowdy, read my novel after I'd given it to her to blurb but instead returned it with editorial suggestions. The book was weeks away from being sent to the printer, but Barbara rightfully called the manuscript unfinished and said it would be a disaster to my career to publish it as is. She meant that it read more like a draft than a completed book, but I can't think of it differently ("a disaster to my career") even long after I've fixed it. When I asked my publisher to literally stop the presses, I got an angry email threatening to cancel it. My agent then stepped in and threatened back and I was able to finish the work that was needed but not before pissing everyone off and turning my hard-earned nice-to-work-with reputation into a dumpster fire.

And then once the book eventually got printed, a series of unfortunate events was set into motion.

My author copies being sent to the wrong address should have been my first clue that the stars weren't aligning. On the day of publication I showed up like some kind of delusional self-published maverick in various bookstores across the city ready to sign it, only to be finally, gently told by a goth teenager working at one of the larger chain stores that perhaps it's in the boxes that haven't been opened yet. The way she looked at me told me all I needed to know, but I smiled as brightly as I could and said I'd be back; she nodded with visible relief. Walking out, I wondered if I'd imagined the past six years, if I was maybe in some sort of elaborate long-term psychosis where I believe I write books and that people buy them but in reality I'm sitting at a barred window in paper slippers and a gown tied in the back, looking at a tree.

Yet now that the book is technically here, friends call and write to ask if I'm happy about the launch, some wondering where they can find it since for now they can't find it online. I remain slightly mortified about the whole thing, my entire body burning as the blush creeps from that tiny, fragile pulsing core every artist has inside their heart. The tiny, pulsing core that is both the most beautiful and the ugliest, a place more intimate than a lover's touch, more authentic than a dream come true. The place where I germinate those words and sentences before I release them to be looked at, marvelled at, poked at, ridiculed.

This is the risk every artist takes, every caretaker too when they raise something, teach it and shape it and *show* it. I believe writing—or painting or dancing, et cetera—is a job like any other, that we're not more special than those who don't constantly reach into their cores for a living. But the sensitivity that allows us to show you something that makes you feel doesn't get to punch out at the end of the day.

And what if your creation isn't doing well and every negative thing that happens around it confirms[58] that? It feels deeply personal. Maybe that's why *Possessed*'s failure to launch well is a bit like watching my own full-of-promise kid get disqualified from making the soccer team. Or it goes even deeper, closer to what we go through when we observe someone else's public humiliation, someone we love. There's a body of research that explores this "vicarious shame," and I wonder if I'm experiencing some of that with *Possessed*.[59]

While *Possessed* does eventually get out to readers and reviewers, I never stop feeling awful about it. I give up on self-promoting it in the shameless, unapologetic way most authors are expected to promote their books these days. I look at the cover and no longer see my beautiful, anticipated child but rather something I don't want to be associated with, something that repels me.

And the less I want to call it my own, the more I'm convinced it will probably fail.

---

[58] Apparently we're hardwired for negativity. Studies have found that the amygdala—responsible for regulating emotions—responds with greater activation to negative than positive stimuli. And one fMRI study has pinpointed specific brain regions associated with the negativity bias. In other words, we tend to remember the bad more than the good, and we pay more attention to it.

[59] One study that investigated such feelings aimed to understand the underlying mechanisms and emotional responses related to vicarious shame. By having participants respond to written scenarios in which they were to imagine, say, a family member or colleague committing an embarrassing or morally questionable act, the study found that they indeed experienced vicarious shame and guilt, feelings whose intensity was affected by both their closeness to the person and the perceived severity of the transgression. Importantly, the study also showed how empathy and social connection can play a role in influencing these emotional experiences.

But guess what? The world beyond me doesn't seem to think so. The first review, published in the largest and most influential national newspaper, is glowing; an entire front-section page dedicated to it, complete with a large photo of me, an illustration, and the cover of the book. I've come into my own with this novel that the reviewer says "embraces Camus [and] blends Gothic horror elements." Here I experience a sort of dissociation: I'm puzzled by what the reviewer has written; I don't believe he's saying this about *the thing*. I can't even bring myself to open the thing to check if by some accident I was cleverer than I am. I lost whatever confidence I had about it a long time ago. And by now I've collected all kinds of delusional evidence with the help of my negative confirmation bias.

That evening I get drunk alone and later take a selfie lying on the floor with the review, my two-dimensional face from ten years ago fresh and happy next to my actual face, swollen and with checked-out eyes.

Canada's arts and culture coverage—and especially book coverage—has been shrinking year after year, and mid-list authors, a category in which I include myself, are lucky to even get reviewed. So many books launch and sink. Immediately. And yet, despite the hiccups, *Possessed* somehow makes the rounds of newspapers, literary magazines, and, of course, online, including a popular BookTok where a sweet twenty-one-year-old gushes about *Possessed* being a book about cool, unlikable heroines. Honestly, if I could be objective about it, there's nothing to be ashamed of. And yet I am. And this will not go away even after I have evidence that says otherwise.

How I feel about *Possessed* is the opposite of how I felt about *Drunk Mom*. With the latter, no amount of criticism could convince me that I'd created something I should be ashamed of. But now, to flip it, the positive responses to my Camus-Gothic-horror-blend novel also don't seem to matter. The Shame I feel is real because it's private, because I've internalized it so much that it's become part of me.

33.

As if I needed any more reason to think *Possessed* is possessed, I receive an email—timed to arrive on the night of my launch party—from a lawyer threatening me with a lawsuit by a former lover who's decided, without having read it, that he's the subject of the book. Here are the facts: at one point in our relationship I joked that he'd inspired the fuckboy character. Eventually I tried to end things between us, which in turn inspired him to declare his undying love. The letter seems a last-ditch attempt at connecting with me—if we can't be lovers, maybe we can be enemies? I open the email as my journalism students work on writing a scene and another professor sits in the corner writing an evaluation of my lecture. And here I'd thought her evaluation would be the most stressful thing that day. *This is fine*, I murmur under my breath, thinking of that famous meme of a dog having a cup of coffee while his house is on fire.

Don't worry, you did great, the evaluator says, suddenly next to me—I'd been staring so hard into the screen that I wasn't aware of her getting up with her little black knapsack. In my own knapsack are a pair of heels and a slinky black dress I intend to change into before I go to my party tonight. I think how she has no idea about the lawyer's email, how I just found out I might be in big trouble.[60] I think how nobody has any idea about anybody, and those horrible clichés—not knowing what battles others are fighting; what hundred miles their moccasins are walking—start clunking about in my head. I smile brightly at the professor and thank her for her time.

At the launch party that evening I'm in a blackout, this time not an alcoholic one but an emotional hole I've fallen into after reading the letter. The onstage interviewer asks good questions and smoothly guides us into a playful banter that elicits a lot of laughs. The book's gloomy cover photo—a woman reclining on a dark Victorian couch, a cracked and crumbling wall behind her—seems apt for how I feel: as if I'm disintegrating. Outwardly, though, I'm a star, and congratulate myself on not getting shitfaced despite things being a little tense.

There's a box of books at the launch; I can touch them and turn their pages, I can smell their newness, their papery warmth, which relaxes me a bit as I sign copies and pose for photos. I'm sparkly and pretty in the new dress my boyfriend bought me for the occasion. My publisher has sent a new publicist, and, for the second time, a gorgeous bouquet of apology flowers.

Everyone asks how I'm feeling, what it's like to be so celebrated, am I happy with the launch, am I happy with the cover, am I happy? Am I not a brilliant, happy, talented, cool, happy, happy thing? Am I happy? So many people shake my hand, somebody hugs me, I catch

[60] I am not. A friend who's a defamation lawyer suggests I write an article about the letter "for publicity," and I do. It's the only nice thing I go out of my way to do for *Possessed*, my leper child.

sight of an ex I used to pine for slinking out the back, my sister and her partner, my editor for *Drunk Mom*, my boyfriend, and friends and everybody else. Their faces are smiles, their eyes are bright, they're happy for me, happy for me being happy and I think how this has been the biggest professional clusterfuck of good and bad. I'm so glad when it's over, I mean the night, I mean I'm glad the book is out, my face feels as if it's about to split in two from laughing so much.

34.

But my son doesn't care about any of that, nor should it have been an excuse. He is thirteen and he needs a mom and not an unmedicated bipolar roommate, and he's been crying at school and some kids and the teachers have noticed. Do you know what it's like to be a thirteen-year-old boy and be caught crying to yourself at school? I don't but it's not hard to imagine.

Thinking back, I see my son three weeks before the book launch, on the couch as always, on his phone watching TikTok or playing video games. But that's only a decoy. I imagine his ears pricking up as though he's a hare in the grass with a wolf nearby. His enormous brown eyes—my eyes—following my back around the apartment, trailing after my footsteps like lasers, watching to see whether my feet ever fall outside the lines.

He doesn't say anything about anything—except an occasional request that I not go out for another cigarette—and most nights there's been no reason to say anything. But as it got closer to the launch date I became more frantic, I slept less, I talked more, and I hid a small mickey in a box of cereal.

Everything I've learned in the various groups I attended alone and with my son—about children of addicts whose ears are hare ears and whose eyes are lasers—I conveniently forgot. The kids who can tell the state their problem parent is in by the way she closes the door or by the way she shuts the engine off, the kids to whom boxes of cereal aren't boxes of cereal, whose moms' dancing and singing and insisting on taking funny selfies isn't going to translate into a happy memory but a nightmare. Even something as innocent as talking a little too loudly on the phone is an alarm going off in the head of such a child.

To an addict active in their addiction, whatever it is that people around you complain about—that has to do with how you're behaving—seems a gross exaggeration because, truly, everything is fine. Addiction is the great disconnector. When you're in it, it moves you so far away from those who love you and from your real self that it's no longer possible to experience the healthy shame[61] needed to stop

[61] Although research specifically focusing on "healthy shame" and its direct impact on preventing relapse into addiction is limited, some related psychological concepts shed light on its potential role in addiction recovery. For example, the sort of self-awareness I possess should help me confront my addictive behaviours. Self-awareness allows us to acknowledge the consequences of our actions, recognize the negative impact on self and others, and understand the need for change. Healthy shame is believed to serve as a catalyst for seeking help and initiating behavioural changes. The discomfort associated with shame may push a person to seek therapy, support groups, or treatment for their addiction, which can be essential steps in the recovery process. One study found that people who experienced healthy shame were more likely to seek treatment for their addiction than those who didn't. Additionally, research has shown that people who experience healthy shame are more likely to partake in behaviours that promote their overall well-being, such as seeking social support or engaging in self-care activities.

Finally, shame can act as a counterbalance to denial, a common defence mechanism observed in addiction—since when shame is present it becomes harder to

behaving selfishly. Every time you hear the little voice begging you to stop or not start, a louder voice yells some variation of *It's fine! Nothing is happening! No one can see!* That yell overpowers the whisper of reason. And if it isn't enough, if the whisper is too loud, you just drink more over it. You are the drunkard on your own planet.

35.

When my son's teacher approaches him one afternoon he tells her he's anxious. For him, the anxiety lives in his stomach and takes his appetite away. He learned to recognize it in one of the groups I used to take him to, and he's well-versed in describing what's happening to people close to him. Except that afternoon he also tells the teacher about the reasons for his anxiety—and this is a teacher he doesn't even like very much.

It's the day after Halloween. He's due to stay with me that night; our schedule is two nights on, two nights off. He tells the teacher he doesn't want to stay with me and I don't know what else is being said but I do know that, not surprisingly, this teacher, like most of his teachers, is aware of my addiction (if only because they've Googled my name). Over the years a few teachers have let him know that they've read my memoir, but no one has ever made him feel bad about it and he hasn't received any special treatment.

---

rationalize or justify addictive behaviours, making you more open to facing reality and seeking help. In another study researchers found that those who experienced higher levels of shame were more likely to acknowledge the negative consequences of their addiction and seek help for it, even after controlling for other factors such as age, gender, and severity of substance use.

Besides, I've only ever shown up to school drunk once and it was a long time ago. And yet they're on alert. Imagine?

My son is a bright, kind, well-spoken kid who sometimes gets in trouble for socializing too much and who can be a pain for his English teachers when he corrects their grammar. But overall, he's considered well adjusted and well liked. This year he's gotten close with a girl and has been teased about it; he's even lost some friends over it. It's a brutal age of social selection, with everything under a magnifying glass, from your brand of shoes to your associations. And yet he insists that this isn't why he's feeling anxious.

The teacher tells the principal who tells my ex-husband who tells me. By that time my son is at my ex-husband's place, having come home from school early that day.

He'll stay with me indefinitely, my ex-husband says to me on the phone or in a text, I can't remember. But I remember panic and protest. The panic that this time I've *really* done it. And the protest that every addict is familiar with when people finally confront them, the *How dare they!* that flashes in our stupid heads when the words ring true, the words that strip us instantly of any argument.

This will die down, I think to myself. We've all overreacted. I neither call nor text my son. I don't dare. In any case, I don't know what I would say.

I know I don't deserve him and it's pathetic but my building despair over his rejection stops time as I think of everything that he is. He is a million, billion seconds filled with sweetness, and laughter, and sun-dappled shallow kiddie pools, and impromptu kitchen dancing parties, and soccer, and fast race cars, and *Tintin* and *Thomas the Tank Engine*. I think of his beauty, his love, and his pain, too—the pain of his sadness over me, my pain over my inability to stop causing the pain—and his forgiveness, the immensity of it. I think of a poster I bought him after the separation with the injunction to “Love Your Extraordinary Self.” He once said that to calm himself down sometimes he stops whatever he’s doing and tries to find different words in “extraordinary,” which—the word and his game—is the definition of what he is to me.[62] I think of his honey skin, his sleep breath, and his mornings—he once told me he *always* wakes up happy—and the overall miracle of his existence, the flesh and bone of a being that wasn’t but that came to me after a whole lifetime of waiting and that made it all make sense. I think of moments that define the complicated love I’ve created for us, the high stakes of it. Like the time we almost missed the train in Gdansk, how a look passed between us—not a second to explain—and how he ran up the stairs on his little legs, his face determined, his body toddling with the weight of his backpack but pushing forward, and we torpedoed into the train a moment before it closed its doors. We sat down breathing heavily and giggling and when we finally calmed down he looked at me with those big brown eyes and his face crumpled and he told me he’d peed his pants while running up the stairs. I told him he was like a real soldier, and he closed his eyes smiling proudly to himself, his head on my lap as the train rocked him to deep sleep.

I know already that there is no power in this universe that can take back the transgressions I’ve committed against him because of my addiction. No books with dedications telling him I’m sorry, no

[62] You can make 3,628 different words out of “extraordinary.”

heartfelt apology can now make up for my taking his mother away and replacing her with a walking corpse. What my boy needs is love in action, not Shame and remorse, as useful as they might be when we have the luxury of time and space for reparations. I don't send him a message because there are no words big enough to substitute for a mother's acts of love.

I don't send him a message because I am simply too ashamed.

Except that on the third day, on a supervised walk my ex-husband has cobbled together for the three of us, I say things. And make it worse.

My son reluctantly walks off with me after saying goodbye to my ex-husband, who leaves us alone, finally. He's got my ex-husband's Pentax camera slung around his neck; he's recently taken to photography, and his eye is my eye exactly: shapes and the sky and the in-between beauty where you least expect it. He takes some photos of an old metal playground apparatus and he's aloof toward me, the beginning of a smirk on his face whenever I say something that doesn't sound casual at all despite my trying very hard. My voice shakes. I say something idiotic about mental illness and how compassion—

You have a mental illness, eh? He smirks openly now.

—and then I'm too embarrassed to continue. I look at his hands that suddenly fill my entire vision, his unique, incredible hands, the first thing I zeroed in on after he was born. My son has a congenital condition called complex syndactyly that he's inherited from his father. His left hand looks almost like your left hand except the middle and ring fingers are permanently bent and stuck together. His right hand is a Picasso. It has the joints of six fingers but only four actual fingers. It is the most beautiful hand that's ever existed, and I am a lot more of a handicap in his life than that hand.

This is not the right time to beg for pardon on account of mental illness. Or to use mental illness as some sort of excuse—something I never do and that now just sounds fake and desperate, amounting to a *She'll say anything* approach, eliciting not sympathy but pity.

He sighs and says, I don't mean to laugh. You know I laugh when I'm nervous.

I nod. I know.

Show him that you're okay, I repeat in my head—something my ex-husband said to me before the walk. It sounded condescending and I rolled my eyes at it but now I wish I could just arrange my face and my brain into whatever okay is.

My son says, I feel two emotions. I'm angry with you. And I'm also angry with you because I really miss you.

Internally, I pat myself on the back for never shying away from talking about things that hurt; if I've done one thing right, it's making him feel safe where emotions are concerned. But beyond that I fail, and I fail now, too. What he said hurts. And I'm aware that my tears are a mistake, that I should be strong and cool-headed and that I should "Show him . . ." (I'm okay! Okay! Okay?)

When are you going to come back to me?

I don't know. Maybe this weekend, he says flatly.

Why not tonight? I snap, and my son looks at me with cool curiosity.

I don't want you to pressure me, he says.

I'm not pressuring you, I say, pressuring him and feeling more and more desperate—*Show him you're okay*—the tears now pushing against my eyelids, my voice shaking, my mouth shaking too, lower lip, uncontrollably, the way it does before I have an anxiety attack. My hands go numb and suddenly I cannot stand to be around my son. I don't want him to witness this, I don't want him to see how *not-okay* I am, I don't want to be judged by my quivering lip, by my tears, by my shaking voice, by pleas. Yet at the same time he can't leave, this is ridiculous, what does it mean he can leave? I'm his mother, and tonight is our night together, and I really want him to *not* go, and I also want him to fucking get lost. I can't stand how he's staring at me and I finally say, Why don't you just go home with Daddy?

And he tilts his head and smirks again. Sure, he says. Then he runs off, shouting, Daddy!

Daddy! Like he couldn't wait for this moment, like I finally gave him one thing today that he found acceptable.

36.

My son is my main witness. I don't have to be right with the world, but if I'm not right with him I'm not right with anything. We all have them—or had them, those less fortunate than I—our main witnesses. Whether those are our children or our partners or our parents, there's always a person whose joy and, equally, whose disappointment in us matters the most. The one person (or people) who we know sees not just what's beneath our facade but even beyond that, the person who can see what even we might've lost the ability to see, whose one poignant look can snap us back to reality, mirror the ugly thing we're ashamed of so deeply that it blinds us, arrests us to the point where we can't look away—at least for a moment. This is who makes us hold on, who makes us *want*—want to one day be who they believe we are or who they remembered we were, who they witnessed when we were at our best. This is the person who can know all about our Shame. And who can also forgive it.

Forgiveness can be an important step in overcoming Shame. We might be too weak or too far gone to forgive ourselves, but having someone in our life who can might be the necessary push we need—we've been seen and we've been ugly, and yet our main witness hasn't turned away. By experiencing their compassion, we too might consider its possibility—and feeling compassion toward ourselves reduces feelings of Shame.

It takes courage to forgive because it involves letting go—of anger, resentment, and bitterness toward the person who's wronged you. It requires the forgiver to confront their own pain and vulnerability, and to choose to respond with understanding instead of anger or revenge.

Finally, forgiveness involves risks—the risk of being hurt again, the risk of appearing weak to others. To face these risks and to choose forgiveness anyway is a tall order, and not something I expect from my kid. And yet, when he tells me he's angry with me because he misses me, I know there's still hope. And hope is the only thing I have.

I didn't have any of those thoughts then; I didn't dare think that far into the future, to hope. If I'd learned anything about addiction and recovery, it's that there's no rushing how this process goes for those who love us addicts. There are many week-sober addicts who get frustrated with their loved ones when they're reluctant to celebrate their supposed change; after all, one week sober equals seven in human years. But considering how many promises get broken and how much pain our addiction causes, we're fortunate to get even the smallest glimpse of grace.

Ira Byock, an American physician, author, and palliative care advocate, has described how the famous anthropologist Margaret Mead responded when a student asked her what she considered to be a first sign of civilization. Mead said that in ancient society the first evidence of civilization was a broken femur that had healed. She explained this further: In the animal kingdom, when you break a bone, you die. You can't run away from danger, you can't walk up to a stream for a drink of water, you can't hunt for food. *You* are food. No animal can survive a broken bone long enough to let it heal. A broken femur that has healed, then, is evidence that someone took the time to pick you up after you fell, someone attended to the wound, someone brought you to a safe place and took care of you. Helping someone during a difficult time is where civilization starts. "The first sign of civilization is compassion," Byock writes.

I'm lucky to have a main witness, whether my son was going to be ready to forgive and offer compassion or not. Before anything, all I needed to know was that he exists—that he's in my life even though he's not in my apartment.

Most of us aren't drunkards on a drunkard planet where we're seen and heard only briefly by a little prince who's passing by. Or if this is where we are, there are still witnesses in our head, those who we still think about and who would want us to be well. A witness could also be someone who needs us to be well—someone who might depend on us. Being needed is being seen, being witnessed.

Hold on to that witness, whether they're still in your life or a memory that comes back when you wake up from your Shame wondering how you'll ever walk again with your broken femur.

37.

I wish I could say that knowing I was losing my main witness was what made me stop. It would serve the story to have a neat timeline like that, but I think we know by now that neither his birth nor a smash into a concrete wall could stop me. Yet the fact that he is my main witness and that he does still need me is enough to make me want *to want* sobriety.

For now, my son's rejection is a dull distress over which I drink the way I drink over anything that makes me feel—good or bad. I have an ongoing argument with nobody in my head about this. How am I supposed to show him I'm okay, how am I supposed to be okay when I'm very much *not okay* and the reason I'm very much not okay is that he's left me and I'm drinking in order to cope with that because what else am I supposed to do? I have no other coping skills, and, also, to hell with coping skills—how is a mother supposed to cope with her child not wanting her? You would drink too. But even if I wasn't drinking, how am I going to prove it if he's not here to see? And how am I supposed to fix whatever else is going on with my brain that I can't seem to shut down, that makes me agitated and sleepless and sad?

When I say I'm drinking over this pain, I mean I'm just drinking as I have been—still not every day and still only a mickey—but now I give myself a justification for it.

I don't even want to drink, to be honest, and I don't want not to drink in the way that has allowed me to stop before, those rare moments that weren't exactly spiritual but that were gentle, like a suggestion from a mildly disinterested angel: Maybe today you could not?

Maybe I could not. But what else is there to do? I'm a mother without a son, I'm a writer with a failed book, I'm a poster girl for sobriety who drinks. So I do what I know to do: I go out and buy red-capped mickeys. I have no witnesses, nobody gets upset, nobody threatens to leave. My boyfriend works late and has long ago given up on trying to encourage me to stop. Some nights I ask him to pick up white wine and he does; he brings it home, resigned, and I pour us each a generous glass which he sips and which I down.

And on it goes.

Beyond my teaching work, nothing else is meaningful. Time stretches and compresses, morning, afternoon, evening, night, counting down till I can check out for a few oil-razor vodka hours, maybe spend them on some dumb online banter with another drunk up at midnight like me—you know who you are; there are quite a few of you out there and we've had many unrepeatable conversations.

Every day I check in with my son and with his father to see how everybody's feeling, and every day I'm told he's not ready yet. We've made a few attempts to have him come and stay over, but on the day of each visit he feels sick to his stomach at school and doesn't come. I try and fail to reason with my ex-husband about mandated visits. I study custody laws and pretend this isn't a consequence but rather some injustice. He mostly just responds with "Call your lawyer and

I'll call mine," meaning he'll speak to his girlfriend who's a lawyer, meaning fuck right off.

At home I walk past the fold-out sofa where my son used to sit with his phone or his video games, the fluffy gang of stuffies he hasn't yet relinquished perched untouched, unloved, the clueless, blissed-out face of a giant plush sloth—I got him as my son's "pandemic buddy"—just asking to be punched in.

When he does come over it's an in-and-out visit that's tense and that neither of us enjoys. Every time he shows up, he discreetly—*not* discreetly—and systematically removes his favourite clothes from the dresser, the precious soccer jerseys I bought him in New York, the cool vintage T-shirts we found on one of our thrift-shop hunts.

Day by day, no matter how many lights I turn on, everything dulls more and more inside the quiet apartment, matched by the outside as the first snow falls and the world fades to white.

Some mornings I wake up and stare at the ceiling for hours, just the way I used to do after moving to my first post-separation apartment. Such indifferent walls, so much dust—magnified, absorbing the sound.

Tomorrow will be the same as today and the day after will be the same as tomorrow. And so on.

I put a red period between each day, in a Smirnoff font.

38.

I can pick up the puppy in Montreal on the weekend, which is good news, but the window to do so is only a few hours. The problem is that the friend who arranged this whole thing and who's offered to drive me can't now. The breeder messages that she can *put the puppy on a plane* instead, which strikes me as ridiculous and hilarious, but at this point I've spent enough money that another four hundred dollars feels absolutely reasonable.

I sign various PDF forms and make a number of e-transfers and finally, after everything's set, I am me except I am happy. In fact, I'm more than happy—I am anticipation herself. I'm me at five years old, Christmas, shaking a brown-paper-wrapped box and knowing it's Lego. Or I am me at thirty-one and my son's heel is wedged in my side, under the skin, after he's turned upside down—an announcement of his imminent arrival.

I am me at forty-five, sitting in the grey waiting room of a cargo warehouse, my sewing-machine legs the one big clue to what's happening inside me. I arrived in an Uber at a vast, desolate warehouseland four hours too early after three sleepless nights and I still ran into the building as though I were on fire.

The puppy is the first thing I've anticipated, the first thing I'm responsible for, in months. I've left absolutely nothing to chance; I am waiting for this dog the way people wait for a baby. Inside the warehouse the forklifts' *peep-bleep-peeps* make my heart jump every time as I peek to see if it's finally him. It's not him for a long time but the beeping is a beautiful sound; it confirms that something is happening; it's better than the silence at home.

When my puppy shows up he's quiet.

Hello sweetheart, I whisper to him as we lock eyes for the first time. Hello, my love. I tear up and he seems to be crying too or at least that's what his little face looks like, worried and unsure. You're okay, you're okay, sweetheart, I say to him and wipe my face.

He's a chihuahua, the size of a large snowball, and for all intents and purposes he is a snowball, with large black eyes, floppy ears, and a nose like a stamp. A soft blue blanket with white stars lies inside his carrier and a packet of puppy food has been taped to the top. I take a picture of him and his pleading eyes, sign forms, and call an Uber.

What I don't know is that I'm bringing home another important witness, but one who doesn't need me to be a certain way because he needs me only to *be*. To him I'll always be perfect; to dogs, we're the entire universe. Drunk or sober, it doesn't matter: just be. If there is no I, there'll be no puppy; he's completely dependent on me—for food, for my protection, for my warmth.

For now we're new to each other, and I don't want to overwhelm him but right away I love him hopelessly. Hopelessly, because I'm also full of fear that I'll somehow lose him too, that *he* will overwhelm *me*. And that I'll do what I do with all the things I care about—break them.

When I hear him whimper that first night I get up automatically, half asleep, like thousands of years and billions of mothers before me—like me thirteen years ago—and pick him up. I lie down with him snuggled up in my armpit on my son's pull-out sofa. He whimpers quietly to himself but soon he's asleep, moving his little paws, sighing contentedly, dreaming puppy dreams of his brothers' and sisters' soft warm bodies and his mother's warm milk and maybe the warm hands that picked him up and held him as soon as we got home.

39.

My son names him Clifford after a favourite cartoon character from his childhood, a big red dog who grew to the size of a house. He lies down on the floor holding the trembling puppy on his chest until the little animal calms down and starts licking his face, which makes him giggle. This is the most intimate, emotional moment we've had in a long time.

I ruin it by taking a picture—you never take a picture of a teenage boy without asking him first.

But he doesn't leave. I pass him the phone and he deletes the picture. Then he crumples a piece of paper and plays with the puppy, who's both brave and shy, lunging at the paper ball or running away from it when it's thrown, tumbling over himself.

I'm not denying that the puppy is partly a bribe, but we make jokes about it, how cliché it all is. My son has no qualms about telling me how mildly pathetic I am, that the puppy doesn't mean he'll be ready to trust me again. In fact, if anything, he says offhandedly once the jokes die down, this is manipulative.

It is and it isn't. The puppy is for me, too. I don't want to tell him—I'm too embarrassed to tell anyone—that I've finally reached a stage of loneliness that's dangerous.

I often catch my son looking at me with longing, but if he catches me catching him he instantly grows scales. An entire armour that protects him from my complicated love. Usually the one or two hours he spends on his fold-out sofa, visiting, feel like a painful experiment I've willingly signed up for. I don't know if I should talk to him or leave him alone; I watch how I speak, move. I haven't drunk around him once since the night before Halloween, but my sobriety hurts—it feels like punishment, or maybe just a lack of the anaesthetic I feel I need to survive this particular situation. Today, though, for the first time in weeks, it feels almost nice.

When the puppy gets tired I put him in my lap and he curls up and falls asleep. I have the most ridiculous thought: how even his size seems a mistake, as if I couldn't even get us a normal dog instead of this hamster with a high IQ.

Yet, unbeknownst to me, he will open my heart in such a massive way that I'll be left with no choice but to turn all that hopelessness around.

When are you coming back to me? I say to my son.

Don't ask me that. I'll let you know, he says. He pats the puppy on the head and gives me half a hug.

I'm not one of those parents who are overly dependent on their child. My son is the point, but I've always had other points in my life—my work, my relationships, my writing. Yet he's the only one who's been a constant, a reassurance that I have something good to live for. And someone to get better for, too.

And there are reasons other than me why he left. He worries about his father, who's dealing with some health issues. The social worker tells me my son has said as much. She explains how children of divorce often feel responsible for their parents' happiness, how they become little parents in their own right, wanting to ensure that their two most important family members are in a good place.

Neither my ex-husband nor I want or expect our son to make us happy, but he's a sensitive, naturally empathetic boy.

People who know about his leaving assure me that this is normal for boys his age, wanting to "identify with the father." They mean well. They send quotes and links to articles about teenagers and fathers and hormones. One friend tells me about her twelve-year-old, who stopped speaking with her for a year and moved in with his dad; another friend's teenagers live with their father permanently, unhappy with her moving to a smaller house. She reminds me of this whenever I start to whine too much.

Kids are difficult, boys are difficult, puberty is difficult, it's just their age, it's not you, it's them. I hear it over and over.

I haven't told anyone why he left. This is another Shame.

I think about other mothers, even the ones whose children abandoned them—and I always come up short. Our apartment is small, I'm a bad cook, I don't drive, I'm not wealthy, I'm mentally ill, I had postpartum depression.[63] Except, of course, my son doesn't care about any of that; he cares only about having a sober mom. Yet I frequently blame myself for all those things too; they're a source of Shame as well. I never invite anyone over, worried as I am about being judged—and not for my drinking, since I hide that well, but for the size of my kitchen.

[63] Or postpartum euphoria, "baby pinks," a relatively new term used to describe the intense feelings of joy and happiness that some women experience after giving birth. It's often characterized by a sense of elation, increased energy, and a heightened sense of well-being. In my case it was most likely an onset of hypomania, which led to an almost instant rollercoaster crash and possibly to my subsequent relapse.

People often compare themselves to others, of course, and rejection can amplify feelings of Shame if it seems others are being accepted while you're not. When what they do—the opposite of what *you* do—seems to work and bring happiness it seems almost personal. To me it does, in the state I'm in. So I watch and envy the mothers on social media with their Instagram stories of sun-dappled afternoons goofing around in home pools, in Alpine snow, kayaking on a Muskoka lake, dancing in large kitchens, their cheek-to-cheek hugs in massive rec rooms.

And like it or not, the wealth of others is a great shamer. I might roll my eyes at a post with seven photos tracking the progress of a soaker bathtub installation, but the bathtub also signals that this is a mother who can provide for her children. As bohemian as I feel myself to be, I'm not immune to the portrayal of wealth and luxury in others' social media displays, and it does shape my perceptions of what constitutes success.

Social comparison theory, introduced by psychologist Leon Festinger, delves into how people evaluate themselves by weighing their abilities, opinions, and attributes against those of others—a process that serves to gauge our own self-worth and make sense of the world. And since it involves looking both downward and upward, to those better off, it can influence self-esteem and motivation.

Because of the Shame I feel over my parenting and my lifestyle, the way I look at those posts only deepens my sense of inadequacy. I'm even ashamed of feeling ashamed about this, since I'm supposed to be an artist and above it all. But fuck, life is just easier with a soaker bathtub, no?

My son has never demanded anything. He *always* stresses how happy he is—and that he feels proud of his weirdo, artsy parents. So this is just about how I am. And when I feel particularly dark about his leaving I add that insecurity to all the others. Would having a big house make my other shortcomings, my mental illness especially, more bearable? Would a personal soccer coach help even out an occasional wobble? None of this is fair or intelligent, but in the mood I'm in all aspects of my life seem to contribute to the feelings of failure.

I fixate on surfaces and appearances and somehow forget the hundreds of readers who, over the years, have written to me about their own demons, their own drinking—readers from all walks of life.

40.

Addiction is a disease of secrets and Shame, and a disease of loneliness. It's a Great Disconnector that demands all our attention, jealous of every moment we spend not in its service. It's impossible to be active in addiction and keep people close—keeping them close is a threat (to *it*). Addiction doesn't share time or space. The worst thing that can happen to an addict is to be interrupted; secrecy and hiding/isolation are needed in order for it to flourish, or rather, fester. As lonely as we are on our hellish drunkard planets, most addicts just want to be left alone.

Leaving: This is what addicts are best at. Leaving, disappearing. I don't mean only the junkies, the sex addicts, the twelve-step meeting attendees, the overeaters, the undereaters. I mean all those who worship at the altar of obsession, whether it's with vodka or work or working out. Or watching TikTok for hours. I'm talking about those of us for whom addiction can be defined as the thing that interferes with our life to the point where we're no longer able to be in our life. To the point where we see our loved ones only in reluctantly scheduled intervals—during the holidays, say. (If we see them at all.) To the point where most of our social engagements get cancelled in the name of wanting to—or having to—hide with our thing. Where the thing demands so much that we have to sacrifice all others—the things we love, that used to bring joy—to serve it. To the point when we not only leave but when we're finally also left; alone.

In that way, I got exactly what I worked so hard for, and for so long.

My addiction is half the reason for my loneliness. My Shame is the other. Compounded, they've locked me in a loop, and although there's a key, I'm here to tell you that I've swallowed it.

People who experience Shame are more likely to be lonely and disconnected from others. This is because Shame makes us feel unworthy of connection and causes us to withdraw from social situations—we believe that our true selves are unlovable or unacceptable, and we fear that others will reject us if they see who we really are. If who I really am is a woman who drinks straight from a mickey of vodka, who has a whole ritual of marching into a liquor store like some sort of funny ninja—sunglasses, a hoodie, drawn shoulders—and then ducking into the next empty alley, do I really want anyone knowing this about me?

Of course I don't. And yet because I still have Shame, this might be, paradoxically, my cure. If pain is a warning our body gives to tell us something needs attention—an injury, an underlying condition—Shame too can be considered a protective mechanism that alerts us to potential or actual damage to our psyche.

41.

Looking back, I believe another part of my motivation for getting the puppy was to show my son that I'm getting better. And that I do have it in me to be a responsible caretaker—a responsible mom. I've had an instant connection with the little animal, a milder version of the sort of intense, protective love I've experienced only once before. I feel guilty about this too, and worry that my son will ask why I'm a mother for this puppy I couldn't be for him. Of course, he doesn't say anything like that. But he does tease that I'm becoming obsessed with the dog.

He's not immune to Clifford's charms either—they play a ridiculous game where the puppy licks his face, including his mouth, and my son gently pulls on the puppy's tongue with his teeth. When he does that the puppy's tail becomes a little windmill and they break apart, clumsy paws, joyous giggles, and all.

As for me, I carry the puppy inside my coat whenever I go out, his little face next to mine. When I lie on my son's sofa bed to write, the puppy lies asleep in my robe pocket. I teach him to sit, to shake a paw, to show us his belly. I know I'm biased but in the squished-face-bug-eyed chihuahua lottery our little guy has had incredible luck. He's not one of those dogs with an Instagram account documenting his overbred genes. There's no permanently stuck-out tongue, no proptosis eyes, no weird warts growing out of his muzzle, no over- or underbite. He's perfectly proportioned, cartoon cute. My son says he looks like one of the evolutions of Pokémon.

Our conversations revolve around the puppy. This shift in focus gives me a quiet excitement I'm careful to keep to myself: finally we have something to talk about other than what's wrong, or what was wrong, or how to fix it. Nor do we talk about my son coming back to live with me. It's not that I don't want that to happen, it's that I accept it might not; that this might be a new version of us. And with the puppy around, I hate this version less.

In these early days I keep thinking how the puppy's presence feels magical—how my son and I are writing a fairy tale about an enchanted mom, a boy's broken heart, and a little white chihuahua who helped to mend it.

42.

The new puppy is in a little dog bed next to my own and he's awake, staring at me as if I'm food. I pick him up for a cuddle, his soft, floppy body with its little lungs, its tiny brain with that famous dog's emotional intelligence, its puppy soul with the purest unconditional love.[64] It's the most marvellous miniature design.

I'm fine, I tell him, and cry for some reason when I hear the tremble in my voice.

[64] Dogs don't experience love in the same way humans do, owing to differences in cognitive and emotional processing, yet their responses do indicate a deep attachment to, and affection for, their owners. For example, oxytocin—often referred to as the "love hormone"—is released in both humans and dogs during social interactions, particularly positive ones. Studies have shown that gazing into their owners' eyes can trigger an oxytocin release in dogs, similar to the way it happens between human caregivers and infants. And the presence of a familiar, trusted human can reduce a dog's stress levels, indicating a sense of security and comfort. Dogs can also demonstrate empathy by responding to their owners' emotions—they may offer comfort when their owner is sad or distressed. The fact that they've evolved along with us gives them this incredible ability to read our human cues—facial expressions, body language—which contributes to their social bonding.

I kiss near his stamp of a nose and he starts licking my face and I'm sure our oxytocin[65] is at an all-time high, except that at the moment I'm not thinking about hormones: all I know is that this is awesome. Nothing has changed and I'm still officially in the dumps, but unofficially, improbably, I feel good.

In the most paradoxical way, I think giving up is another reason why I feel good. More specifically, it's being able to lean into my son's leaving. The puppy's presence dials down the ongoing hum of desperation, along with the fear—of not having anything to look forward to—that I only now realize I've been living in. I don't know how exactly that change occurred, or why now. It just happened. I'm going to be okay even without my son living with me. I still have him; there's still a possibility that we might repair what I broke. But if not . . . I pick up the puppy and whisper all the words I want to say to my boy.

Or maybe they're words I say to myself. I've found a new way to talk to the universe. Instead of the intangible ear of God, I have the soft floppy ear of a dog.

The words are not profound; they're simple.

Actually, they can be summarized in one word: Please. Like prayer, "please" recognizes that there's something beyond oneself, that there's a dependence on a higher power. *I need guidance. I need*

[65] When oxytocin is released it can have a calming effect on the body and help mitigate the physiological responses associated with stress. Like dopamine, oxytocin has been shown to activate the brain's reward system, associated with feelings of pleasure and positive reinforcement. The release of oxytocin during positive social interactions might contribute to reducing discomfort and enhancing well-being, including the ability to deal with pain.

support. It acknowledges that we're not entirely self-sufficient, that we sometimes need help, that our own means aren't enough. "Please" and a prayer share a language of seeking, whether it's a simple request or a profound spiritual plea.

I'm not asking the puppy to save me. I'm just telling its little ear that I want. *Please*. I just *want*.

What do I want? For now, I just want this to last, this feeling good or whatever this is, and I also want to not be afraid of it. I don't want to treat this state of contentment as a credit of some kind I'll have to pay for later. I also want a day. Just one day. Just one day when I don't think about drinking, when I don't wrestle with myself over whether I *should* or *should not*, when I don't look at the clock to calculate which liquor stores are still open in case I decide to drink that night, last minute. When I drink, clocks are dangerous till ten p.m. So I want a day where ten p.m. is just ten p.m.

I need to start small. I cannot overwhelm the universe with my demands. The universe is only a puppy; it weighs only two pounds. Two pounds can't carry too much. A day, and beyond that—we'll see.

43.

Is it possible to experience Shame all on your own, without others present? Absolutely, although our internal judgments and beliefs are always shaped by other humans, even if it's our own perceptions that give rise to the emotion of Shame. Shame is brought on by the belief that *social* norms have been violated. This is impossible to test, but of all emotions, Shame is the one that wouldn't exist if it weren't for other people.

A feeling of Shame is the first consequence of rule-breaking in the Garden of Eden. After eating the forbidden fruit from the Tree of the Knowledge of Good and Evil, Adam and Eve became aware of their nakedness and felt Shame. Up until that moment their nakedness felt natural and right—but once they'd transgressed, that nakedness became something else.

What's significant here isn't just that Eve tempted Adam or even that they disobeyed God, but that they needed each other to bear witness.

Just as we need witnesses to experience Shame, we also need them to get rid of it. Or at least to help us make it smaller.

If Shame is brought on by the fear of being seen, Unshaming is brought about by being seen.

That means being witnessed—allowed the space and time to disclose something about ourselves that stops us from feeling good, or even, if you prefer the self-helpy vernacular, from being our true selves, from realizing our full potential. I like just feeling good (for now, occasionally, sometimes). For me, the typical self-help assurances can feel overwhelming, creating yet another portal to Shame. Any book that shouts promises at me, or that suggests I need *it*—because I'm shy, or a worrier, or quiet, or disorganized, or imperfect, or maybe too perfect—is the last thing I want to pick up. Sure, I still walk away wondering if I'll be fucked if I don't get this or that self-help guide.[66] Yet these books carry an expectation, and therefore the potential for disappointment if that expectation isn't met. Because doesn't that mean you must be doing something wrong? If you're not getting *it*?

[66] Although there's a popular self-help book that says I shouldn't give a fuck.

The first self-improvement book I read in recovery was *Alcoholics Anonymous*; its numerous decrees stressed me out, creating yet another place where I ended up feeling inadequate. Still, the popular reading that many AA meetings close with, known as "The Promises,"[67] used to be a balm to my beat-up romantic soul. I'd feel as if I'd stumbled onto an incredible treasure, and would picture some sort of Transformer version of myself: all-powerful, confident, wealthy, popular, sober. All this would be mine if only I did the program the way it was meant to be done (a mystery to this day).

Consider just these three assertions: "We are going to know a new freedom and a new happiness." "That feeling of uselessness and self-pity will disappear." "Fear of people and of economic insecurity will leave us."

Who wouldn't want that? Except whenever I got depressed or bored or frustrated, the Promises would start to sound like mockery, like a time-share spiel. And whenever I returned to the rooms of AA after a relapse, the Promises turned out to be yet another thing I wasn't doing right. The niggling feeling of failure would

[67] It goes like this: "If we are painstaking about this phase of our development, we will be amazed before we are halfway through. We are going to know a new freedom and a new happiness. We will not regret the past nor wish to shut the door on it. We will comprehend the word serenity and we will know peace. No matter how far down the scale we have gone, we will see how our experience can benefit others. That feeling of uselessness and self-pity will disappear. We will lose interest in selfish things and gain interest in our fellows. Self-seeking will slip away. Our whole attitude and outlook upon life will change. Fear of people and of economic insecurity will leave us. We will intuitively know how to handle situations which used to baffle us. We will suddenly realize that God is doing for us what we could not do for ourselves. Are these extravagant promises? We think not. They are being fulfilled among us—sometimes quickly, sometimes slowly. They will always materialize if we work for them."

become bigger and bigger until all that was left was frustration and self-reproach.

I understand that the Promises are there to create a sense of hope—especially for new initiates—and that there's no actual time limit on when those things might happen ("sometimes quickly, sometimes slowly," which when read out loud is often pronounced "slooooowly"). But maybe instead of promising anything we could just agree to strive toward feeling . . . better. And there actually is an AA adage that helps many people relax about it all—the Promises, the rules and regulations. It's this: "Progress, not perfection." This to me acknowledges that maybe we shouldn't take it all so seriously, that we're all just stumbling around trying our best. Or not even our best. But at least we're trying.

The one wisdom of AA that *has* appealed to me as possibly the most authentic and realistic is "One day at a time." In other words, instead of worrying about the future or dwelling on the past, consider just what is. And remember that we can control our actions only for today. I've felt the power of that maxim a few times—and on day two or three when I hadn't made alcohol my focal point, the relief I experienced was greater than any edge I would have taken off with a drink.

For now, as I cobble my little universe back together, with my little puppy in it, I have my one day at a time. A strange non-desire. Some sort of liminal space where I don't think about whether I have the desire or not. I don't know if it's my talking in the dog's soft ear, but our connection opens something in me. And, being the addict that I am, I want more. I need a witness. A soft puppy ear is a start. *Please* is a start.

44.

Confession involves openly admitting one's actions, thoughts, or emotions to oneself or to others—an act that can lead to a sense of relief, self-awareness, accountability, and connection. Many writers and thinkers have explored the theme. In his *Confessions,* St. Augustine reflects on his spiritual journey and his conversion to Christianity, emphasizing the value of confessing one's sins to God and the transformative effect it can have on the soul. And in his novel *Crime and Punishment*, Fyodor Dostoevsky explores the psychological effects of confession through his main character, Raskolnikov, who struggles with guilt and inner turmoil after committing a crime. His eventual admission to Sonya, a character representing innocence and redemption, becomes a turning point in his psychological healing. In his own *Confessions*, Jean-Jacques Rousseau considers the power of self-examination and self-disclosure as a means to understand and confront one's flaws and contradictions. And another writer and philosopher, Albert Camus, investigates the theme of confession in his novel *The Fall*, whose protagonist, Jean-Baptiste Clamence, reveals his moral failings and hypocritical behaviour to a stranger he meets in a bar, grappling with guilt and seeking a form of redemption. Finally, Sigmund Freud's psychoanalytic theory involves the concept of free association, whereby patients confess their thoughts and feelings without censoring themselves. Confession in therapy, Freud believed, allows clients to gain insight into their unconscious motivations, helping them confront unresolved issues.

The first time I ever talked about Shame was with God. I was eight years old and getting ready for my first communion, a Catholic ritual where a child receives the body and blood of Christ in the form of bread (and sometimes wine). In this moment, the child is said to become closer to God, strengthening their faith.

As I remember it, there was a white dress involved, a host wafer that got stuck to the roof of my mouth, presents, a big family celebration dinner, and lots of preparation in our catechism classes. I was allowed to walk to and from church on my own to attend these classes, and once they were over I'd repeatedly cross the street, back and forth between the church and a little park, as a way to make up for all those times my parents walked me to catechism classes, years and years of having to hold stern hands and obey the rules before being delivered to yet another place with yet more rules. As for the classes, we had to not only learn prayers and all the kneeling-standing-bowing gymnastics of the special first communion mass; the girls—as presumably the more naturally sinful bunch—had to sign a document promising no makeup, dating, or swearing—setting us up right there for a life of failure.

The day before communion we had our first confession, where we told our worst secrets to a man in a dress sitting inside a wooden box. For those still not sure what qualified as a sin, we were told it was anything you didn't want anybody to know. The man in the dress had to know because he had to tell the Catholic God.

I didn't learn about being *seen* during the Catholic confession. I learned the opposite—I learned about being exposed. Exposed in a way that a small, terrified animal feels when dragged out of a dark corner. My biggest conundrum at eight years old was my inability to turn off sinful thoughts, ones for which this Catholic God—who weirdly insisted on being told about the things he could see anyway, even inside my head—would grant no reprieve.

There was no running away from the searchlight eyes of the Catholic God and his cronies. Whatever you did or didn't do you'd always fail him. But for all the denunciations, condemnations, and dire warnings, he'd still insist that he loved you—even more than he loved his only son. It was a toxic love. And the Catholic confession was the place to learn even more Shame.

And yet, right after the act of it, upon emerging from the church—through enormous doors dividing its mysterious darkness and the light of the day outside—there came a tangible relief, a feeling of wings at my feet. Now I was free to cross the street fifty times if I felt like it, back and forth, again and again. This is what I really wanted to do, where true freedom lay, not inside the cold-stone-walled, myrrhed-and-frankincensed institution filled with paintings of upset women and half-naked men bleeding out of various holes in their bodies.

I experienced a similar feeling of lightness in adulthood, except more magnified and more powerful, after I joined Alcoholics Anonymous. The difference, of course, was that I'd signed up for AA voluntarily.

In order to recover from the alcoholic obsession of the mind, it was strongly suggested that I do certain things to minimize my chances of drinking again. Admitting to my faults was one of those things. And I didn't need my psychology degree or time spent in therapy to understand how good it would feel to unburden myself to a compassionate and interested witness. In expressing hidden emotions and realities to someone who listens without judgment, many of us will experience not just an emotional catharsis but also reduced isolation, validation, and a deeper sense of acceptance. Sharing secrets offers a chance to distribute emotional burdens, fostering personal growth, trust building, and the release of Shame associated with hidden thoughts.

That's the theory, and although AA isn't therapy and should never be viewed as such,[68] I not only believed in the process of sharing my wrongdoings and "shortcomings," but was eager to do so. At the time I wasn't thinking of Shame—how it underlay my addiction, along with most of my mental, emotional, and spiritual distress—but I did know about the relief I could expect from unloading my pain.

As for the specifics, AA's fifth step entails admitting "to God, to ourselves, and to another human being the exact nature of our wrongs." This step is meant to encourage people to take a thorough, honest inventory of past behaviours and actions, and to share this

[68] Most AA sponsors are *not* trained therapists. There's a lot of controversy about what constitutes good guidance in twelve-step programs, and the "expertise" that some "old-timers"—people with a lot of time sober—wield in and out of the rooms of AA. An overeager, Big Book–thumping old-timer may well give damaging advice; one sponsor I had told me I could stop taking the medication I was on and pray away my depression. The important thing to remember is that, no matter how long some people have been sober, they have no monopoly on recovery; they're there only to guide you through the process—and should do so with little judgment and with the understanding that you might need professional help with problems that are beyond the scope of twelve-step teachings.

information with another person. The goal is to help people gain self-awareness, take responsibility, and prepare to make amends for any harm caused to others.

It's not usually the step you take upon joining the program,[69] yet I remember reading through all the steps for the first time and getting stuck on number five, wanting to know when this confession was going to occur and when I could move to step nine, which involved making amends. I wanted to forgive and be forgiven. I wanted a formula, a guarantee that I'd never drink again. The Promises told me that I could then flourish even more, move far beyond those desires. I was twenty-seven and sitting in a car in a church parking lot before my second meeting. I was with Terrence, my fun new lover—I found AA through sin—urging him to tell me how important it was to do the steps in order and get an absolution. He laughed and told me I first had to tell all my wrongdoings to someone.

A few months later I sat with my first sponsor, Ruth, and read out loud my step five—a long list of my "defects of character,"[70] my resentments and my transgressions, my fears, my pain—all those things that usually made me want to check out, that had the potential to make me drink. Ruth—who later became my closest

[69] The only requirement for AA membership is a desire to stop drinking, meaning you join the program the moment you say you've joined the program. You don't even have to be sober from alcohol or attend a meeting, although it does tend to help.

[70] AA's version of the Seven Deadly Sins: negative personality traits or behaviours that can contribute to addiction and cause harm to oneself or others. Examples include selfishness, dishonesty, resentment, fear, and anger.

friend—listened for hours, occasionally stopping me to explore a concept or help me through finding "my part in it."[71]

After I finished, it truly felt as if I'd flushed out most of the dark gunk, not just my drinking but almost every ugly thing that had ever attached itself to me over the years. Ruth and I said a prayer and wrapped it up. (Now it was time to go home, reflect on what had been said, and move on to amends—a list of people, places, and things based on what I'd felt bad about in step five.)

That evening I'd vibrated inside. During those long hours in Ruth's beautiful study, with its low, warm lights, its open windows letting in a breezy, jasmine air, I told her some really embarrassing things, admitted to being petty and broken. But she never flinched, never snickered or showed shock, and not once made me feel bad about myself. She was hugely pregnant at the time, a real-life goddess glowing from within, her hair golden and electric, her impossibly blue-green eyes full of kindness and compassion. Looking at Ruth's soft pink robe stretched over her belly, I thought of miracles—of birth and renewal; I thought how lucky I was to be partaking in something miraculous.

[71] Every defect of character and resentment is thought to include your part in it, whether you were an active participant or not. For example, I once had a sponsee—a person I took through the twelve steps—who got stuck on her part in a sexual assault. I broke the unspoken AA rule and "absolved" her from it, not seeing how an eight-year-old child would be even partly responsible for what happened to her—or how she reacted to it even years later when dealing with the after-effects of that trauma. Later I was advised that I should have consulted my sponsor to help me figure it out. My sponsor, Ruth, said fuck that shit, which was exactly how I felt about it too. We absolved ourselves from having to absolve ourselves.

But there was one thing I didn't tell her, one Shame I held on to. I couldn't say it out loud, especially to a woman who was with child. So although I was relieved when we ended our session, on another level I was devastated. Still, it was eleven p.m. and I had no words to say it. I knew I'd always think of it, though—it was the only thing left unsaid, and if you think about something long and often enough it can drive you crazy. Maybe crazy enough to drink.

I walked home in the hot, quiet Toronto night and thought how I hadn't done it right. I still felt alone. I hadn't let myself be fully seen. But then, right before I turned the key in my door, my phone rang. It was Ruth, asking how I was.

I blurted out what I thought was my worst Shame.

That's what you were worried about? she said. I didn't have to make amends for what I'd done, she told me; in fact, no woman had to. It was bad enough that some viewed it as a crime, and that my Catholic God believed it was murder.

Ours was a simple, brief conversation. But it brought on a profound feeling, the same wings-at-my-feet relief I'd had as a child upon leaving the church. Except now it felt authentic, and now I understood the point of confession.

This episode taught me that there are people out there who will hold space for you without judgment. I learned that trust feels like a risk, but it's a risk you must take to break your Shame.

45.

I did a few more rounds of step five over the years, and every time the feeling afterward was the same: as if I were no longer flesh and blood and bone but just a silly little soul, pure and sober and . . . ready to sin some more. And to apologize. And to be forgiven.

If step five is confession, your sobriety is your communion.[72] If you're alive, you will screw up and you will have Shame to confess about. And if you hold on to it for too long you'll risk going to hell, which in AA is right here on earth. Too much—resentment, defects of character—or not enough—meetings, prayer, God—will most likely lead you to that hell, to drink.

I'd like to think these step fives lead to more permanent changes than a Catholic confession does, especially one from a confused child who's mostly interested in avoiding God's wrath. With step five you understand the reason for it, and instead of some abstract afterlife punishment, you know exactly what the punishment is. Because AA is understudied—with most of the research relying on self-reports—it's impossible to say how this impacts everyone, but I know from my own experience that step five has been a beneficial practice; much like therapy, it has allowed for more self-reflection to identify some of the patterns that tend to get me in trouble or cause misery.

I associate writing with work—even the sort of writing that pulls my guts out—but there's research[73] suggesting that journaling is a great

[72] One definition of communion: "a close relationship with someone in which feelings and thoughts are exchanged."

[73] According to one study, the benefits of journal writing are more pronounced when participants write about emotionally difficult experiences rather than neutral topics. The study found that people who engaged in expressive writing about their deepest thoughts and feelings enjoyed a variety of benefits, including reduced distress,

practice for exploring and expressing one's emotions, including feelings of Shame.

Back when my ex-husband and I attended couples therapy, we had a lovely Jungian therapist who insisted on both of us journaling, which neither of us did. The word itself was enough to make me shudder; it was akin to "scrapbooking" and "rom-com." But what I did do was write unsent emails to "Dr. College" (he was American and referred to post-secondary education as "cah-lege" in a delightful, non-rhotic drawl). This was something he suggested when we bristled at journaling: that we write to him, without sending, all the things we wanted to say out loud but couldn't, in therapy or otherwise, for fear of embarrassment or of angering each other more. He also suggested we reread the adversarial emails we'd written to each other in the recent past in order to learn something about the dynamic that had brought us to his office in the first place.

As reluctant as I felt about journaling (writing *not* for a living), I also knew from all my step fives how helpful it is having things set out in front of you—if only because memory is a great liar, like a buffer overflow in computer science: a quirk that emerges when a program

---

improved immune system functioning, improved working memory, and improved social and academic performance.

In another study, participants were asked to write about a traumatic or stressful experience for twenty minutes a day for four consecutive days, with the researchers using fMRI to measure changes in brain activity before and after the writing exercise. The results showed that expressive writing led to increased activity in the prefrontal cortex—a brain region associated with cognitive control and emotion regulation—and decreased activity in the amygdala, a brain region associated with emotional processing. It was concluded that expressive writing may help us regulate emotions and improve cognitive functioning.

scribbles data,[74] extending its reach beyond the memory it was assigned. It's better to have records that won't disappear into glitches.

The weekly couples therapy became an event I started to look forward to. We still made fun of Dr. College, and I know my ex-husband was never sold on any of the writing part, but things started to improve between us. It was as though we were finally adjusting the lens we'd trained on each other's faults. Even when we'd try the corny "What I hear you say . . ." statements, we cringed just a little less. I remember that period as calm and hopeful. A year later we were pregnant, and we've often talked about how out of the three therapies we tried, Dr. College's was the only relatively successful one.[75]

The action of putting thoughts and feelings into words helps us see them better, often from angles that are inaccessible when we keep them inside. Imagine that your Shames are pieces of some exotic mineral,[76] a chunk of meteorite you've swallowed the moment each Shame hit, and that as you disclose your Shames—in words only and only to yourself—you're reaching inside to examine these pieces as you describe them on the page. Having words and a story helps us view our experiences more objectively and will hopefully minimize them, turning their meteoritic strangeness into something we can digest better, break into smaller pieces, or obliterate altogether.

[74] In computing, a buffer is a designated area of memory used to temporarily store data while it's being transferred from one place to another. It acts as a sort of waiting area where data can be collected before it's processed or moved to its final destination.

[75] Emphasis on relatively; we separated later.

[76] Or maybe shame is a spiritual teratoma, some sort of dark material that contains immature or fully formed sorrow, including tears, teeth, and pulled-out hair. Something you absolutely do not want to carry inside.

When I was asked by the media about whether I felt a sense of catharsis after writing my memoir, my instinct was to laugh. But looking back, it's obvious that it did help me release and alleviate the emotional distress I had around my drinking with a baby in tow. I have no way of telling whether, during the process itself, my Shame-related emotions lessened in intensity, but I do remember writing in a sort of paradoxical state: frenzy combined with utmost calm.

I started the memoir as a work of fiction, and while I was still drinking. In fact, I wrote because I couldn't talk and I couldn't talk because I was too ashamed. For a time, I even referred to the narrator—of that "fictional" work—as an "ordinary villain."

But wasn't the whole process of writing *her*, of writing her story—and along the way examining the origins of her Shame, her triggers, her associated thought patterns—another aspect of journaling?[77] Writing about *her* and not me meant I could put my emotions and experiences on paper; I could externalize them, make

[77] Other benefits of journaling include identification of patterns over time. By writing things down and later reading what we've written, we can try to identify recurring themes, situations, or triggers that lead to shame. Even something as simple as "I always" is valuable information: You always what? When does it always happen? This sort of awareness can aid in developing strategies to manage or avoid such situations.

Journaling is also said to provide us with a sense of control and agency over emotions, whereby seeing words on a page allows us to see where the big emotions tend to live, what it is we do about them, and if we do anything about them at all. Let's say you often feel stressed about one of your cousins visiting, and during the writing process you discover that she always seems to judge how you live. This could offer you an opportunity to reframe that Shame-inducing experience, develop a more compassionate, self-accepting narrative, and come up with a way to avoid the stress—perhaps by suggesting you meet in a restaurant until you work out those feelings. Or just ditch that particular cousin and avoid that stress altogether.

them seem less overwhelming. In other words, I could introduce a sense of distance from my own feelings.

46.

Back when I got sober after a relapse of almost a year, the actual moment when it began was insignificant. I was hungover, bruised from falling off my bike the night before, limping along with a stroller. As I described earlier, I was also concocting a story about having had a concussion, a story I would present to my ex-husband to prevent him from kicking me out. Instead, I told him the truth.

Was everything building up to that moment of clarity? Probably—there'd been three different outside interventions: an in-patient rehab, a series of ultimatums, and a baby who kept growing and whom I kept trying to raise and love without alcohol around. But the actual moment was nothing special. Yet in that instantaneous, blurted-out confession, I gave up all I had.

This time around I don't own a home I can lose and I haven't been to rehab, nor has there been a single ultimatum. I don't even have witnesses, save for my son, whose semi-return is still uncertain—so I'm not sure if I haven't lost him too.

My boyfriend is away most days, working long hours. We never talk about why he prefers to sit in rented offices all over the city and eat out instead of coming home to dinner and to—well, *who* exactly? Neither of us knows.

Sometimes me and sometimes my ghost. He never lectures about my drinking, and the mornings when I "feel sick" and stay in bed longer he's attentive and loving and we both play the pretend game in which I possibly have some sort of Covid-related ailment where I'm sweating too much and my body aches. Since I've had two serious bouts of the virus, this is plausible.

I don't know whether he's become resigned to our situation or too exhausted to do anything about it, but sometimes he reminds me about growing up with his white, alcoholic parents, especially a father who raged and would pour booze into his morning coffee. Once, on the way to school, he didn't notice that the car door opened as he made a turn and his six-year-old adopted son fell out and rolled onto the road. Which is to say, there isn't much I can do to trump my boyfriend's childhood trauma with my mostly uneventful drinking. We often talk about what happened on the island as though it's a fairy tale, one that we need to recount and piece together.

I don't know if we do this to make sense out of something that was senseless and traumatic, or to remind ourselves that we have that special bond, that he'd possibly saved my life, and that I might need him around to save my life again. Or is this something we talk about because it needs to be resolved so that we can go our separate ways? I do know that it's replaced our old story, where he used to tell me how we met in the spring and how in the summer he saw me cross the street one day in a halter top, long hair bouncing against my bare back, and he said I moved with such grace that he froze watching me, and that as I passed him I said, "Hello Jules," with a smile that he said blinded him. This, he claimed, was when he fell in love with me. I've always wondered if he'd confused me with someone else, but I never told him. I adored the way he described this woman, and I was in love with her too.

It's hard to say whether my accident on the island was when he realized he was responsible for me, that he was now stuck with me, that there was no escaping me. That the summer girl from back then was nothing more than the rusalka I'd told him stories about, the mythical Slavic creature that appears in the body of a young woman to lure her male victims underwater.

The closest he gets to scolding is when he tells me sometimes that "the puppy needs you to be well." But I tell him that the puppy is perfectly happy, and this is true. I take Clifford with me everywhere—wrapped inside my coat in one of his cute sweaters and coats on long winter walks alone or with a friend, parting from him only when I head off to teach, never for more than a couple of hours. Because of the snow and his delicate little pink paws, I also take him for long walks in the downtown underground shopping tunnels that spread for miles under banks and shopping malls and condos and that are mostly deserted after six p.m. This is the only time he's allowed out of the safety of my coat.

I'm sober on those walks, the little creature trotting along as if attached to my ankle by an invisible string. I don't notice the fact that I'm actually sober a lot more frequently—some of it has to do with my son coming by more often, some of it's because of my teaching, and a lot of it is just being generally psychologically exhausted by my own drunk self and her demands. Every time I pass a liquor store without stepping inside is a small triumph. Conversely, the couple of times I do walk in are full of Shame, same as always, until that first magic gulp at home that often makes me simply say who cares, out loud and to no one in particular, to all of you who would judge and feel disgust and pity were you to see me.

And like my baby in the past, the puppy has become the dependent little creature who's unaware of why my energy suddenly shifts.

But all that happens less and less, although I continue not to notice and not say anything about it—I've said enough about quitting to last seven alcoholic lives.

We have a nice sober Christmas. My son stays over a couple of nights in a row, we have a family lunch with my ex-husband, I spend some time with my boyfriend, and I get away for a weekend with Ruth.

My son comes over for New Year's Eve and we stay up till midnight and light sparklers and take pictures of Clifford, whose fur reflects the tiny bursting silver stars.

47.

A few things happen in the new year. First, my boyfriend—who had to leave town suddenly during the holidays to attend to his mother, who's had a bad fall—has to stay longer in Calgary to get her into a home. Second, the puppy eats something poisonous and then knocks a glass of water onto my laptop while vomiting blood. I find out about the last two when I wake up and the puppy is nowhere to be found, but there's a small puddle of gelatinous red phlegm beside the laptop that's lying on the carpet by my bed, an empty glass and a chewed up power cord next to it.

The irony is that the night before was *not* the sort of night that would've led to these emergencies—I didn't leave pills around or chocolate, and I didn't drop my laptop as I passed out drunk. I went to sleep like a good girl, the way I've been experimenting going to sleep for more than a few nights now. For a drunk, going to bed sober and waking up without a hangover are momentous occasions.

And they do seem like experiments indeed, like something exotic one does for their health, like a loofah scrub or body cleanse. Whenever I get sober I'm astonished at how fantastic I feel even when I feel shitty. All the stories you've heard about interrupted sleep, anxiety, sweating, depression—all alcoholic withdrawal side effects—are 100 percent true. "My worst day sober is better than my best day drunk," as they declaim in the rooms of AA, is a popular expression for a reason. It's not that I didn't have a great time while absolutely blasted—the instant euphoria of taking a drink is why alcohol is sometimes referred to as the nectar of the gods. What they don't say is that drinking what's meant for the gods is bound to result in serious punishment for us humans.

This morning I have no reason to get punished but I do feel cursed as I finally locate the puppy, who's cowering in the corner, looking even smaller than usual—and apathetic, too, his large ears flattened against his head as I ask him what's wrong, hearing my own voice grow in panic, which makes me panic even more.

I'm not mad at you, baby, sweetheart, I babble. Are you okay, are you okay? I pick him up, touch his nose—dry—and open his mouth—empty—and cradle him to my body.

He's going to die but I cannot let him die; I will die if he dies. *I don't know what to do,* my mind says, and then goes blank. I don't know who to call: my boyfriend is in Calgary, my sister is at work, my best friend is in another town, and I don't know my neighbours.

I call my ex-husband and he picks up instantly; suddenly we're ten years younger and back on Wallace Avenue. I tell him I can't breathe; I ask why can't I breathe and his voice is soft and loving and very, very calm as he tells me to sit down on the floor, take a deep breath, breathe slowly, slowly, and then he asks me very stupid but necessary questions, such as what am I looking at, what colour is it, how many, what time is it, where am I sitting, what is the puppy doing, where is the vet, am I dressed, did I brush my teeth . . .

He's been through a few anxiety attacks with me, and he's pulled me out of them, too.

Once I settle down he asks me about the vet again and explains that the vet is very close, I can walk or he can walk with me if need be. I say it's fine, it's just a couple of blocks, they'll know what to do, they'll help, the puppy will be fine, it's probably nothing. He's vomited already; he got it out, whatever it was. My ex agrees and so I get up, get dressed, get the puppy dressed, walk out of the house, turn right, turn left, get to the lights . . . I do exactly what he told me to do.

It's raining outside and I didn't bring my umbrella. The puppy is bundled up in his blue blanket with the stars, and I don't dare move my lips from the soft spot on his head, covering him with my hair as the rain falls on me. We are a miserable sight, I'm sure, as I walk-run, clutching my little bundle, and finally burst into a nice, warm, clean vet's office where a kind nurse takes the puppy from me gently and sets him on a little scale—2.6 pounds—and invites us to an exam room. She comes back a few seconds later with a little portable heater that she asks me to hold against the blue blanket and I feel like a rotten dog mom, dragging him out in the rain and cold, and I say I'm sorry some more and she tells me everything will be fine. My puppy looks subdued but he's probably okay, the vet will be with me shortly. Clifford doesn't shiver but he cuddles up to where the heater's touching the blanket and I make a mental note to get him a heater like that.

When we get home—with special food and some medication—I lie down with the puppy and wait for him to fall asleep. He's fine. A little upset after the invasive checkup but otherwise fine.

What isn't fine is my laptop, which I turn on and which turns off immediately. I plug it in and it doesn't charge. I call Apple support and walk through all the troubleshooting steps but it turns out my computer's brain is fried and needs to be replaced. So I call my ex-husband for the second time that day and ask him if he can watch the puppy so that I can grab a taxi to the closest computer repair store, drop it off, and have it serviced for what will amount to my entire paycheque that month.

On my way back from the store I pick up a mickey of vodka and drink it in a Starbucks bathroom, straight. I proceed on foot all the way to my ex-husband's house to "walk it off," but not before making another similar stop. I deserve this vodka, and you'd drink too if you'd had the sort of day I had. I don't know how many days sober I just annihilated but it doesn't matter because I never said I was going to quit, did I?

48.

In Polish there's an expression, Urwał mi się film, which roughly means "The movie was interrupted," the movie being your life and the interruption being the (usually alcoholic) blackout that made its frames impossible to decipher. The only interesting frames I can decipher from that time are the ones where I need to be sober:

the day before and the day of my son's visits, which have now settled into two times a week.

I am militant about those times. The day before, I hole up in my apartment with food and watch endless reality shows about stupid people doing stupid things for money. The day of, I try not to overwhelm my son with suggestions of fun things to do. I avoid talking about emotions because I know he doesn't like it. And I certainly steer clear of asking him if he's going to come back for sure now.

He's his usual sweet, mostly kind self, sharing funny stories about school and occasionally revealing something that's making him anxious. I can tell he's just testing whether we can get our old connection back but his steps are careful on that particular bridge and he shuts things down if he senses anything above base-level excitement in me.

I'm not going to get my boy's trust back for a long time. So I too step around him as gingerly as I can—the roles having been reversed, as though I'm now the child of an alcoholic trying to test the atmosphere, feel out what's safe to express.

He watches me carefully. Once, when I start to sing along with the music playing in my headphones, he asks me to please shut up.

I shut up.

I know that despite his inherent kindness he'll try to hurt me, that even in his kindness he'll say things intended to put me in my place. I accept it because I deserve it. I won't take it forever; we'll have to snap back into our roles eventually, but the truth is I still have a secret and it's the one that has destroyed us before. It's my guilt, my Shame over that secret that makes me small, that makes me feel like a little worm underneath my son's shoe.

On the nights he's not staying with me I drink out of a huge, supermodel-beautiful bottle of vodka I seem to have ordered on Uber Eats. I've never ordered alcohol through an app before, and one night when I get sushi delivery to avoid leaving the house I test the option and somehow land on a litre bottle of Grey Goose. Only the best for baby. Believe it or not, I choose this brand and that size because neither is my preference and in my alcoholic logic I figure this will mean I'll drink less, more responsibly, and more guiltily too, considering the price. I'm guessing my odds are about 50-50: either I'll start drinking less or I'll start drinking and never stop.

Normally I'd rate the odds at 10-90 in favour of the latter, but considering the regime I've worked out with my son's visits and my prior little stretch of sobriety, I believe I can probably afford the gamble. The first bottle around. I don't know about the second or the third . . . and that I'm even considering a second or third tells you all you need to know.

Yet somehow I manage to make the first bottle last. I get into the habit of drinking before sleep while watching my reality TV shows, diluting the vodka with water so that I don't black out. Then somehow, some nights, I just don't. Drink. Even if my son isn't coming the next day there are those nights when I'm able to apply what I've been told to do in two in-patient rehabs and what I've heard in meetings over many years: I play the tape through.

I used to force myself to do this but now I do it instinctively upon uncorking my slick blue-silver goose—cork in hand, I see it all. I give myself a sneak peek of how the night is going to go. It's always the same, the same shows, some vodka, more shows, some online chats, followed the next day by feeling groggy, nauseous, exhausted, and thirsty. It's not that I'm afraid of those mornings, it's just that the repetition takes away whatever false excitement I used to derive from being buzzed. Unlike with past relapses, I don't try to "take advantage" of my godly state of drunkenness; I don't make social plans, and I don't wander the city in search of adventure the way I would have twenty years ago. Gone are the drinking buddies because I'm not drinking. My world has been reduced to a few blocks around my house and the seventy square metres of my apartment as I count down the hours till I can go to bed.

Over and
over and
over and
over and
over and
over,
same
same
same
same.

Nobody interrupts this, not my boyfriend, son, ex-husband, worried sister, or AA sponsor. And every night I pick up the small, warm puppy and take him to bed with me, hold him in the crook of my arm as I fall asleep. I cry and whisper in his soft giant ear *Please* or that I'm sorry. His big black eyes glisten in the dark and I feel guilty for giving him all this sorrow. I'm also sorry for everything else, for how tiny my world has become.

When I get to the bottom of the bottle I order another, convincing myself that I've finally been able to drink like everyone else—a little nightcap here and there with barely any blackouts.

The bottle arrives; I stick it in the pantry between two cereal boxes and get on with my day. The ease with which I can now order alcohol is terrifying; it feels as though I've crossed yet another line—that my suicide is literally at my fingertips now, that I don't even need my feet anymore or to have to make a decision to walk the wrong way home and find myself in front of a liquor store.

49.

One night, slightly buzzed and feeling particularly social, I accidentally dial a woman I used to know from AA meetings. Nancy reaches out occasionally, mostly to appreciate social media posts about the puppy—like me, she's a small-dog mom—and we have friendly exchanges via Facebook Messenger. We never talk on the phone, but when I dial she answers immediately, greeting me as if we've set up this call and she's been waiting for it.

I decide not to make up some bullshit excuse about having to run out to pick up my kid, and suddenly I'm in a conversation. And as I give her updates on the latest, something unlocks inside me. I tell her about my problems.

I say nothing about drinking. I just remark that every day is the same, that maybe I'm a little suicidal and don't even know it. I'm alone a lot, I say. I say, I don't know how to change my situation. I mention my son choosing to live with his father and hint at that being my fault; I talk about not taking the medication for my bipolar condition; I talk about a fuck-up with my last book. I have no way of knowing whether she thinks I'm full of it. When she asks if I've been drinking, I lie. She suggests that I check out a meeting anyway—one in her hometown, an hour away by train.

Tomorrow morning, she says, bring the puppy with you. We'll go to the meeting and then we can hang out with our dogs; it'll be great. A chance to get to know each other better.

Okay, I say, shocked at having agreed to something that in the past would have sounded absolutely torturous. But suddenly I'm actually excited to be getting up at seven a.m. to make the train for the ten a.m. AA meeting. It'll be my first in years. And it's not even the meeting; it's the fact that I'll have something else to do that Saturday other than nothing much; that I'll maybe make a new friend and see another dog.

And that is all. I don't think about what else could happen or what it all means. Nancy says to call her in the morning to confirm and I hang up the phone, elated for the first time in a long while. I'm not surprised at how I unloaded on this near stranger, although I am embarrassed that I spilled and spilled and didn't ask her about herself.

I'm aware of the theory that people may feel more comfortable sharing their problems with strangers, who are less likely to judge or stigmatize. It is, after all, what makes therapy successful—having the attention of a kind, unbiased professional who creates a safe space in which to be vulnerable. For me, it was Nancy's ease and her old-school, tough-love manner that instantly coaxed things out of me, things I haven't dared to say in their entirety to anyone.

I'm so inspired by what's just happened that I call my last sponsor, Cate, who's having a bath but stays on the phone with me for an hour.

We talk here and there and love each other dearly, but between the pandemic and my relapses, I haven't been the best at keeping in touch. Still, like Nancy, Cate doesn't ask why I'm calling so randomly. She listens and shares things about herself, too—our conversation is almost two-sided but we both know, and don't say, that this phone call is not so accidental on my part.

I code my Shame in ways that hide the fact that I've been drinking. Again I talk about the sameness of my days but without detail; I stop short in any stories that would include my nighttime ritual, fewer and farther between as they are.

Cate's voice is calm as always. When she jokes about her toes pruning from lying in the water for so long I ask her if she needs to get out and she says, Absolutely not, this is nice.

I don't have a name yet for what occurs that night, or what I feel after we finally say our goodbyes.

When I'm off the phone at last it's late, almost midnight. I'm no longer buzzed, but I am energized in a completely different way, as if after a long run, full of healthy endorphins.

I sit in my blue velvet chair, my usual drinking spot, but I don't drink. The little puppy is curled up and asleep in my lap; I touch him gently, feel his warmth, his little heartbeat beneath my fingertips. Then I caress my own arms as if I were someone else, someone new to myself, a marvellous being that lives below all those scales. I take the glass filled with half vodka, half water and don't empty it in the sink. I'm wary of symbolic gestures, I'm wary of jinxing things, I don't even want to hope.

Yet.

I put the glass in the fridge.

50.

In John Berger's book *And Our Faces, My Heart, Brief as Photos*, a brilliant poetic treatise on, among other things, love and disconnect from home, he writes, "And the naming of the intolerable is itself the hope."

I haven't named it yet—not quite—but something shifts as I wake up at seven the next morning and dress the puppy and myself and set out on my adventure.

The weather is bonkers, with high winds and a strong whipping rain, but I grab my plastic see-through umbrella and go outside, march against the wind that assaults the umbrella and twists it so violently that at one point I'm suddenly encased in it like a giant condom. I should turn around.

The puppy is safe and warm inside my coat, asleep, but I worry I'll slip so I walk as slowly as I can, the back of my coat getting soaked as I continue.

The umbrella moves again, all around me, whatever's left of it, occasionally getting stuck back to my face. I grind my teeth but I don't turn around.

There's another saying in AA: how an alcoholic "will go to any lengths to get it." The it, of course, being sobriety. My walk to the train is no longer about meeting Nancy, or about breaking out of my pattern of sameness. It's about proving to myself that I'm serious. Serious about what I don't dare think. But I tell myself to pay attention, to notice and appreciate every violent slap of the air and the rain and the plastic in my face. To be present.

Even with my martyr-like tendencies, this is next level. And yet it's exactly how it needs to be: turning back would mean turning back on what I don't dare think is happening.

Twenty minutes later, soaked, freezing, but determined, I get on the train and go all the way to Hamilton, where I'm supposed to meet Nancy.

When, after an hour, she doesn't show up, I turn around and go home. I'm disappointed and a little annoyed and I wonder if this was some kind of prank. But the annoyance doesn't last. I'm feeling weirdly accomplished and forgive Nancy for whatever it is that's made her a no-show. When I get back to Toronto it's past the lunch hour, and without thinking much about it I Google "Zoom AA" and click on the first link that comes up. Then, as I dry my hair and feed the puppy the fresh chicken I'd baked for him, I settle into the preamble[78] of a traditional meeting.

When I finally hear back from Nancy, she's full of apologies. Not surprisingly, she'd assumed I was drunk the night before, and when I didn't call in the morning to confirm my arrival, she slept in. I'd sent texts but she'd had her phone set to silent.

After twenty years in the program, she'd learned to attend to her own needs first rather than to those of temporarily inspired

[78] The preamble begins this way: "Alcoholics Anonymous is a fellowship of people who share their experience, strength and hope with each other that they may solve their common problem and help others to recover from alcoholism. The only requirement for membership is a desire to stop drinking . . ."

potential newcomers. She knew full well the attrition rate of certain types in the program.

I know this from experience, having been a Nancy in the past and wasting hours and sometimes days waiting for various women who'd promised to be somewhere at some specific time but would change their minds and decide to continue doing whatever had made them call me in the first place.

When I tell Nancy that it doesn't matter, that I went to a meeting anyway, she says, "You are exactly where you're supposed to be." And for once this doesn't feel like patented AA jargon, which is what it usually sounds like to me. It's true.

I am exactly where I'm supposed to be. Logged into Zoom and anonymous, my name spelled phonetically, listening to people from San Francisco or Paris or Barrie talk about the usual stuff they talk about in meetings.

Within days I find an agnostic group after growing increasingly alarmed at some of the almost comically old-school meetings where people talk about Jesus and God so much that I start to get distracted as to why I'm doing this to myself in the first place. But even those meetings have been fine—I appreciate the plain fact that people have gathered during a set time for the same cause.

I first share at a virtual agnostic meeting out of Montreal. For a moment I worry that I'll run into someone I know, but, again, that's just one of those cons outweighed by the pros, all part of what I'm doing here. What am I doing here?

My name is Yoveeta and I'm a person with a substance use disorder, I say, following another person's lead in using the more inclusive introduction. The Zoom people in their little squares—most of them with their cameras on—say hello, Yawayta. Even with my phonetic spelling and clear pronunciation, my weird name is a problem. But not for me; I don't care, and would introduce myself as Avocado if that's what it took.

The next time I introduce myself I say, My name is Yoveeta and I'm an alcoholic from Toronto, Canada.

Waves, thumbs up.

I adjust the puppy in my lap and say how I'm back after a long break where I was doing some "research," a euphemism for relapsing. I talk about being a chronic relapser, too. But then I pause, think for a moment, and say, I don't want to call myself anything, give myself labels. If I tell you I'm a chronic relapser that's what I'll become to you and that's not what I am. I'm many other things. Which is also why I used to balk at "alcoholic" because I didn't like how I had to identify myself by my . . . pain. But it's fine, I can reclaim it in a positive way—this is what we do these days, don't we? Reclaim our shames and turn them into strengths or something.

I go on and on, and when I'm done the host thanks me. A few people comment on what I've shared despite the no-crosstalk rule. Rules are generally looser in agnostic meetings, and in all my time attending them I've never been taken aside by some old-timer and scolded about breaking one. If anything, the agnostic members poke fun at the rules, although not so much as to undermine the general structure and goals of any given meeting. What I like most about these meetings is that they seem more evolved generally, and that they welcome change—including changes to the traditional texts, which are often considered sexist and borderline religious-sounding.

Ultimately, it doesn't much matter where I park my alcoholic ass and whether it's online or otherwise.[79] I just need somewhere to go to be among people who understand more about Shame than any other group I've ever encountered. I could recite my favourite *Little Prince* passage and most of them would probably mouth the words along with me, or at least nod with a knowing look on their faces.

At some point early on I decide to force myself to share in every meeting I attend. This is so much easier than it used to be while sitting in a room full of flesh-and-blood people—people who'd turn around and frown or smile or make noises while I performed my shares, women I'd try to convince to be my friend, men I'd try

[79] Like everyone else post-pandemic, I've gotten accustomed to online life. I'm brand-new to AA Zoom meetings, but it doesn't take me long to appreciate them, especially the convenience of not having to leave the house. The list of agnostic meetings I was given has almost seven hundred entries, some of which are further customized to welcome more specific groups, among them men only (cis and trans), 2SLGBTQIA+, and women only (cis and trans). Some are combined with other twelve-step ailments: emotional codependency, Sex and Love Addicts Anonymous, Overeaters Anonymous. There are even listings for Satanic Recovery, which I attend once out of curiosity and which has an assemblage of the most gentle, soft-spoken individuals whose only possible connection to Satan is their goth vibe and slightly nihilistic shares.

Many people say something similar to what I said the first time I shared: "I'm a person with substance use disorder/addiction issues/difficulty staying sober." This is different from the early 2010s meetings I attended, even the agnostic ones that were already much ahead of their time.

I know this reads like an ad for agnostic AA meetings, but it isn't, I assure you. There's plenty wrong with these meetings, too, but by now I understand better than ever that it's the people who make the meetings, and that sooner or later someone or something will fuck up. There will always be an issue of some kind, just as there always is when two or more people gathered together call themselves a group.

to seduce with clumsy cuteness, assholes I'd try to offend, secret *Drunk Mom* fans with starry eyes I'd try to ignore. And sometime later, all these people, whether real or imagined, every single one of them I'd have to lie to. Because I could never share about my relapse, because I could never tell them that I couldn't wait to get the hell out of whichever sad room we'd be gathering in so that I could hide with my secret—that the sad room wasn't a haven but rather a place exactly two blocks west or one bus stop north or a twenty-minute bike ride away from a liquor store.

I used to miss meetings because I had to work late, or because I was at home with my son, or because I just didn't feel like spending hours in transit and preferred to not "go to any lengths to get it" if it meant I'd get to sleep in a few extra hours or see a friend. AA would say that my effort to make it to a meeting should at least equal my past efforts to get drunk. And that such arrogance and laziness on my part is probably a character defect and the reason why I drank again. But really, it's because I *drank again*.

The online meetings bring people together from all over the world at any time of day or night. Meaning I'm having a hard time coming up with excuses for why I shouldn't attend them. As long as I have the time and enough energy to click a couple of keys on my keyboard I can join one, which means that the only excuse not to join one is that I'm sleeping or that I'm dead. For the time being, I go to at least four meetings a day. I even have a chart where I write notes about what I liked or didn't like about each one, with stars next to the ones I want to repeat. I begin attending one semi-regularly, a daily nine p.m. meeting that calls itself "Sane Heretics," plus a Sunday meeting out of Los Angeles.

I try to figure out when to part with the half litre of Grey Goose I still have: Should I pour it down the drain, should I make a ceremony of it, or should I just give it to one of the lovely, stumbly people on the street who need it more than I do?

For now I keep it in the pantry, understanding that this is akin to keeping a bomb in the house. I'm simply not sure I want to say what I'm doing yet with going to those meetings.

But at the same time I don't hide my new pastime when my son comes over, explaining who the strangers saying weird things on my Zoom screen are. Right away he's curious about seeing grownups make fools out of themselves, going so far as to ask me to turn my camera off so he can watch.

You might hear something upsetting, I warn him.

He thinks about that for a moment. OK, boomer.

My son doesn't pressure me, and as much as I'd like to use this as an opportunity to show him that Mommy is okay—this time for real, for real—I'm glad we didn't turn this into something I'd probably end up mocking just to suck up to him.

Back when I first got sober and would attend meetings, his father used to refer to AA as "Happy Clappy," and we'd share jokes about the program between us. Looking back, I wish I hadn't gone along with that, and instead tried harder to get him involved. I did try in the beginning—brought him to meetings, introduced him to my new sober friends—but he found the whole thing alienating, which I guess is fair enough. We settled on the fact that it was a thing I did for myself, the way one of his former girlfriends did yoga and another took acting classes.

51.

My cover's blown one night at Sane Heretics when I get a private Zoom message from a member asking if I've published anything since *Drunk Mom*. Secretly, I'm flattered. The meeting goes at its usual pace. One woman's uncle has been in hospice for weeks and she shares what she shares every night, which is that she's going to be devastated when he dies. Then everyone proceeds to share about their various losses and past griefs. I've obviously hit some sort of compassion fatigue, or maybe I'm just bored, because I can't seem to pay attention. And what I want to share doesn't align with the theme—not that there are themes, except there are, and the theme is grief.

Distracted, I look for a link to my ugly book baby, *Possessed*, and send a message back to the member who recognized me. For good measure, I attach a glowing review. Then I think about what to say when it's my turn to share. Something has been bothering me lately, so I want to talk about how uncomfortable I've been over feeling joyful; how I've woken up many mornings now feeling even better than just good or fine. Some mornings I'm *overjoyed* to be alive. But I'm wary of appearing arrogant about not feeling today's particular theme. And like a big baby, I also feel a little indignant that I'll probably have to tailor my share a little bit.

In the end, however, I don't tailor anything. When it's my turn, I say, To my greatest horror, I'm discovering that I might be an optimist.

This is a fun line I've been saying aloud to myself every time I wake up the way I wake up. Now I get to practise it on my audience.

But bad stand-up lines aside, it's in sobriety that I rediscover one of my greatest fears: contentment. I don't mean its usual pitfalls: boredom, or lack of drama, or finding comfort in discomfort. It's not even thinking I don't deserve it, that I'll be punished for it. Rather, in sobriety I'm always aware that there's nowhere to hide. In other words, clear-eyed contentment is so very different from the happy oblivion of drinking. I believe it takes great courage to allow yourself to be *actually* happy—and I'm not courageous in that way.

I don't say any of that during my share, nor do I voice my mean thoughts about others' stories of grief.

Once I'm done talking I turn to the Zoom chat window, only to discover that I've messaged the link to my new book—and the glowing review—not just to my admirer but to everyone. And now I have a couple of replies reminding me about AA not being a place where we market and promote our work. One even warns me about getting banned if I do such a thing again.

My face and hands go numb; I'm suddenly hot and cold and nauseous; I take big, desperate gulps of air to stop myself from throwing up. I am beyond embarrassed, furious at the guy who messaged me, and mad at myself for letting my ego overtake my need for privacy and walking right into the universe's clever little trap designed to thwart the very thing that really matters to me. My cursor arrow hovers over the Leave Meeting icon; I blink at the camera; I move the cursor to shut it off.

I don't leave. I decide to sit with this discomfort. I will not bolt from it, I will not let it stop me from doing what I'm supposed to be doing. Which is to face it, however it manifests.

With shaking fingers I send an apology to the group, explaining how my original message was meant to be private. Hearts and thumbs-up emojis instantly roll in.

Although I still want to throw up I remain sitting there, frozen in mortification, until the closing. I promise myself to come back the next day, and I do.

52.

My boyfriend returns from Calgary after his mother settles in to a new assisted living home. When I regale him with tales of the Zoom AA meetings he's kind and a little distant, saying, as he always does, that he supports my new sobriety. I make him promise to never listen to me even when I twist his arm to bring home some white wine or to "go out for oysters," which used to be our thing when we'd get dressed up and try to be civilized about my drinking.

I tell him I can't possibly apologize for the past few years. My apologies will have to take the form of what's known in AA as "living amends," meaning a living proof of change, meaning just being a decent person to him.

Day by day, gradually, I'll have to show him—as I'm trying to show my son—that things are different.

He nods and says he believes in me. He's always believed in me, but when I look into his eyes I see that he doesn't quite believe *me.* Still, I tell him that I'm grateful and that I'm sorry, however inadequate that may be.

You have nothing to be sorry about, he says. You don't need to apologize to me. But you do need to apologize to yourself.

This stumps me.

Our relationship isn't perfect; it hasn't been perfect for some time. I feel that, after my accident on the island, we lost each other in some way. I don't know whether we can recover as a couple, and I don't even know whether either of us wants to. For now, though, we're both here. And his support of my recovery is unwavering, even if we both have to pretend that for each of us it's not tinted with skepticism.

I tell him what happened in the Sane Heretics group, explaining how in the end it was a good thing, that it helped me confront something that before I would have run from.

In that case, I'm proud of you, he says. It's nothing to be proud of, I respond. And yet it is. And it's the first change I can identify—feeling a little proud of myself.

53.

In Greek mythology the Hydra is a terrifying water creature, often depicted as a serpent-like monster with multiple heads. She emerges from a deep cave in murky lake waters, and with her poisonous breath and a deadly scent she terrorizes nearby villages. When Hercules encounters the Hydra and draws her out of the cave for battle, he discovers her astonishing ability to regenerate—when one head gets cut off, two new heads grow in its place.

I think of the Hydra's symbolism: how if you don't deal with problems effectively, they'll only multiply. The same goes for Shame: how if it's not instantly cauterized it'll tend to compound.

Hercules doesn't defeat the Hydra by himself. Once he realizes the monster's secret power, he enlists the help of his nephew, Iolaus. As Hercules cuts off the Hydra's heads, Iolaus burns the wounds, stopping them from growing new heads.

Eventually Hercules gets the better of the Hydra by decapitating her entirely and burying her immortal ninth head under a large rock. This too, to me, is symbolic of how Shame is—even when defeated and no longer threatening, it's not dead.

The small incident at Sane Heretics turns out not to be so small at all. It grows inside me—not as an unattended Shame, but rather as a clue.

If I were more spiritually inclined I'd say it was a message from the universe that I'm having a hard time decoding. That something's knocking on the door of my subconscious—a vision that's blurred, a fogged mirror.

Or maybe it's just a pressure I need to identify, and in so doing relieve myself of its weight.

What's my biggest Shame? What has kept me from getting sober?

My come-to-Jesus moment happens at a one p.m. Saturday Zoom AA meeting for women. It's a hybrid, meaning it's held not only online but also in a physical room with physical people.

Lately I've been spending my weekends with my son and the puppy, going for walks together and playing various games of fetch and tag. The snow has mostly disappeared and the earth is rich and moist in promise, tiny green buds popping up everywhere despite the chill. But spring is in the air and the puppy is ecstatic as he runs in the sunshine. I've read that chihuahuas love the sun, whether on account of their Mexican heritage or because their small bodies are continually seeking heat. I'm almost as ecstatic as the puppy, watching him tearing around outside, ears flapping, little face smiling as he fetches and runs off with his new favourite toy, a squeaky little football. I can't wait to show him the summer. He's learned a new game where we throw him the ball and he runs away with it as we try to catch up. First he dashes around in circles, and then he suddenly changes direction, zips between our legs, stops and waits for us, then bolts just as we're getting close.

I'm amazed at how intelligent this simple game is and how he's clearly having fun. My son is having his own enormous fun, running after Clifford calling his name, shouting *I will getcha!* as the puppy roars off, squeaky ball in mouth. Eventually he drops it, one of us throws it again, and the chase continues. We almost never manage to catch him.

Today my son has an early soccer practice and a visit with a friend. So, instead of puppy time, I check out new meetings, which is how I end up at the one I'm in.

I don't turn my camera on, the way I never do when I attend a meeting for the first time. My name is spelled phonetically, the way it always is.

There's a Lead Share, a typical *Every-day-is-a-good-day-because-I'm-sober* speaker, which I don't mind. I've become one of those people too, sharing about my own joy, probably pissing someone off in the process.

I don't know if it's the Lead Share's self-deprecating but optimistic talk, or the share that follows by a mother of two who has a lot of guilt about raising her children while drunk, but I'm suddenly hot and my heart is beating fast. That new pressure inside me becomes more intense, as though I'm being filled with fire that absolutely must escape. I click on the little hand-raise icon even though I have no idea what I'm going to say. For once I haven't prepackaged my emotions, although I feel them so close to the surface that if I don't release them I'll have to claw them out.

I listen to an older woman, a pretty, white-haired witch with a cackling witch laugh and jangling bracelets and crystal necklaces, who talks about her grown children who've only recently trusted her with babysitting her granddaughter. She is twenty years sober. I listen to another woman whose daughter, older than my son, has told her in therapy that she'll never trust her. I watch a bawling mom who had her children temporarily taken away. In an almost-whisper, she says she hopes her daughter is still young enough not to remember. Finally, a woman shares about going through post-partum depression, saying she needed to hear what she heard because right now only the fear of becoming a drunk mom is stopping her from giving up.

When they get to me I turn the camera on, begin to speak, and everything that's been building inside me blows up. It's the most beautiful explosion—so much fire that it cauterizes whatever Hydra heads might threaten to emerge.

I tell the group that I'm not just an alcoholic and a mom, but that I told the world a prolonged lie that trapped me in my Shame. That I am a hypocrite. That I hid.

I say that I relapsed twenty times.

I tell them my son has refused to stay with me since Halloween.

I don't name-drop the book but I do tell them about it, and about the Sane Heretics meeting and how it's probably going to be impossible to pretend forever that I'm "Yoveeta"—if only in my own deluded belief that more people know about who I am than actually do. It doesn't matter. That Shame is alive and well until I name it, and if I'm right about my delusion, then even better.

I tell them about the puppy, and how the puppy needs me. How I've been waking up full of joy.

I tell them how this is the first time I've said out loud everything there is to say. Which is the truth. I search inside me to see if the fire has been extinguished, and it has. In its place is a wide, open space, a calm like deep sleep.

And then I'm done. It's as if I can finally breathe again. I feel humbled—not humiliated, as I thought I'd feel. I'm humbled because everyone smiles and sends private messages that say "Thank you" and "Welcome," and for that one afternoon I'm finally known as I really truly am.

54.

I plan to go back to the meeting the next weekend, and so I arrange with my son to come in the late afternoon. This represents another tiny win—it's the first time in a while that I've dared to ask for something, when I've risked having him ditch me as a mother for good.

Which, of course, doesn't happen. The worminess I feel is my own; it has nothing to do with him. When I tell him about the women's meeting he's happy to oblige, and makes plans to see a friend again.

And then he texts, I just want you to know I'm proud of you lol.

Lol, I text back. And cry a little, of course.

When I log in to the meeting a few of its members send me private messages saying they're happy to see me back. "I loved your share last week," one writes. Another says "I've loved your book." I swallow air a few times before simply *heart*ing back.

I share again, this time about how I shared last week and how I've changed my name back to its original spelling, which is maybe the first step toward combining all these scattered parts of me into one whole. I stutter as I run out of profound conclusions. Then I end my talk and listen to others.

After the meeting, and with a few hours to spare, I decide to take my nervous joy outside—I know by now that highs and lows are both dangerous, attached as they both are to an energy that needs to be spent. And for me, the easiest way to do that is physical exercise.[80]

It's an afternoon like any other in the typically gloomy, steel-blue Canadian April weather, when it's warm enough to go for a walk but too cold to sit on a bench. I'm wearing my favourite wool coat and Clifford has on his favourite sweater: blue, black, and white stripes with a cute penguin face sewn on the back. When I lay it out

[80] Engaging in physical exercise, including walking, has been shown to reduce stress levels and promote relaxation. Exercise increases the release of endorphins, natural mood-elevating chemicals in the brain. Walking specifically can help establish a connection between the body and mind. Focusing on the physical sensations, the rhythm of the steps, and the breath can divert attention from stressful thoughts and bring a sense of grounding and presence. This mindful walking practice can be calming and help cultivate a sense of peace and mental clarity. One study found that walking was associated with reduced risk of depression and improvements in cognitive function. Walking also stimulates blood circulation and oxygen flow to the brain, which can not only contribute to the sense of calm but also improve cognitive performance.

on the floor and say "Put your sweater on," he's learned to nudge underneath and try to wiggle his little body inside it. It's the sweetest thing. I help him put his paws through the openings, praise him for being a good boy, then put on his own winter coat, complete with a little hood. He's always wearing his handmade collar with his vaccination tags, his name, and my phone number, and then the harness with its retractable leash.

A friend joins us and together we trek all the way to High Park. At one point we briefly sit on a bench with Clifford napping on my lap, his little body shivering in his sleep. The sun is a pale yellow stain, our talky faces zapping in the brisk chill, so we don't linger for too long. On the way back I alternate between letting the puppy walk and putting him inside my coat, which he's a little unhappy with, trying to wiggle out here and there. I say goodbye to my friend and pick up some oranges and grapefruits from the fruit stand near my house. You wouldn't be able to tell it's spring already considering how cold the air feels, but the sun is high and the stand is selling its first tulips, their tight rubbery stems holding up clenched turban heads of pinks and yellows and reds. I'm inspired by their nerve, their bold announcement of a new season coming, so I pick out a bunch of fuchsia ones.

A woman in the lineup compliments me on Clifford, calling him a sweetheart. And unusually he is one, not barking but rather putting his big ears down and letting her pet his tiny head. I kiss his little head too, and tell him how much I love him—so much. He looks at me with utmost devotion and licks my nose.

On the way out of the store I put him down on the ground to adjust the bags and move the tulips. As I do I drop the leash; the plastic handle makes a startling sound; I bend down fast to pick it up but somehow the puppy is gone, running next to the moving wheels of an SUV. I lunge forward, screaming; now he's running next to the giant front wheel of a bus, the red leash dragging behind him, something dragging behind him, how does he walk attached to the front wheel like that, there's no way, there's no way, I scream again or there is a scream, a baby cannot die, a baby shouldn't die, a baby cannot die—

The cinematic oranges and grapefruits rolling onto the street, the tulips smacking against the curb, my body collapsing like the body bag I've become. The woman from the store is next to me, saying *Oh no, oh no*. There's another woman with a hand to her mouth across the street, the bus driver stumbling out of the halted bus, her face is twisted as she says sorry over and over again. Cars stop, everything stops, the woman from the store is out on the street with a black garbage bag scooping . . . I cannot look so I don't look but I see it all, except for what goes into the garbage bag—little lungs, a heart, so much love, all that love, how does it fit inside? Who can we call, call someone, oh no, let me give you my number, please call, I need to go, I can't, I need to go, just take the number, okay, go, go, I understand, the black garbage bag, and I put the oranges back in my tote, and I'm clutching the tulips and the handle of the leash, no, no leash, just the tulips, and I go up up, I want to go down down, but the bus driver is crying, so many people standing, looking, wailing, someone's wailing, I'm wailing, and then suddenly I'm vertical and I go up, float all the way to the sky, I float above the street, and the sidewalks, and the buildings, I float all the way to my apartment, my son on the phone, my son's wail in the background,

"Oh no, oh no," pure despair, pure child's misery in two words repeated, Oh no, oh no, I'm sorry, I'm so sorry, everything shakes, I shake, the penguin sweater, I can't see anything, I collapse, I'm on the phone, I'm at home, my boyfriend's angry, What happened, what happened?

What happened?

What was she putting in that garbage bag? What was that?

We need to find some water for the tulips, a vase, we need to put them in the window so that they can open up.

My boyfriend does what he did for me and my smashed clavicle and face—he takes care of what needs to be taken care of. He goes and gets the garbage bag with Clifford's little body inside it. I didn't mean to leave—he says it's okay, he kisses me on the mouth. It's going to be okay, he says. I'll be right back. I love you.

My ex-husband's girlfriend calls me and says she'll wait for me in the little park between our houses. We're always on our best behaviour with each other; she knows I won't say no to her. I will listen to her the way I wouldn't listen to my ex-husband. So I leave and we go over to my ex-husband's house. Our son is there and he laughs when he sees me and then his face twists and falls and he is all tears. We hug tightly, I am so sorry, I am so sorry, we say back and forth. Are you going to be okay, he wants to know, and I tell him one thing, which is the only good thing I have to tell him, the only good thing I have other than him, now.

I'm going to be okay.

I don't tell him what I mean, which is that across from the fruit stand is my old liquor store, full of red caps and relief and also despair, and failure, but also nothingness. I need nothingness now. No instant solutions. I don't tell him that my feet haven't even tried to go right toward it, that instead of turning left I floated above sidewalks and landed at home. I hope that my "okay" contains all that and his pleading brown eyes tell me that he knows what I mean when I hold him by the shoulders and repeat it: I'm going to be okay. You're going to be okay.

I pull him close to me again and hold him, count my breath backward, ten, seven, three, two, one, think of nothing, I am a rock, I am steady, I don't float. I am as solid as I've ever been, my entire body is a ground onto which he can fall if he needs to; I am a lap where he can lay his head, my arms are only for him, my arms are his mother's arms, nothing else. We stand there for an eternity.

My ex-husband and his girlfriend wait in the living room. I leave their family where my son is safe, where he's not going to be required to do anything other than mourn his tiny best friend, his little brother. When I leave, I leave steadily, calm, with a dry face.

We're going to be okay, I say, and everyone says *I'm sorry* and I say *Me too.* But we're okay.

I hold my strength until I can give it to someone stronger. When I get home, I do—I collapse again and my boyfriend holds me up. He holds me for hours and lets me cry. Where is he? Where's the puppy? Where . . . He says he's in the basement, in the black garbage bag. My boyfriend put his blue blanket with the stars and his squeaky football and his bear inside it to keep him company for the night.

He will take him to the island tomorrow. He will find him a spot. He will make sure he's happy. He's happy now, my boyfriend says. He's happy because he knows you loved him.

Did he think I pushed him, I say, and I see the turning wheel, the penguin sweater, the little trot, the strange image I cannot make sense of.

He would never think that. He just thought he was running toward you.

When it gets really late my boyfriend takes my clothes off and takes his clothes off and we go to bed and I pull him inside me and we let grief make love to us. I float again and he with me, all the way up to the sky, past the clouds and right into the stars where a little white chihuahua is jumping over a rainbow bridge. When I look at him he looks back and he doesn't know so I don't tell him. I just tell him he is a good boy and my body shudders and releases so many tears that back on earth I drown and sink and finally settle somewhere on the bottom of silence. Maybe I sleep, I don't know, but I rest and breathe. That's the best I can do and there are big, safe arms around me never letting me go.

55.

The next morning my boyfriend takes the black garbage bag to the island. He walks to a spot where Lake Ontario is calmly brushing against the stones at the shore and he sits there all day, the white puppy spirit next to him. When the sun goes down my boyfriend buries my baby in his soft blue blanket with the white stars, with his favourite white bear and the squeaky football, in a beautiful, hidden spot near a small forest. He sets down a big stone on which he's written "Here *lives* Clifford." Next to it he positions a card I've written with my son. Later he will tell me, again, about Clifford running happily in the stars, and he will tell it to me as though I'm a child every time I ask—where Clifford is, as my mind tries to make sense, and cannot for quite some time.

Once I can think clearly I'm horrified by my own shock, and that I left the puppy's body behind, although I don't feel guilty about it. I realize that staying could've brought on even more heartache than I already have. I've avoided that heartache by having my boyfriend commit to the painful and necessary task of the aftermath, and of creating an event and a place where closure would be possible.

I'm a person whose greatest sorrow has always been a lack of anchor. Going back and forth between two countries, two languages, and the parallel worlds of writing and living, I'm an expert in leaving and longing. It's an affliction of transience and I don't know how to ground. Grounding never feels safe when your life has been one of uprooting. But I need it just as everyone does, and I'm lucky to have someone in my life who understands this about me, who can anchor me, at least where the death of a loved one is concerned. It's not just a poetic device when I say I floated above it all after the accident, and my boyfriend's kindness allows me a place to land once I'm ready to acknowledge what happened.

56.

I don't let the grief fester, not even for a moment. I don't sit alone with it for too long. As I see it, I've sat with darkness all by myself long enough. The people in my life understand something about me because they keep creating little nets into which I can fall, smaller and bigger kindnesses.

I also don't let my grief develop into something else. The question I've been asking myself is *Was it my fault?* As impossibly painful as it's been, I've gone over each moment, all of them stopping cold at the fallen tulips. The plastic handle of the retractable leash I used to train the puppy made a sound that caused him to bolt. I research the leash and learn that it has a bad rep—mostly to do with the cord, which is very narrow and can easily get wrapped around fingers or legs, causing injury—but there's nothing about the handle in particular. Still, I wish I hadn't used that leash, I wish I'd attached a regular leash to a belt tied around my waist—something I'd planned to do but hadn't. I wish I hadn't stopped at the fruit stand. Or I wish I'd asked my friend to wait with the puppy as I stopped at the fruit stand. Or I wish I hadn't noticed the flowers. I wish I'd carried the puppy inside my coat. I wish I'd avoided busy streets. I wish they'd have finished the construction and gotten rid of the buses in that area. I wish we lived in the country. I wish we lived in Mexico.

I wish I could stop wondering if the puppy thought I pushed him.

But I don't linger with my wishes. I don't let them develop into rot that will eat away at my conscience. I say them out loud, the nonsensical ones included. The guilt—which doesn't always follow logical reasoning either—never goes away. But now that I've been practising telling people and allowing myself to be seen, it's impossible to hide the way I instinctively want to—or maybe no longer instinctively because what I want to do instinctively is shout about it. There are seven hundred Zoom meetings I can connect to. Every hour on the hour I can click Join on the screen and can talk through the pain. I need to let it out—and I can. For the umpteenth time in my life I think how being an alcoholic in recovery means I'm luckier than most. I used to bristle at such pronouncements, find them corny and disingenuous, but it's true that having ready access to meetings is an enormous luxury everyone should have.

Finding witnesses isn't hard these days with social media. As weird as announcing one's pain on X or Instagram seems to some, for many it's a way to lessen the burden. There's a whole world out there of people streaming their entire existence online, broadcasting various aspects of their daily activities, experiences, or thoughts, eating, sleeping, and playing in real time. I'm hardly alone with my exhibitionist tendencies.

When I join the meetings I raise my Zoom hand. This time it's me who gives meetings a certain theme—with other people chiming in about their own pets dying, about their own pets keeping them sober, about guilt, too. I mention all the ways in which I torture myself with my wishing, and although no one actually says *You're absolved*, many say they understand.

Many people also say—or message—that I should forgive myself, give myself grace; others say I should just let myself feel everything. Some agree that getting another puppy isn't a terrible idea; they laugh, too, when I make jokes about how that's a typical addict solution, trying to find an instant fix. And so what? Addicts in recovery start small, with one day. Then we add to it—only as much as we can carry, but gradually our small, isolated lives become larger. We add days, activities, people, but most importantly we add love.

Where I am now, it feels I'm ready to take more on—more love, more life. I'm far too enamoured with being conscious again to succumb to loss. I say to my boyfriend, I don't know what to do with all this love; I have to put it somewhere. I search for "white chihuahua puppies for sale." My heart is breaking and expanding at the same time. But I do not drink.

People keep telling me, "If you got through that sober, you can get through anything sober." Yet I still don't want to make any pronouncements, to see anything as a guarantee. If it's anything, it's a triumph of unshaming and connection, but again, it's not a definitive conclusion. The moment I start believing I've fixed this thing—Shame and addiction—that's the moment I let my guard down. Addiction doesn't go away. Just as Shame doesn't. For now, all I know is that I don't want to stop—living.

As long as we're on this earth and as long as we have pain, we'll have to deal with that pain—however we do it, and with whatever resources. I'd like to think that talking about my grief with others—my guilt too—is what helped prevent my succumbing to all the impossible wishes I could never fulfill, if only because time doesn't go backward. We're still here, we still have to keep moving.

I'd also like to think Clifford's arrival in my life is what helped sustain that momentum. Many wisdoms are passed on to people new in sobriety, and not starting a romantic relationship in the first year is one: getting a plant before getting a goldfish before getting a dog before getting a boyfriend. That's because every addition carries a risk of loss—and being addicts, we're experts in losing—so we need a cushion to protect us. I believe meeting Clifford was what protected me. The love I had for him didn't disappear with his death; it's still there; it's what propels me forward. Love grows exponentially; it increases at an accelerating rate. And so, although grief seems a threat, it's love that provides the structure and emotional foundation to endure it. It's one of those magical love maths.

With Clifford, I'd relearned some things: how to care for another being, how to care for myself since he depended on me, how to adhere to a routine, and how to be happy, too. I would cry and whisper my "Please" prayers into his ear when there was no one else who would listen or understand. There was no judgment, and in his big, devoted puppy eyes I saw myself reflected back as a good person. Maybe that's all I need for now: to be seen in a different way from how I used to see myself.

PART 3

Poland 2.0

(2023)

57.

I wake up from a pleasant nap, remove my ear plugs, eye mask, and neck cushion, and place all three in a special zip-up bag inside my purse with its well-organized compartments. I feel stupidly proud of having these items, of being so well prepared for the flight, as if I'm a real adult. I am a real adult. But I'm also a kid, the way every newly sober addict is a kid when they have to learn or relearn the ways of other adults, when small things like having a neck cushion and ear plugs bring small joys. There's no relief like the relief of a former messy drunk when everything goes as planned, when no phones go missing, when you're rested because you took a nap. I'm still so fresh in my sobriety that this turns into disbelief at how orderly and easy things are. When the announcement comes through urging us to put our seats in the upright position as the plane prepares to land in Warsaw, I sit up like a good girl, scan my close surroundings, pick up my trash (a tiny ball of paper), and fold the plane blanket. If they gave out gold stars for nice passengers, I would've earned one.

Once the seatbelt sign is off I get up to leave the plane, politely and slowly, my hair brushed, my face refreshed with a clean wipe from a cute clean-wipes container I carry in my purse at all times. I smell my perfumed wrist discreetly to mask the bad, sweaty plane smells of a nine-hour trip and I smile good-naturedly at parents with small, fussy children, wait patiently for dishevelled stragglers blocking the aisles while trying to dislodge their carry-ons.

In the baggage claim my brand-new pale green suitcase is one of the first to emerge on the carousel, gliding majestically toward me. It was a surprise gift from my boyfriend, who said he couldn't let me go on the trip with my beat-up Samsonite that I'm pretty sure immigrated with me in 1992. He brought the green suitcase home a couple of days ago and urged me to open it; when I did, another gift lay inside, wrapped in Hugo Boss tissue paper.

You need a travel dress, he said.

And I said, What's a travel dress?

He pointed to it.

I'm wearing it now, an elegant, long-sleeved, dusty blue number cut to a straight fit with V neckline and a string belt. It comes with a short blue slip that feels cool against my skin. My boyfriend has expensive taste and has always been generous with presents, but the ridiculousness of the reason—"You need a travel dress"—for this particular one made me both laugh and tear up in gratitude.

My thoughts often run along the "I can't believe I'm doing this" and "I can't believe I get to do that" lines. I'm experiencing the world as if for the first time. I can't believe I've landed in Warsaw, I can't believe I'm wearing this dress. The dress makes me feel as if I'm Nicole Kidman. I lift my suitcase and pull it effortlessly along, the same way I imagine she would have. Lately everything makes me feel as if I'm Nicole Kidman: perfect, elegant, and happy and lucky.

I'm also freaked out about these nice feelings, but not because they're unfamiliar—this isn't my first sobriety—but because I know they're short-lived. And I want to keep them forever; like every addict, I'm greedy. It's also hard to believe I won't be somehow punished for being this happy. But I try to stay in the moment, especially this one; it's a good moment when I make out my uncle's sweet, familiar features amid a sea of faces.

He gives me the usual awkward hug and I give him the usual air kiss on both cheeks. Then we're off, tracing the usual route to Ogrodowa Street through a city that looks both extremely familiar and confusing, a dream of a place I used to know. The pinball machine in my head lights up as we hit landmarks—grey and white stone, thick-columned Socialist Realism structures, rows of communist blocks with their sad pastel-paint facelifts, glass buildings blending into the sky. And in the distance and then quite close, rising above it all like a compass needle, is the Palace of Culture and Science tower.

Two years ago I swore I'd never come back. Today I can laugh about how in my alcoholic delusion I'd blamed everything but myself for my woes.

58.

"It's in Elektrownia, the same restaurant we went to with Luke," Agata says when I ask her for specifics. "The Italian place," she adds, which isn't helpful.

Like me she's just arrived in Poland, except from Germany. The dinner is for all her female family members, and I'm invited the way she always invites me, as an honorary sister.

The problem is I don't remember where we met with Luke on my last trip to Poland. On my phone, however, are photos from that night two years ago—in one, I'm smiling brightly but my eyes are gone, shot out into the sky of oblivion. I also have a vague, somewhat blacked out memory of dancing on a wooden stage and someone saying they loved how I moved. But I don't know where the night started or where we met Agata. Or where we lost her, and whether it was right away. Thankfully, the former power plant complex (Elektrownia) narrows things down a bit, so I say *Sure, sure, I'll be there.*

I could fess up and tell her I was drunk that night, and maybe she'd laugh and say something to make me feel better about it. I could say *I was just going through a hard time, you remember, it was a weird summer, we were all weird, it was the pandemic* . . . But I don't want to remind her of 2021 and there's a chance I'd just upset her. Agata cares almost neurotically deeply about the people she loves, so it's also possible that she'd cry.

The way she cried in the voicemail she left after my summer 2021 tour so that I'd receive it upon landing back in Canada. Actually, she left three. The first was probably meant to ease me, bait me, with her describing a funny workout she just had and how her cat was trying to climb onto her belly when she did crunches—she giggled that familiar giggle that would immediately bring one out in me too. The second began with a sharp intake of breath and suddenly Agata's rushed, serious voice saying *I don't know how to help you* as she launched into a speech about how she worried about my . . . health, and to call her if I needed anything, and was she failing me as a friend? And then how she hoped I could maybe take some time off, maybe I need a real vacation, maybe I could call someone, maybe I could go to *a meeting.*

She was listing what she'd probably heard of or seen in movies, or maybe what someone had suggested on a Facebook forum; perhaps she was even reading it off some influencer's viral post: *10 Ways to Confront Your Blotto Bestie*.

In the third of the three voicemails she was crying a bit and she apologized again and said that someone had noticed, someone in her family, and I remembered her nephew's watchful eyes in the rearview mirror as I happily plopped into the back of the car at the gas station with sweet vodka coursing through my veins.

The phone was hot and burning in my hand as I heard my childhood best friend's voice break and her breath catch. I felt so ugly and exposed in the first moments as I listened, but I didn't hang up and let the feeling pass.

That's not how *she* saw me, Agata continued. If anything, she saw my beauty or at least something worth saving. *I'm sorry, I'm sorry* she said too many times. Her voice was almost a whisper, as if she were trying to make it all smaller, small enough to sweep it into the phone, get it all over with, make it sound light and yet urgent, too. The way she spoke sounded rehearsed, and so pained, as though it were part of an oral exam, as though she were reciting one of those Polish epic poems we had to memorize to graduate from elementary school. Which is how I knew instantly how much this was costing her.

This is what I thought about when I got her messages. How she'd now joined the exclusive circle of my confronters. How sad it was that this circle was expanding, but also how I'd never had a real group intervention (my largest one having been my sister and my ex-husband back in *Drunk Mom* days). How, if I were to add up all the people now in on my big dirty secret, I could fill a small gym. Also, how sad it was that I'd sullied even my childhood best friend with that *thing* and how maybe this was good, how I had fewer places to hide now.

An addict amid their addiction is no different from a person standing on the edge of a skyscraper about to take a step forward. We're lucky when we have people in our lives who still care. As I listened to Agata I thought of the show *Intervention*, with its addicts who'd lash out against their loved ones and friends, grown-ass men and women running out of some beige hotel room in some forsaken Ramada Inn where relatives and friends would gather in their Sunday best with letters they'd read out in shaky voices to the about-to-bolt indignant party.

As ugly as this is for everyone involved, I'm all for interrupting someone who's trying to kill themselves. Especially an addict who hates being interrupted—because it's just fucking annoying to have to watch this, and addicts invite everyone to their show whether they like it or not. No addict is an island, and even that guy wrapped around the parking meter on Front Street isn't invisible—he's a character in this book. Sometimes when you see an addict it looks desperate but often it isn't at all. Sometimes it's just an eccentric old friend whose backpack clinks suspiciously and who wobbles a bit and bickers with your husband and makes your daughter laugh hysterically with Pop-Its.

But just as it might look desperate but isn't, it might not look dangerous but it is. As dangerous as death in slow motion. Even if interventions aren't exactly effective, never doubt that what you're doing is an act of love and that, as ugly as it might look, it's an act of bravery. Still, I know it's not fair, that it makes you feel gross and horrible, that sometimes you even hate *yourself* for having to do it, and that you're angry.[81]

My childhood friend didn't sound angry in her voicemail. She sounded exasperated and terrified. Sheer distance meant she hadn't been corrupted by my addiction like the other people in my life, versed as they'd become in the lingo of confrontation. Maybe it was that innocence and her obvious discomfort that made me pause, that stripped me of whatever protest I had left.

I replied in a long voicemail back, stumbling over my words, trying to explain that I was unwell but thankful for her concern, that she had nothing to apologize for. I never mentioned drinking, and like her I used words like "healthy" and "stressed" instead of "dying" and "desperate." I remember shaking afterward, my body clammy with sweat, my cheeks burning. Although I was alone, I'd been exposed, and yet also seen. Thank God I was finally exposed.

I didn't drink for four months. If I'd relapsed twenty times, then this was my nineteenth attempt to get sober. Which means that I

[81] And I'm here to suggest from the other side that you practise loving detachment with the addicts in your life. While there's no rule as to how many times—three or fifteen or a hundred—you should try to help before you give up on your addict, I'm just saying don't give up right away. Take my friend Ryan, for example, who is a lovely person but in and out of recovery and when he relapses he breaks the law. My one boundary is that I won't answer his calls past midnight because he never calls sober that late. Boundaries are crucial; and they're love, too. And if it wasn't for Ania and her boundaries I'm not sure I'd even be here, as I believe her kicking me out contributed to all the information I needed to finally confront my Shame, the foundation of my drinking. Healthy detachment means caring for the person without enabling their addictive behaviour or becoming overly entangled in their problems. It's a balance between showing compassion and taking steps to protect your own well-being.

drank again eventually, that the intervention didn't work. Except that I'd like to think it also means I had hope again.[82] That I got another chance. I've long surpassed cats with their nine lives, and if that doesn't make me supernatural—the way every addict is supernatural—I don't know what does.

Right now I put on my favourite dress, a dark silver See By Chloé I'd bought on sale for my first book launch and then kept in the closet for years waiting for another momentous occasion. But at the beginning of 2023 I started wearing it to most social outings, since as it turns out life is a momentous occasion. Tonight I pair it with my beat-up grey Converse x Commes des Garçons PLAY sneakers, which I also bought to wear to something important. And seeing a woman who has saved my life, and her family whom I last saw while standing on the edge of a skyscraper, is mightily important.

I feel giddy and beautiful like a princess when I arrive at Elektrownia. I got here by walking across Warsaw the way I always do, updating the map in my head. And now, in 2023, this map has expanded and become more detailed than ever—I'm constantly uploading, arranging streets and buildings and the stories attached to them. I'm now in possession of my past as much as my present and future, too, as I create new memories and add new places. The life of a drunk is all holes and 404s, streets permanently under construction, moving targets. But this is a sober map, and I finally understand the directions.

[82] And "Hope is the mother of the stupid," as the Polish saying has it (Nadzieja jest matką głupich).

When I get to the Elektrownia complex I walk toward a restaurant whose blond wood walls look similar to the ones I made out in photos from 2021. And bingo, there they are—a bright, chatty, laughing table of girls and women I've known all my life. Agata's mother and sister and their daughters, no husbands or nephew, bright eyes looking up as I approach, waving and smiling.

Agata gets up, squealing, and says I look like Thumbelina in my princess dress. She makes me turn around and twirl, and as I do she takes a picture. She herself is fresh from a photo shoot she arranged for herself and her daughters, with perfect makeup and hair and a gorgeous crocheted top. I walk around the table and hug every person, absorb their warmth and perfume and the joy emanating from seeing one another. I sit down. For a short while I'm nervous; I notice my voice breaking a few times, my laughter sounding a little forced. I imagine Agata's mother looking a little too closely at me, at least until she asks if I think our server is taking his time. I breathe with relief and lock eyes with the waiter, who rushes over with menus and apologies.

Soon we busy ourselves with happy updates on our summer so far, the weather, the city, our upcoming weekend at the Masurian Lakes, where I've also been invited as the honorary member of the family. When Agata's younger daughter asks me to draw our portraits I jump at the chance, wanting to redo the last time, at another restaurant, with a drunken pencil swirling wildly on the page as I cracked jokes to her hand-clapping delight. Sober, I'm more restrained, worrying I'll disappoint people who know me as fun and spontaneous. Still, it's not hard to tap into the childlike part of me that doesn't need alcohol to draw silly pictures. I might be quiet about it—not waving the page in people's faces, asking them to admire it—and the portraits are less flamboyant, but I pass the test. The daughter folds the sheet, saying she'll add it to her collection. I've half a mind to tell her to throw away the one from before. But why? This fun auntie was also that fun auntie, and I can't dismiss the fact that the one from before makes me appreciate this one so much more.

At one point I give Agata a copy of my last novel. She tears up at seeing her name in the acknowledgments; then, giggling through her tears, she asks, But what are you thanking me for? What did I do for this book?

It would take too long to explain, I say.

I can't readily express what that voicemail from two years ago did exactly. What her not rejecting me *then* meant and continues to mean. What her inviting me to join her family means *now*.

Unshaming triumphs are often small, unspectacular. Ask any sober addict how it feels when for the first time they've been able to get through a Christmas dinner without worrying about having to take a drink. What it's like to go on a bike ride on a beautiful summer evening *just* to go on a ride. What travelling feels like when you wake up from a pleasant nap as the plane lands and remember to collect all your belongings. How sweet it is to hold your child's hand and feel it squeeze you back when you signal with your squeeze that you love them.

No one at the table knows what my sitting with them means, but what it means is that I'm worthy of it. I take a weird and secret pleasure in being absolutely normal.

—

A week later Agata picks me up with my backpack; I wedge into the back of the VW next to her niece and off we go to the Airbnb in the Masuria Lakes. Once we get to the lovely cottage by a lake I help prepare a meal and then sit down with everyone else at the table as Agata's niece heats homemade wild blueberry pierogies with fresh sour cream.

After dinner, in the bruised dusk of the evening, I go for a walk with Agata. We fall into our familiar pace, her small steps and my longer strides, her arm hooked over mine.

It's a little cool tonight, and drizzling. To our right, the quiet lake echoes with children shouting far off in the distance; to our left, a tall evergreen forest stands on a rich carpet of moss and ferns, absorbing the sounds of the rain. I've a flashback to being eleven years old, two scraped-kneed girls at Scouts camp, on some mission to win a badge in a forest just like this one. As we walk Agata tells me a secret she hasn't told anyone, relating it in that familiar urgent whispery voice. I feel honoured, as heavy as her secret is, or especially because it's that heavy. I wouldn't say her trust is unearned, but I'm elated that I haven't destroyed it, and that she knows I'm strong enough to hold a space for her. What she doesn't know is that it was her grace and her acceptance of my ugliness that helped me eventually get here.

59.

The scold's bridle, or the "brank," was a form of punishment and humiliation that originated in England and Scotland in the late sixteenth and early seventeenth centuries. Although both men and women had been subjected to torture, branks were predominantly used on women—the kind labelled as talkative, argumentative, or otherwise disruptive within their local communities.

The most basic form of the device was essentially a muzzle[83] consisting of an iron framework placed around the wearer's head, with a plate that fit into the mouth to prevent the woman from speaking. More sinister scold's bridles included spikes or sharp edges on the mouthpiece that would be triggered every time the woman moved her mouth, adding an extra twist to the torture. Other contraptions with a more artistic bent would feature inscriptions or images intended to illustrate the supposed crime, or they'd be in the form of animal-shape masks meant to hint at their wearers' transgression—pig for gluttony, dog signifying unruliness. Once secured within the brank, women were led through the town or exhibited openly in public, where onlookers would hurl refuse or spoiled food.

I remind Ania about the contraption when on one of our many Krakow walks we come to the conclusion that we've spent literally days talking. Too much talking.

Somebody should just muzzle us, I say, and we talk about people who've tried. The scold's bridle is on my mind after a morning researching various public-humiliation devices[84] meant to ridicule

[83] Perhaps its most famous contemporary version is worn by Anthony Hopkins's Hannibal Lecter character in *The Silence of the Lambs*, making him the most atypical recipient of a torture reserved almost exclusively for women.

[84] The wearing of a scarlet letter as a form of public shaming for adultery was a fictional concept popularized by Nathaniel Hawthorne's novel *The Scarlet Letter.* Although public humiliation was a common form of punishment in Puritan society, there is no historical evidence to suggest that the wearing of a scarlet letter was ever an actual penalty.

people. Actually, there's now a pile of topics that I throw the scold's bridle on top of, a clanking junkyard of fascinating Shames that keep multiplying the more I research the theme. And the more I research, the more I realize that if a topic is even vaguely related to a human being,[85] Shame will be connected to it.

Ania brings up Darek, who fell in love with her free spirit and her spontaneity, and who loved her as though she were an exotic flower. The handsome, sensitive Darek who not only paid for expensive trips to Portugal and Spain for the whole blended family but who also meticulously planned their outings, including finding the best benches to rest on. Darek, who ate dinners with important people in Dubai, who understood perfume, and what went well with concrete and glass, and what shoes to jog in. I ask Ania what his hobbies were, and she remembered how he'd bought himself a whole woodworking shop, with the best high-end table saws, jointers, and planers, and how he would force himself to spend hours

---

Besides the scold's bridle, a device called a ducking (or cucking) stool was used to punish women accused of being scolds or gossips. The accused was tied to a chair or board and repeatedly dunked in water, often in a pond or river, before a heckling audience.

For both genders, the most well-known forms of public shaming are probably the stocks and the pillory, wooden devices that restrained, respectively, a person's feet or head and hands, leaving the accused exposed to humiliation and abuse from passersby, who could taunt and throw things at them. A simpler version was the wooden whipping post, to which individuals were bound and then publicly flogged, and in some cases made to wear masks or hoods with humiliating symbols or caricatures; the drunkard's hood, for example, was a mask with a piglike nose.

85 Or a dog. Two dogs in since I lost Clifford, I still disagree with Dr. Alexandra Horowitz, who says dogs only perform shame. I've decided to rely on my own anecdotal study of dogs and shame and conclude that they absolutely feel it.

there trying to fulfill a long-ago fantasy of restoring old furniture. In reality, his only fantasy was to be a husband again, and a good father to his young teenage son.

As for Ania, it turned out that being a stepmom and housewife to a handsome, wealthy, cool guy—who would gently and patiently nudge her to get up early to make breakfast, who urged her to spend weeknights playing house instead of going to protests—was Ania's brank. Darek wasn't a tyrant—he loved her spark. But when he learned he couldn't quite bottle and buy it, it irritated him. She kept sleeping in and making art and wanting to sit on the wrong bench in Cordoba.

Urwał mi się film, Ania says about the two years when she couldn't be her true self.

Me too, I laugh, except my own interruption is captured in the saying's classic meaning: an alcoholic blackout.

I'm in awe of us—of how we've reconciled after my disastrous visit two years ago. How natural and easy our friendship is again, even when we talk about hard topics—Poland 2021 included.

Ania reached out some time last year after Darek abandoned her during a health crisis. I wouldn't have reached out first—I was still too mortified. And for a short while I was indignant, too, about what happened with us, indignation being a drunk's forte. But I was touched that she trusted me with her broken heart. Maybe I wasn't such a piece-of-shit friend after all? Maybe this was the way forward for us? And it was; we started talking.

In the summer of 2023, Ania is a brand-new homeowner, having bought a gorgeous ruin of a prewar tenement apartment in Krakow, and I'm writing a new book about not feeling shame. In a way we've each found a home, one tangible and one not, but both feeling like the place where we're supposed to be.

We walk and talk, and sit and talk, and see art and talk, and eat and talk. We talk before sleep, and when we both wake up early Ania slips into my bed—bleary, messy-haired, and swaddled in a blanket—and we talk again. For the past year or so we've been leaving each other lengthy voicemails on WhatsApp that we call "podcasts," after Ania joked that she'd once cleaned her entire apartment while listening to one of them. After that, we recorded them intentionally long to keep each other company during chores.

I don't consider myself a talker and I don't know if Ania does, but we've tapped into a dialogue that seems practically Socratic in nature—staying with a given concept for a long time, developing it by asking more questions, building on it, refining some of its ideas. We frequently conclude that we remain in constant discovery—that nothing is certain or wrapped up for good, that we don't really know anything.

Some of the conversations Ania and I have revolve around complicated men, our kids, our mothers, and the domestic renovations you'd expect from two women talking (I joke), but they often evolve into larger themes of home and longing and love and happiness and art and beauty. And the good life, the quest for fulfillment.

Whenever we arrive at an unsolvable topic, especially one that's unpleasant, we call it "information"—we collect it; approach it as if it's all part of a program we're continually trying to download and improve. I'm familiar with the idea of looking at life as a series of lessons; I know that wisdom comes from conflict as much as it does from things working out, but in the summer of 2023 it's as if I finally have some tools to understand what it's all for and how some of it goes rogue despite my intentions to fix the glitches.

Perhaps it's the geographical distance between Ania and me, along with the unusual nature of a friendship that began with a shared art project, that has taught us to be intentional. Here we are, talking freely, but our podcasts have taught us to distill our thoughts, to remain aware of the time and space. Or it could be the fact that we've always treated the man who first connected us—my teenage years' lover and her ex-partner—not as a focus but as a fun fact. Because, although we do talk about men a lot, they're not central to who we are or how we define ourselves. At our age their presence or absence is just . . . information—evidence of something that has more to do with us than with them: this one was a father figure, that one a child. Ania concludes that, for her, they've all been projects. But this is changing, she promises. Her new apartment is proof: she's no longer waiting.

Shame. During my five weeks in Poland we take a few breaks as I visit with other friends and family, but when we reconnect Ania reports new Shames she's observed. For example, the Ukrainian guy who, an hour into their date, asks her what Poles really think of Ukrainian men. He speaks Russian with his mother, who doesn't speak Ukrainian but has remained in wartime Kiev—their communication is loaded, painful, he tells Ania. I imagine it's like spitting glass. Ania wonders if he's ashamed of being considered a deserter, especially by men his age in Poland (who would probably run too).

These conversations I have with Ania happen all over the city I once considered a locus non grata, an ex I vowed never to speak to again but know now I've never stopped loving. If I'm like Warsaw, broken but renewed, embarrassing at parties but still getting invited, then Krakow is my poet lover, his dark eyes watching me broodingly from a corner of the room before leaving to do his own thing. I follow him out, rediscover what made me fall for him in the first place.

We enter unassuming iron doorways and walk through dark, tunnel-like passages to surprise gardens, tables pushed close together or half hidden by trees, vines snaking around stone walls and fairy lights, a smell of cloves or tobacco in the air, conversations and laughter, the clinking of glasses. These sorts of places are where we end up on most of our walks, scooping hummus and smoking cigarettes and drinking prosecco, that last one for Ania, not me, as I try not to note that I'm not drinking prosecco. Whenever I'm in drinking situations I remain always aware that I am very much not drinking. This will fade eventually as sobriety becomes my new normal.

Sometimes we're joined by Ania's friends, this summer most often by the pretty dark-eyed Ela, who the first night shows up with her star-crossed lover. He's an observant Israeli Jew and she's not; they can't marry. But they can have sex and they can pine for each other and they can hide from their families, especially him with his Orthodoxy. Sometimes they meet in Krakow, sometimes in Paris; sometimes they don't talk for two years as they try to unlove each other. I don't dare ask Ela what it's like to be someone's Shame; I don't know whether she actually feels that way. She does make a joke once about how many years she needs to wait before all the members of her lover's family die of natural causes.

60.

On my second to last day in Krakow, Ania and I loop around the city that, as always, swarms with tourists, who in the scorching heat seem even more disoriented and frantic, like confused insects. We weave between them, lost in conversation as usual. After walking through the Central Square, we head to one of the area's famous streets, with its famous churches; in other, smaller squares we pass more groups of tourists, nuns and monks, and teenagers trying to hand us flyers advertising houses of mirrors and wax museums. We're semi-lost but also not, and we're not in a hurry. We're sweaty and hot but giddy with our mission. There's something otherworldly about our wandering, as though we're in a different time, on a different plane from what's happening all around us. On this plane we discover each other, patiently and lovingly, flawlessly taking turns listening and responding, connecting without end, an infinity between two human beings becoming deeply known to each other.

Not for the first time I point out that what we're doing is, in practice, unshaming. Ania and I aren't trying to cure each other of Shame, or to engage in some sort of experiment of mutual therapy, but it's inevitable that by revealing our authentic selves to each other we're cultivating a sense of security[86] that enables us to divulge Shame in the first place.

Without trust, without feeling secure, you can't easily disclose your experiences. The root of Shame often lies in the fear that revealing your authentic self and telling your story will lead others to view you less favourably, thwarting your innate desire for acceptance. This is why it's essential to recount your narrative to people who will lend an empathetic ear without passing judgment. After hours and days of talking, Ania and I have created an environment vital for embracing vulnerability. Many psychological theories view

[86] Safety is paramount for well-being, creativity, and forming connections with others. According to Dr. Stephen Porges's polyvagal theory, or "science of safety," safety starts with two—in other words, we all need someone else to create an environment conducive to co-regulation, a process in which two or more people work together to regulate their emotional states and physiological responses. Safety cues are conveyed through such avenues as body language, tone of voice, reassurance, active listening, and consistency (the last of which Ania and I had to rebuild after our 2021 fiasco). These cues help pacify the autonomic nervous system, thereby fostering secure and trusting relationships. Conversely, when your nervous system detects danger, it triggers a shift from connection to self-protection.

Shame attempts to shield you from others because it erroneously believes that revealing your true self would result in disapproval. Your task is to reassure your nervous system that it's safe and acceptable to share your story, reaffirming your likability and worthiness. For many, though, this isn't so straightforward—for some of us attempting to break free from Shame, the prospect of opening up results in an internal resistance manifested as negative thoughts and bodily reactions that insist it's unsafe, even when surrounded by supportive people. This response is rooted in trauma, and requires skills to soothe and manage it. I've been very fortunate to have had a lot of safety "training" in AA, for example, especially with my first sponsor, Ruth. Significantly, I've also shared about my relapses—and about the drunk mom–sober mom farce in that women's meeting before coming to Poland. And, in the summer of 2023, I'm also regularly seeing a therapist, my other safety net.

Shame as more than just a *feeling*—its complexity and entwinement with self-worth bring Shame closer to the state of *being*, meaning instead of feeling shame one is Shame. When you establish a connection that allows you to talk about Shame, saying it aloud removes it from you and makes it an external entity. You are no longer it. You can now release it.

On learning this theory, I think that a helium balloon is a nice metaphor for it, letting go of a string and watching your Shame go up, up, up into the sky. Except that every time I think about how Shame *becomes external* the balloon becomes a turd, which strikes me as a better metaphor.

By the time Ania gets to the Shame that lies between us, it's neither a balloon nor a turd but merely a footnote to be acknowledged.

We've talked about it already. A while back I left Ania a voicemail on WhatsApp promising to address it before my visit. And in response, Ania left me a message saying she needed to apologize for kicking me out.

But then came my heartbreak over my son's temporary departure, then there was Clifford, then there was life. The truth is, that huge Shame that made me swear off Krakow became so insignificant that we kept forgetting about it.

And so today, when we finally say it out loud to each other in person, it's more like a burp than some cathartic outpouring. It goes something like this:

I'm sorry I kicked you out.

You have nothing to apologize for: I was a drunk.

And then we laugh. And stop for ice cream.

For each of us it's the first ice cream of the season, near the end of the season. On this hot day we're already childlike, on a special mission, and so the ice cream seems fitting. In any case it's almost impossible not to have ice cream in summertime Poland, a country obsessed with everything dairy. There are ice cream shops on every corner, most claiming their wares are handmade and based on a recipe that's five hundred years old.

We spend some time admiring and assessing the flavours, a serious matter. We discuss how blackcurrant is superior to sour cherry, gelato to sorbet, sugar wafers to plain. We're on the same page about extras—sprinkling candy or peanuts over ice cream is sacrilege. Topping it with gummy bears makes us shudder.

We stop again when we pass a wedding, a tableau of well-dressed, stiff-haired, sweaty strangers posing for group photographs, smiling grimly on the steps of a fat Catholic church. They seem to have been at it for some time: the photographer shooting from across the street looks exhausted, and the bride, stuck in her pearl-studded corset, is red in the face. Ania giggles and suggests we photobomb the scene. But the photographer has suddenly had enough: she breaks away from her camera and leans against a wall with her eyes closed. Wordlessly, Ania and I do the same thing at the same time: take a picture. Then we continue on our way.

I'm down to the bottom of my cone when we finally find the place we've been looking for. Józef Mehoffer's lovely one-storey, Secession-style cream-white house is a museum now and a café. Without waiting for Ania I charge ahead through an arched white passage, my tongue against the wafer's walls as I scrape out the last of the blackcurrant's deep sweet silk-sour flavour.

Then I'm out in a garden and inside a painting. I look up Mehoffer's rendition of it on my phone and it looks the same, except for the white lace-wire tables where visitors are sipping tea and munching daintily on tiny pastries with cream.

The little orchard I'm walking toward isn't exactly the one from the *Strange Garden* painting I love so much; but at the same time it's recognizable to me on a cellular level, its fruit planted by the artist whose brushstrokes I've had tattooed in my mind since childhood.

I sit on one of the two worn-out benches and look around at the small, stooped trees, heavy with apples already, some of them on the ground rotting, giving out a sweet, fermented scent that mixes with the buzzing of August insects.

In *The Strange Garden* the apple trees are exaggerated in size and form a cathedral-like arch above the lady and her maid. Here, though, they could maybe tower above the blond child—the child I once interpreted as the universe's whisper that I too would one day have a golden-haired son.

I pick up an apple from the ground; when I bite into it I taste the sun.

What makes this moment even more special is that I'm not alone. My talking companion, who's witnessed both my Shame and my unshaming, is about to join me. She's lingering by the house; I don't know whether she stayed behind to give me this space or if she's just being Ania, endlessly curious about everything she experiences.

For a minute, I feel briefly possessive of my private cosmos, wondering whether my friend's company would interfere with its purity, its secrecy. I have half a mind to bolt, to hide in the bushes.

Except the reason we're here at all is that a couple of weeks ago when Ania visited Warsaw, I made her come to the National Museum with me to look at *The Strange Garden*. I felt nervous about it, conflicted about my easily pleased tastes, my love for something so instantly lovable, the way I used to feel embarrassed around my father as a little girl when he tried to explain why abstract art was more serious, more rewarding—more akin to solving a math problem than admiring the pretty and the obvious.

At the museum, Ania and I rushed through the rooms, pointing to a significant painting here and there, nodding toward others as if they were good friends we had no time to stop to chat with but needed to acknowledge.

The Strange Garden used to have its own partition wall in the middle of the gallery; as visitors approached it many would stop in their tracks, as if unsure whether the dragonfly had somehow broken out of the painting and was coming at them.

I didn't realize I was holding my breath, but when we finally got to the painting it was as if I'd risen to the surface. I exhaled. I felt the tightness in the bridge of my nose and throat that signalled tears, so I let them out, too, mostly just to get it over with.

I thought of my son, the last person I'd brought to look at the painting, in 2018. I photographed him next to it, with his untameable bushel of golden hair, standing only a few inches away from the blond boy—the flesh, the premonition.

I told Ania about that premonition, a story that seemed corny, and maybe it is, but it's true and so I told it anyway. Ania grabbed my hand and squeezed it. And then she came up with the idea of visiting the painting's real-life version, explaining about Mehoffer's house in Krakow. We squealed, giddy with the possibility, like two children who've just discovered the opposite of childhood's end: that everything they'd thought about magic was true.

I stay put in Mehoffer's garden. I wait for Ania on the little bench as she approaches, calling in her soft, singsong voice, You found it?

Her "Znalazłaś?" could be the garden, the apple, or whatever it was I was looking for, which is why I instinctively pick up another apple to eat later, at home, or to bring back to Canada, tangible evidence that I've been to a dream and back.

I wave the apple. I found it, I say.

ACKNOWLEDGMENTS

To attempt to write a book about shame is like trying to write a book about love or death or memory—existential and universal and slippery and hard to contain. When I first set out to do this, I had a vague idea that I would have to approach shame from a psychological, philosophical, cultural, societal, historical, and maybe even spiritual angle—but soon, it became apparent that I would never be able to do the topic justice. Not just because of its emotional weight, but because of the sheer scope of it. To write something definitive about shame would require a lifetime of research across some of these disciplines—and across the world—and even then, how would I ensure I was interviewing the correct people and covering the correct angles? At the same time, I started to have conversations about it with friends and strangers; for at least two years, I'd bring it up unasked or when people *would* ask me what I was currently working on—whether in the context of a dinner party or during a panel talk—and I quickly realized three things: (1) People really want to talk about it; (2) They don't want anybody to know (often, these conversations are hushed, almost creating additional shame); and (3) It is a deeply personal topic that starts in an individual's core, wherein lies the universal truth.

So although I couldn't possibly get access to all the scholars and thinkers, read all the studies, or afford a trip to Japan to study concepts like *haji*—the culturally ingrained sense of shame tied to social harmony and loss of face—I knew I had the most important ingredient to say something universal about the topic, simply because I too am human and I too have shame.

I trashed sixty-plus pages of research and background (some of which made it into the footnotes!), and I decided I would test my own theory of Unshaming—getting rid of it by exposing it—through using myself as the subject of this book. Right away, I knew what I was going to disclose: the shame that has been my on-and-off companion through addiction and relapse, the cycle of falling down and getting up again. (And again. And again after I said I would never do it again. And again.)

It was a terrifying idea. And because it was terrifying, it was the best idea.

But I couldn't do it alone. What I had learned in my talks about Shame is that how the space is held and *who* witnesses your disclosure are what is crucial to the success of Unshaming. Conversation is the weapon that destroys Shame. Sharing shame is what weakens it, and me being a writer, I chose *you*, my readers, to help me annihilate it as my witnesses, while also hoping to inspire and encourage you too to begin talking about Shame, a conversation that's both public and private.

But before choosing *you*, I was extremely lucky to have a whole bunch of other witnesses who allowed me to tell this story in its raw, emotional form, before helping me shape it into the book that it is now. If it weren't for these people—who listened and held space—this book would not exist, and my Shame would still stay hidden.

Thank you, from the bottom of my Unshaming:

Eva Oakes—for being the first reader of this manuscript and the first witness of it in its book form. For your loving, professional encouragement.

Sam Haywood—for your endless support and belief in this book. For your expertise and wisdom. For witnessing me.

Doug Pepper (Signal)—for being my brilliant publisher, editor, and guide, but first of all my witness, who understood the importance of this conversation, long before it became a manuscript.

Chip Fleischer (Steerforth Press)—for taking a chance on this Canadian author, for being another witness, for your support and courage. Now more than ever, we need Unshaming in America.

Amy Fleischer—for reading and understanding and supporting this book. For your own interest in and passion for this topic.

Stephanie Sinclair (M&S)—for believing in this book and for your encouragement. A long-time fan, I still can't believe I got to meet you and do this book with you!

Hannah Karpinski—for reading, for your encouragement and support. Pozdrawiam!

Karen Alliston—I have never had an experience where the copy edits made me tear up, but in a good way. Your genius is unparalleled. Thank you.

Erin Kelly—for your enthusiasm and support and for understanding what I'm hoping to do with this book. I cannot wait to see what we do together.

Matthew Flute—for your brilliant cover design and not shying away from a clunky word.

Sarah Howland—for your knowledge, care, and belief in this book from the beginning.

Tonia Addison—for your thoughtful support and for helping guide this book into the world with clarity and intention.

Lorissa Sengara—for your diligent proofreading.

Steerforth Press team—Cate Fricke, Zandra Rose, Devin Wilkie, and David Goldberg—who have been beyond supportive of me and this book and with whom I cannot wait to start Unshaming!

Also, thank you to:

Owikiskichikew—for your love and support, for your witnessing, and for your grace. For keeping me sane (or at least trying to). You are my friend for life, and if it weren't for you, I wouldn't be here, writing these acknowledgments.

Tim Rostron—for all your support, encouragement, and love. This all started with you—if you hadn't taken a chance on me, there would be no books and there wouldn't be this conversation.

Brian McDonald—for your incredible friendship and support, and for always being my witness.

Ken Whyte—for our conversations about the topic, for your encouragement and support.

Barbara Gowdy—for being my witness, friend, and support. For always inspiring me and being present with me.

Agata Miszczynska and the Miszczynska family—for friendship and support. I love you all.

Anna Lawrynowicz—for being such an integral part of my story. For friendship and support. For your tough love and for your gentle love.

Laurka Bydlowska—for all your support and love, and for always trying to understand and make space for me.

John Ross—for all your support and love and your undying grace.

Cat Black—for letting your toes prune in the bath as I told you my Shame. For always being present with me.

Naomi Gaskin—for being my first teacher of Unshaming. For your love, support, and wisdom.

Nancy-Marie Desfois—for inspiring my recovery. For being a friend.

Tory Hetherington—for all your endless support and friendship.

Angie Abdou—for your wisdom, and for inspiring me to take my pants off in the middle of the street, again.

Shannon McKinnon—for being a shamelessly supportive friend.

Bunmi Adeoye—for all your support and love.

Joe C.—for being a friend, a witness, a brilliant support.

Ira Wolfe—for your kindness.

Godless Heathens—for being such an integral part of my recovery.

Alcoholics Anonymous—for saving lives.

Hugo Smith—my son, my heart, my greatest teacher. Your strength, your insight, your forgiveness—these are the gifts that brought me back to life. I owe you everything. This book, this version of me, this